Architectural Knowledge
Architektonisches Wissen

MODELLING THE METROPOLIS
The Architectural Model in Victorian Lo

ARCHITECTURAL KNOWLEDGE
gta VERLAG

Matthew Wells

MODELLING THE METROPOLIS

The Architectural Model in Victorian London

7	INTRODUCTION
21	THE PUBLIC SPHERE
29	Competitions and the pursuit of truth
42	A new model for London
49	THE COMMONS
58	Models as a mode of inquiry
65	THE COURTROOM
69	Producing legal models
75	THE EXHIBITION
85	Edward Schroeder Prior and the model as 'feeling'
93	THE MODEL-MAKERS' WORKSHOP
100	From drawings to models
102	Accidents, empire, and beer: John Thorp and his workshop
119	THE UNIVERSITY
121	Model-making handbooks
126	Education at the Architectural Association
129	Inspecting models outside the Architectural Association
134	Banister Fletcher and technical knowledge at King's College
137	Education at University College
143	THE MUSEUM
147	John Soane and the practice of collecting
153	The Royal Institute of British Architects: Models for the profession
155	Architectural models at the South Kensington Museum
159	The origins of the Royal Architectural Museum
162	Change at the South Kensington Museum
171	CONCLUSION
176	BIBLIOGRAPHY
183	IMAGE CREDITS
184	INDEX
186	ACKNOWLEDGEMENTS

INTRODUCTION

MODELLING THE METROPOLIS

In his 1888 essay on London, the American author Henry James attributed the difficulty of understanding the 'dreadful, delightful city' to its immeasurability. On his journey down from Liverpool by train he encountered the endless terraced houses and miles of viaducts, the webs of roads and mazes of railway signals, all of which left him with the impression of an immense metropolis.[1] Each morning James would set off from his drab hotel in Trafalgar Square to explore a different area, often walking across the city in the rain. From the banks of the Thames he saw London as the 'largest chapter of human accidents … a strangely mingled monster' made evident in the construction of its houses ('without ornament, without grace, without character or even identity'), the location and expanse of its parks, and, above all, its spectacular absence of urban planning.[2] While he recognised parts of the city from lithographs, novels, magazines, songs, and maps, the immensity of London as a whole was impossible to fathom, so much so that James resorted to metaphor to describe his experiences of its buildings and streets: 'She has no time for fine discriminations, but after all she is as good-natured as she is huge, and the more you stand up to her, as the phrase is, the better she takes the joke of it.'[3]

As he walked through the 'murky, modern Babylon', from Chelsea and Notting Hill in the West to Wapping and Blackwall in the East, the city itself was changing. During the nineteenth century, London grew in population and became the global city of finance, industry, technology, and the capital of the

[1] Henry James, 'London', in *Essays in London and Elsewhere* (London: Osgood & McIlwaine, 1893), 1–43, here: 7.
[2] James, 'London', 14.
[3] James, 'London', 23–24.

British Empire.[4] New buildings, new urban spaces, and new networks of infrastructure were required and constructed. FIG. 1 Or as John Summerson put it, London was 'more excavated, more cut about, more rebuilt and more extended than at any time in its previous history'.[5]

Contemporary writers turned to metaphors to describe the horrors and wonders of London: Babylon, the labyrinth, 'the Great Wen'. Architects looked to a specific visual media. *Modelling the Metropolis* examines how architectural models made these changes conceivable as London's past and present were rewritten by the forces of modernity. During this reconfiguration, architectural models came to play a central role in the interactions between architects, politicians, and the wider public across local, national, and trans-regional settings. To take a line from Caroline Arscott and Griselda Pollack on Victorian art, 'the debate was not about a place, but about a process'.[6] Whether employed as educational and explanatory devices in the construction of new civic buildings, used in private debates, or included in public exhibitions, architectural models enabled audiences to visualise different realities, thereby enabling discussions about the past, the present, and the future appearance of the contemporary city.

Within these settings the three enfranchising reform acts of the nineteenth century (1832, 1867, 1884) provided a new context and series of concerns for the built environment, both of which made London the subject of popular and professional debate. These debates often turned on the ability of a model to present an accurate idea of a completed building to the public prior to its construction, with commentators questioning the appropriateness of particular scales, viewing positions, or model-making materials. Equally, models became a part of how new institutions, such as the South Kensington Museum or the Museum of London, delivered public education to their visitors. Equally, by the late 1880s education in the capital's universities had been formalised, and for students of architecture or engineering particular value was placed on models as specimens for the study of ornament, technology, and historic buildings. Meanwhile certain models were used symbolically in civic occasions such as ground-breaking ceremonies or public openings. Likewise, the mid-century expansion of new building codes and legislation in London facilitated a significant increase in building litigation, and a new type of model surfaced in the courtroom, used as a rhetorical tool by architects and lawyers.

---

[4] Major studies of nineteenth-century London that form a background to this book include Dana Arnold, ed., *The Metropolis and Its Image: Constructing Identities for London, c. 1750–1950* (Oxford: Blackwell, 1999); Lynda Nead, *Victorian Babylon: People, Streets and Images in Nineteenth-Century London* (New Haven: Yale University Press, 2000); Martin Daunton, ed., *The Cambridge Urban History of Britain, Volume III: 1840–1950* (Cambridge: Cambridge University Press, 2001); Richard Dennis, *Cities in Modernity: Representations and Productions of Metropolitan Space, 1840–1930* (Cambridge: Cambridge University Press, 2008); Jerry White, *London in the Nineteenth Century: A Human Awful Wonder of God* (London: Vintage, 2008); Andrew Saint, *London 1870–1914: A City at Its Zenith* (London: Lund Humphries, 2021).

[5] John Summerson, 'The London Building World of the 1860s', in *The Unromantic Castle and Other Essays* (London: Thames and Hudson, 1990), 175–92, here: 177.

[6] Caroline Arscott and Griselda Pollack, 'The Partial View: The Visual Representation of the Early Nineteenth-Century Industrial City', in Janet Wolff and John Seed, eds., *The Culture of Capital: Art, Power, and the Nineteenth-Century Middle Class* (Manchester: Manchester University Press, 1988), 191–234, here: 197.

INTRODUCTION

FIG. 1   Jacques-Emile Blanche, *Ludgate Circus: Entrance to the City* (November, Midday), c. 1910

Beyond these parliamentary and forensic capacities, in their representations of historic landscapes, proposed buildings, and new methods of construction, models became a popular way for audiences to interact with the built environment at the major expositions of the nineteenth century. At the Great Exhibition in 1851 architectural models were exhibited within 'Fine Arts', a subcategory that also contained topographic and anatomic examples. Little attention has been paid to these installations, with architectural historians instead focusing on more explicitly architectural examples, significantly those related to the German émigré Gottfried Semper's exhibition design and subsequent theoretical synthesis.[7] And yet among the first objects seen by visitors at the west entrance to the exhibition hall was a model, presented by the Liverpool Architectural Society, which depicted a vast 300-acre portion of the city that included the many dockyards along the river Mersey, each of the city's three railway stations, and significant urban monuments including the Town Hall, the Customs House, and Charles Robert Cockerell's magnificent Greek Revival St George's Hall. FIG. 2 Costing £750, about £60,000 in today's money, each building was modelled with 'great accuracy and care', and the whole ensemble was spectacularly presented in a glass case supported by columns sprouting from sixteen stone elephants.[8] The previous summer local architects and their assistants had surveyed Liverpool, making a set of elevation drawings that were then transferred onto wooden blocks representing each of the city's buildings.[9] When viewed from London's Hyde Park, these scenes transported visitors to an entirely different city. In turn, Liverpool was not simply viewed by the thousands of exposition visitors; it was in fact Liverpool *as modelled* that enabled the city to be understood on a national and international stage. Modelled railway connections and industrial buildings presented Liverpool as part of the British nation, while through the representation of the endless landscape of docks the city was shown to be part of the matrix of global affairs and central to the British colonial project.[10]

---

7   Michael Gnehm and Sonja Hildebrand, eds., *Architectural History and Globalized Knowledge: Gottfried Semper in London* (Mendrisio: Mendrisio Academy Press; Zurich: gta Verlag, 2021).
8   *Great Exhibition of the Works of Industry of all Nations, 1851: Official Descriptive and Illustrated Catalogue*, vol. 2 (London: William Clowes, 1851), 851.
9   'Liverpool Architectural Society', *Builder* 8 (11 May 1850), 226.
10 'Models', *Builder* 9 (30 August 1851), 36. After its display in Hyde Park, the model was purchased by Liverpool Council for £700 and put onto display in the newly constructed Picton Reading Room adjacent to St George's Hall and Lime Street Station. For a discussion on the potential of surveying as a cultural technique and practice see: Matthew Wells, *Survey: Architecture Iconographies* (Zurich: Park Books, 2021).

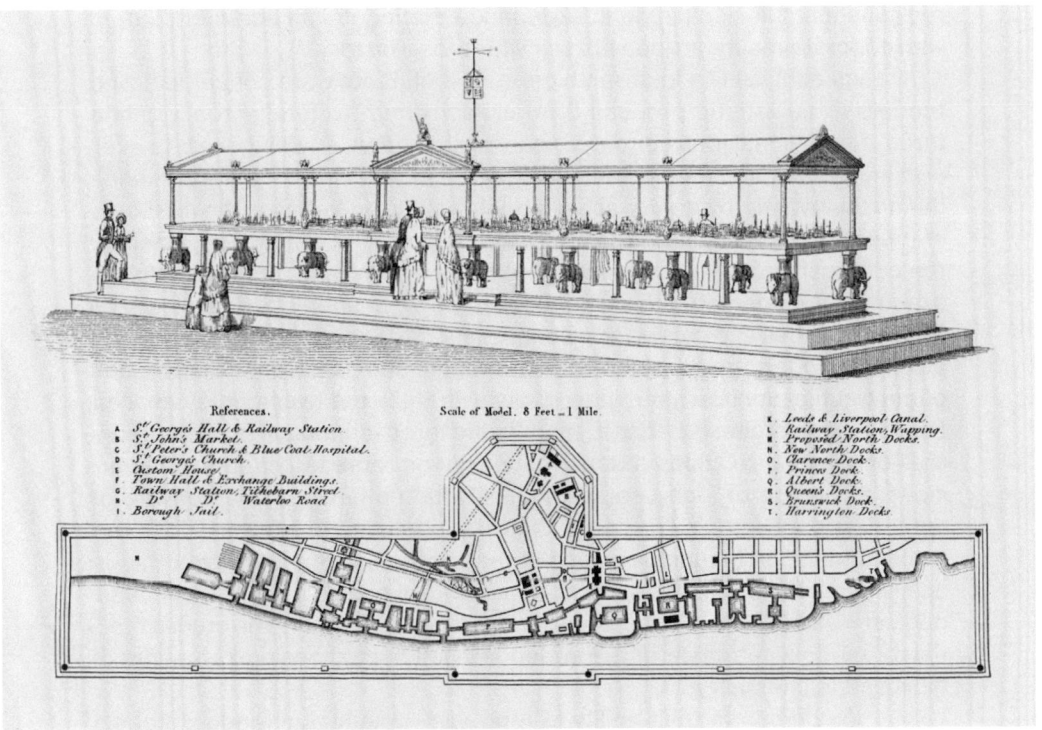

FIG. 2 Liverpool Architectural Society, Model of the Docks and Commercial Portion of the Town of Liverpool, engraving. *Great Exhibition of the Works of Industry of all Nations, 1851: Official Descriptive and Illustrated Catalogue*, vol. 2 (London: William Clowes, 1851), 851

Over the past two decades many historians have explored the significance of architectural models through broad studies that show the clear potential of the topic.[11] Building upon these wide-ranging discussions, recent scholarship by the likes of Teresa Fankhänel shows how the model-maker was active in the translation, interpretation, and transmission of ideas in the creation of buildings.[12] Others have described how certain model-makers played the part of 'intellectual craftsmen' in the production of theoretical and symbolic models for display, particularly those in architects' studios.[13] Most recently, Matthew Mindrup has considered the expansive history of model-making in design, from Leon Battista Alberti's inauguration of the medium as a tool in the fifteenth century, to the emergence of the 'concept model' at the start of the twentieth century.[14] Clarifying this conceptual role is a key concern for many scholars in the field. One view, recently investigated by scholars including Ralf Liptau and Albena Yaneva, is that working with physical models

11 Karen Moon, *Modelling Messages: The Architect and the Model* (New York: Monacelli Press, 2005); Mark Morris, *Models: Architecture and the Miniature* (London: Wiley, 2006); Albert Smith, *Architectural Model as Machine* (Oxford: Architectural Press, 2004).

12 Teresa Fankhänel, *The Architectural Models of Theodore Conrad: The 'Miniature Boom' of Mid-century Modernism* (London: Bloomsbury, 2021). Fankhänel's other major contribution is to identify how the combination of developments in material science and the organization of labour in the workshops of large-scale model-makers contributed to a model-making boom in America during the 1940s and 1950s.

13 Thomas Weaver, 'Model-maker Grimm', *AA Files* 73 (2016), 94–100; Matthew Wells, 'Carpenters and Craftsmen, Architects and Collectors: A Short History of the Architectural Model' in Maureen Cassidy-Geiger, ed., *Living with Architecture as Art* (London: Paul Holberton, 2020) 64–81.

14 Matthew Mindrup, *The Architectural Model: Histories of the Miniature and the Prototype, the Exemplar and the Muse* (Cambridge, Mass.: MIT Press, 2019), 157–202.

provides a tactile, kinaesthetic experience that connects abstract thought with concrete reality, an idea in itself with a long history.[15]

As early as the fourteenth century, architects were conceptualizing models in an artistic process that allowed them to intellectually refine three-dimensional ideas through visual examination, enabling them to exercise judgement and modify their designs.[16] Far away from the Renaissance, during the twentieth century, scale model-making, following in the footsteps of other artistic disciplines, became an artform akin to sculpture, whereby the composition of volumes and the effects of light and shadow could be examined and mediated through photography.[17] In addition to serving a variety of purposes and conveying a complex range of physical and atmospheric qualities, models are considered an immediate and comprehensible means of communication between individuals with different levels of knowledge. This, scholars argue, is because models are three-dimensional objects capable of showing relations that cannot easily be represented in two dimensions.[18] The use of standardized scales, which provide a key measure of control, supports their argument. Whether deployed at 1:50 or 1:500, the scalar dimension in model-making demands the existence of other things against which the object can be compared. This makes models ideal pedagogical aids. Historians of science, for example, have noted the crucial function of models in transferring knowledge and ideas at scale to students of biology and chemistry.[19]

In addition to their ability to represent existing knowledge, models have served as sites of experimentation by many disciplines, from scientists to set designers, and in the nineteenth century even the definition of the word 'model' evolved to reflect these new modes of interrogation.[20] Within the practices of sculptors and craftsmen, modelling was defined as 'working a plastic material into a desired shape' as a precursor 'in the study of an artist's thought'.[21] Following these artistic disciplines, writers proposed that through the process of modelling, nineteenth-century architects would be able to examine the composition and depths of window reveals, the outline of a roof, or the effects of light and shade on a building's facade before construction. A dictionary entry of 1830 describes a model as a moment where 'the sensation [in] which the whole and the parts of an edifice [are brought] together [to]

---

[15] Ralf Liptau, *Architekturen bilden: Das Modell in Entwurfsprozessen der Nachkriegsmoderne* (Bielefeld: transcript, 2019); Albena Yaneva, *The Making of a Building: A Pragmatist Approach to Architecture* (Bern: Peter Lang, 2009), esp. 113–60.

[16] Henry A. Millon, 'Models in Renaissance Architecture', in Henry A Millon and Vittorio Magnago Lampugnani, eds., *The Renaissance from Brunelleschi to Michelangelo: The Representation of Architecture* (London: Thames and Hudson, 1994), 19–74; Andres Lepik, *Das Architekturmodell in Italien, 1335–1550* (Worms: Wernersche, 1994); Amanda Lillie and Mauro Mussolin, 'The Wooden Models of Palazzo Strozzi as Flexible Instruments in the Design Process', in Amedeo Belluzzi, Caroline Elam, and Francesco Paolo Fiore, eds., *Giuliano da Sangallo: Disegni degli Uffizi* (Milan: Officina Libraria, 2017), 210–229.

[17] Davide Deriu, 'Transforming Ideas into Pictures: Model Photography and Modern Architecture', in Andrew Higgott and Timothy Wray, eds., *Camera Constructs: Photography, Architecture and the Modern City* (Burlington: Ashgate, 2012), 159–78. Oliver Elser and Peter Cachola Schmal, eds., *Das Architekturmodell: Werkzeug, Fetisch, kleine Utopie / The Architectural Model: Tool, Fetish, Small Utopia*, exh. cat. (Zurich: Scheidegger & Spiess), 11–22.

[18] Simona Valeriani, 'Three-dimensional Models as "in-between-objects": The Creation of in-between Knowledge in Early Modern Architectural Practice', *History of Technology* 31 (2011), 26–46.

[19] Mary Morgan, 'Learning from Models', in Mary Morgan and Margaret Morrison, eds., *Models as Mediators: Perspectives on Natural and Social Science* (Cambridge: Cambridge University Press, 1999), 347–88; Soraya de Chadarevian and Nick Hopwood, eds., *Models: The Third Dimension of Science* (Stanford: Stanford University Pres, 2004).

[20] Thea Brejzek and Lawrence Wallen, *The Model as Performance: Staging Space in Theatre and Architecture* (London: Bloomsbury, 2018).

[21] 'Modelling', in Russell Sturgis, ed., *Dictionary of Architecture and Building*, vol. 2 (London: Macmillan, 1902), 215.

produce on the mind and the eye'.[22] Echoing this the architectural press focused on process as the source of a model's effect of perception, describing how model-making was akin to designing a hypothetical house through the assembly of walls, floors, and rooms in the mind.[23] But unlike orthographic projection, which required prior knowledge of drawing conventions, architectural models allow almost any viewer to conceive three-dimensional space and form. A volume of the *Penny Cyclopaedia,* aimed at an audience without a formal education, described how a model was made to provide 'a more distinct idea of [a building] than can be obtained from a number of separate drawings ... by those who are unable to comprehend them perfectly, and combine them together mentally so as to figure to themselves a complete and distinct image of the whole.'[24]

Thus many individuals and publications argued that of all the persuasive visual tools architects had at their disposal, the model was best-suited for proposing changes to the built environment, especially to non-professionals. The *Dictionary of Architecture* (1875) explained how a model was 'particularly useful in conveying the effect of a proposed work to an unprofessional eye'.[25] Similarly the *Dictionary of Architecture and Building* (1902) claimed that a model could be used both more effectively and as a substitute for drawing 'to explain to clients the appearance of buildings they propose to erect'.[26] One article in the architectural press claimed, 'Few but professional persons understand or can give due attention to plans and elevations'; for many people, these and even the more accessible perspective drawings failed 'to make the connection of parts and the effect of the whole, as a mass, clear to their comprehension'.[27] Beyond these reports, many significant nineteenth-century architects believed that more than drawings, models could more honestly and fruitfully represent the three-dimensional character of buildings. In this vein the amateur architect Lord Grimthorpe (Edmund Beckett Denison) speculated that even detailed sectional drawings could not give a clear, three-dimensional sense of a building. Instead, he suggested that architects should construct models, as 'I never had a first model made of anything from which it was not easy to see that it might be improved'.[28]

If architectural models first emerged as a part of architectural practice in fifteenth-century Italy, they would not enter into the popular imagination in London until 500 years later, and only through a particular strand of urban culture: the spectacular shows that blended entertainment and instruction through the exhibition of objects to a paying audience. Visitors were rarely divided into poor or wealthy, ill-educated or learned, since by the nineteenth century the cultural interplay between classes stood for an evolving social democracy. Initially, large-scale models of biblical sites were frequently represented subjects and far more numerous than the more expensive to design and install panorama, the sublime simulacrum par excellence of the nineteenth century. Christian sites came to be replaced by models of urban and

---

22   'Model', in Robert Stuart, ed., *A Dictionary of Architecture; Historical, Descriptive, Topographical, Decorative, Theoretical and Mechanical*, vol. 2 (London: Jones & Co, 1830).
23   'Old House Planning', *Builder* 31 (8 March 1873), 183.
24   'Models, Architectural', in George Long, ed., *The Penny Cyclopaedia of the Society for the Diffusion of Useful Knowledge*, vol. 15 (London: Charles Knight, 1839), 294.
25   'MODEL', in Architectural Publication Society, ed., *The Dictionary of Architecture*, vol. 5 (London: Thomas Richards, 1875), 101.
26   'PRELIMINARY STUDIES', in Russell Sturgis, ed., *Dictionary of Architecture and Building*, vol. 3 (London: Macmillan, 1902), 208.
27   'The New Foreign Office', *Builder* 17 (26 February 1859), 158.
28   Edmund Beckett Denison, *A Book on Building, Civil and Ecclesiastical* (London: Crosby Lockwood, 1880), 69.

natural landscapes, such as the city of Rome or the topography of the Alps. At Woolwich Arsenal callers could visit the Royal Military Repository, better known to Londoners as the Rotunda.[29] First erected in the grounds of Carlton House as a temporary ballroom by John Nash, the tent-like structure was relocated and weatherproofed to display models of strategic sites across the British Empire – Gibraltar, Quebec – alongside models of cannons and artillery. Other examples allowed current events from around the world to be depicted in the centre of London. For instance, during the French Revolution when the royal family was imprisoned at the Tour du Temple, a model of the medieval fortress was placed on display in London's West End.[30] Equally large-scale models transported significant monuments from Rome or Venice to Britain. One newspaper argued that a model of the Colosseum exhibited at a gallery on Regent Street gave visitors 'a better idea of [the building] than a hundred pictures' – indication of the medium's potential to communicate ideas about the built environment to an emerging mass urban public.[31] Without a fixed position a visitor was, much like a panorama, free 'to wander and investigate, to bring preconceptions to bear on the work'.[32]

Whether presenting contemporary events or historic buildings, the production of models required the dedicated skill and craft of model-makers, but locating the material to understand the logistics, techniques, and methods of the model-maker is a complicated task. Unlike nineteenth-century architects, government institutions, or prominent builders, these independent tradesmen have no dedicated archives for drawings, personal papers, business accounts, or correspondence. And yet surviving paperwork, advertising, and trade directories, as well as census and probate information, offer a new picture of how London was conceived during its nineteenth-century expansion. Nine individuals comprise the key architectural model-makers of the period: Richard Day and Richard Day Jr, Thomas Dibdin Dighton, John Thorp, the Mabey dynasty (James Mabey, his son Charles Henry Mabey, and grandson Charles Henry Mabey Jr), Stephen Salter, and Charles Newson Thwaite. All were based in the capital, although Thwaite began work from Manchester before moving to London in 1865, and Richard Day Jr left south London for Maidstone in Kent in the mid-1860s. Dighton remained in Westminster before moving to Devon at the end of his career. Richard Day Jr operated separately from his father and had a series of workshops in south London. He inherited tools and commissions following his father's death in 1849. Following the relocation of his business from Manchester to the capital, Thwaite also operated from a workshop in south London before setting up close to the Strand from the mid-1860s. C.H. and J. Mabey were based out of a mews at Storey's Gate, Westminster, from about 1864 to 1889. The Mabey family produced scale models for architects of contemporary and antique buildings, harbours, bridges, exhibition pieces, and monuments in

---

29   Emily Cole, Susan Skedd, Jonathan Clarke, and Sarah Newsome, eds., *The Rotunda (former Royal Artillery Museum), Woolwich Common, London Borough of Greenwich: History, Structure and Landscape*, Research Report Series nos. 251–2020 (Portsmouth: Historic England, 2020), 27–66.

30   Richard Altick, *The Shows of London* (Cambridge, Mass.: Belkamp 1979), 115 cites British Library, Daniel Lysons, *Collection of Advertisements from the Newspapers (1661–1840)*, vol. 2, 197.

31   'The Coliseum', *Weekly True Sun* (3 June 1838), 1991.

32   Tim Barringer, 'The World for a Shilling: The Early Panorama as Global Landscape, 1787–1830', in Katie Trumpener and Tim Barringer, eds., *On the Viewing Platform: The Panorama Between Canvas and Screen* (New Haven: Yale University Press, 2020), 83–106, here: 105.

London, the British Isles, and around the world.[33] Disciplinary background and training were paramount to the business and often determined the approach of the model-maker. Those with a sculptural background, such as the Mabey or Day dynasties, worked exclusively in plaster. Those coming from a graphic or architectural background worked in cardboard or paper applied to a timber structure. In addition to these lesser-known model-makers were the eminent British sculptors Hamo Thornycroft and Frederick William Pomeroy.[34] The latter made models in plaster for several London-based architects including John Belcher, Edward William Mountford, and Alfred Brumwell Thomas. Many of these models were exhibited at the Royal Academy, where Pomeroy's expertise was employed to render the formal massing and outline of a building in a spectacular manner.[35] FIG. 3

Unlike previous model-makers who had specialised in the replication of existing, often antique, buildings of Italy and Greece, which were displayed in the town and country houses of the Georgian upper classes, the work of this new generation centred on making models for new buildings in London.[36] Commissioned by architects and paid by private clients or institutional committees, the model-makers advertised their services in the architectural press, displayed their work independently at exhibitions, and supplemented their income with other activities when commissions were not forthcoming. For the Mabeys, architectural model-making was a secondary source of income at best; their primary employment was the production of sculptural reliefs for buildings, from public commissions to ready-made ornamental elements in plaster and cement, which architects and clients could view at their premises.[37] There were also occasions when the sculptor-model-maker produced both the architectural model of the building and carried out the work for the sculpture on the exterior of the building.[38]

33 A printed advertisement from the early twentieth century lists their sculptural work by programme (Hotel, Bank, Tomb, etc.), as well as the scale models for architects and engineers, as follows: Liverpool Exchange (T. H. Wyatt), Admiralty and War Office (Leeming and Leeming), Barry Docks (John Wolfe Barry, Thomas Forster Brown, Henry Marc Brunel), Parthenon (James Fergusson), Harbour of La Guaira, Venezuela (Punchard, McTaggart, Louther & Co.), Mersey Docks (G. F. Lister), Tower Bridge (J. W. Barry), Putney Bridge (John Wolfe Barry and Henry Marc Brunel), Blackfriars Bridge (John Wolfe Barry and Henry Marc Brunel), Erechtheion (George Aitchison), Institute of Chartered Accountants (John Belcher), Model of the Alhambra, Crystal Palace (Owen Jones), Organ of St Paul's Cathedral (F. C. Penrose), Powerscourt (F. C. Penrose), Crystal Palace, Russia (Charles Barry), Models of the Houses of Parliament (Charles Barry), Eleanor Cross, Charing Cross (E. M. Barry), Temple Bar (Horace Jones), Auction Mart and General Credit Company, Tokenhouse Yard (G. Somers Clarke), the Rosetti Memorial (J. P. Seddon), Entrance to Burlington House (Sydney Smirke), University Observatory, Oxford (Charles Barry), Institute of Civil Engineers (Charles Barry), North Mymms (Ernest George and Harold Peto).
34 Pomeroy, previously a Royal Academy Gold Medallist for Sculpture, was active between 1881 and 1924, and worked on a wide range of free-standing and architectural sculpture.
35 E. W. Mountford, 'Sketch Model: South-West Angle of New Museum and Technical School, Liverpool', *Catalogue of the Exhibition of the Royal Academy* (London: William Clowes, 1898) no. 1804; John Belcher, 'Model of a Dome: Electra House', *Catalogue of the Exhibition of the Royal Academy* (London: William Clowes, 1902) no. 1598; A. B. Thomas, 'Model of a Monument to the Late Marquess of Dufferin and Ava, Belfast', *Catalogue of the Exhibition of the Royal Academy* (London: William Clowes, 1906) no. 1615.
36 For a discussion of this and their effect on British architecture see Frank Salmon, *Building on Ruins: The Rediscovery of Rome and English Architecture* (Aldershot: Ashgate, 2000), 73–5.
37 'Advert: James Mabey', *Kelly Building Trades' Directory* (London: Kelly & Co, 1870), 47.
38 One example of this was Charles Henry Mabey Junior who made a model for the County Hall, London, in 1911, and later completed the architectural carvings for the exterior to the designs of Ralph Knott between 1910 and 1922. See Hobhouse, Hermione, ed., *Survey of London*. Monograph 17: *County Hall* (London: Athlone, 1991), 47.

FIG. 3 Edward William Mountford (architect), Frederick William Pomeroy (model-maker), Southwest Angle of New Museum and Technical School, Liverpool, 1898. 'Architecture at the Royal Academy, 1898', *Architectural Review* 6 (June 1898), 10

INTRODUCTION

In addition to the makers who pioneered new ways of representing the built environment, models of this period were also used to communicate technical knowledge about new and existing methods of construction. In Britain, changes to the division of labour in the building trade following the Napoleonic Wars saw the emergence of subcontracting practices and managerial roles, with precise instructions for construction now delegated from drawings and oral instructions to written contracts and specifications.[39] In turn, both the content and use of models was responding to the changing economic and organizational demands faced by architects in the nineteenth century. The transition away from traditional construction techniques and tradesmen, along with the emergence of new technologies for heating, lighting, and ventilation meant that architects required new types of technical knowledge. On the one hand, this could be gleaned from the specialised and interdisciplinary collections of technical models and specimens of the latest building products housed in London's universities and museums. On the other hand, these new branches of knowledge were connected to the emergence and formalization of architecture as a profession in Europe.

Prior to professionalism, various factors posed challenges to the intellectual credentials and socio-economic position of the architect, from the decline of aristocratic patronage and the expansion of the modern state, to the increase of construction following the Napoleonic Wars, and the emergence of rival disciplines such as engineers.[40] In a British context the formation of architectural societies was significant, culminating in 1834 with the foundation of a professional body known as the Royal Institute of British Architects (RIBA). Professional organizations are the key mechanism from which particular groups can constitute and control a market for their expertise. They can determine who is qualified to perform a defined set of tasks, prevent all others from performing that work, or control the criteria by which to evaluate competency.[41] Within Victorian London the formal structures of the RIBA were a primary way in which the interests of its members – chiefly architects – were collectively expressed. These organizations, their buildings, their meetings, and their printed output in magazines and journals became sites for the presentation of new technical knowledge and artistic production through architectural models, as well as places where individuals gathered to discuss the practical and theoretical implications of architectural practice.

The aim of this book is to combine the study of objects (architectural models) with a new historical reading of architectural practice – one that takes into account the emergence of professionalism in the construction of Victorian London. The study of models in the nineteenth century has been neglected in the field of architectural and art history. Any analysis of architectural models in the long nineteenth century has concentrated on the

39 For discussion of this topic see Howard Colvin, *Biographical Dictionary of English Architects*, 3rd ed. (New Haven: Yale University Press, 1995); Brian Hanson, *Architects and the 'Building World' from Chambers to Ruskin: Constructing Authority* (Cambridge: Cambridge University Press, 2003); Conor Lucey, *Building Reputations: Architecture and the Artisan, 1750–1830* (Manchester: Manchester University Press, 2018).
40 Andrew Saint, *The Image of the Architect* (New Haven: Yale University Press, 1983).
41 See theoretical discussions on professionalization in: Valérie Fournier, 'The Appeal to "Professionalism" as a Disciplinary Mechanism', *Social Review* 47, no. 2 (1999), 280–307; Elliot Freidson, *Professionalism: The Third Logic* (Chicago: University of Chicago Press, 2001); Magali Sarfatti Larson, *The Rise of Professionalism: A Sociological Analysis* (Berkeley: University of California Press, 1979) xii–xvi.

history of acquisitions and the individuals involved.[42] Meanwhile, the circumstances of model production and the use of models by architects in education, design, and construction have largely been ignored. Equally, unlike previous scholarship, the methodological approach taken in this book combines object-based study with the investigation of archival material. Many of the architectural models discussed in these chapters have not been subjected to prior, in-depth academic analysis. New types of objects, such as legal models, are explored to further an understanding of contemporary debates around the built environment. To articulate this object-based study, the story of the architectural model in Victorian London is supported by individual, museum, and governmental archives; diaries and letters, newspapers and periodicals; books, pamphlets, and exhibition catalogues. Print culture from within and outside of historic architectural communities offers an innovative understanding of use of the model in nineteenth-century society. This society was one in which the public sphere was seen as a place for critical debate, a realm mediated through newspapers, journals, and pamphlets. New techniques and technologies of production, combined with tax reform, enabled cheaper production and circulation of illustrated journals, newspapers, and magazines.[43]

With regards to this idea, whether discussed in print or experienced first-hand, architectural models enable social and politico-economic interactions to happen in society. This book uses these interactions and their debate, discussion, or presentation to question the more traditional understanding of architecture as a discipline defined primarily in terms of authorship. Instead it offers a new perspective with a cast of characters – architects, model-makers, the models themselves. All of these people, processes, functions, and objects present a rich and multifarious picture of a modern metropolis shaped by many hands, one that challenges the conventional notion of design as the sole activity of the profession. The most striking contribution of architectural models to existing understanding is the wide range of situations in which they were deployed, examined, and discussed while the authority of the profession was being established during the nineteenth century.

The book is thus organised spatially into seven chapters in order to highlight the intersecting and nomadic nature of the architectural model across the metropolis. Whether in a lecture hall or a courtroom, key themes such as truth and reality, education and training, spatiality and materiality recur at various moments in the long nineteenth century. In the popular press or in parliamentary records, adjustments to the use of models came about in light of Britain's vastly expanded democratic franchise, and how architects and statesmen asserted their authority in public life. When in the public eye, debates around the absence or presentation of architectural models provide new understanding of significant nineteenth-century buildings. The presentation of models, whether in exhibition halls or in the courtroom, describes both changes to the legislative framework of the built environment and the conceptual authorship of architectural practice. Returning to the idea of a cast of characters, different spatial settings show the logistics of production and sub-contraction in the process of design. Alongside these examples,

---

42 See for instance: John Wilton-Ely, 'The Architectural Models of Sir John Soane: A Catalogue', *Architectural History* 12 (1969), 5–38, 81–101; Fiona Leslie, 'Inside Outside: Changing Attitudes Towards Architectural Models in the Museums at South Kensington', *Architectural History*, 47 (2004), 159–200.

43 As a result, between 1836 and 1854 the circulation of English newspapers tripled from 39 million to 122 million. Arthur Aspinal, 'The Circulation of Newspapers in the Early Nineteenth Century', *The Review of English Studies*, 22, no. 85 (January 1946), 29–43.

architectural models were mediated not just through exhibitions and photographs, now-typical sites for architectural history, but through student handbooks and the promotional brochures of model-makers, to name just two. Drawing on familiar episodes from a new position and unacknowledged actors, the book demonstrates how the architectural model became a central part of both professional practice and public life, and how through these objects Victorian London was conceived, contested, and constructed.

Tracing forward to our present condition, it is not difficult to see parallels as similar debates play out in popular and technocratic disputes over architectural competitions, planning applications, or the 'correct appearance' of buildings across Europe and further afield. Despite advances in computer-generated images physical models are still used today to record lost monuments and project future ones in exhibitions or marketing suites around the world. When displayed by museums models contribute to the afterlife of monuments through the canonization of buildings and the transmission of cultural identity. By recording buildings of the past or depicting remotely located structures a model enables its viewers to transcend the boundaries of time and space. Furthermore by controlling the relative quantities of scale or material, architectural models hold the potential to place particular buildings and the societies that produce them in a privileged position. As a result of their miniaturization, the model attracts, hold memories, and captivates because of the satisfyingly perfect world it presents the viewer.

In this sense, architects not only model physically in cardboard or timber, but also in different media. Modelling as a cultural technique manifests itself in a variety of ways. Whether to provide a baseline of certainty or to show the implication of theories in concrete situations, models are always autonomous, representations of both theory and world. They represent both theoretical structures – new designs, new ways of living – and existing realities, subject to new concepts. Whether in Victorian London or in the present, new modes of life emerge, first, in models, then, in reality.

THE PUBLIC SPHERE

On 23 February 1833, the *Literary Gazette,* a London-based magazine of significant influence, published an elevation of a proposed building on Trafalgar Square for 'public inspection'.¹ FIG. 4 Wedged between two articles was a two-storey Neoclassical building with a central portico and two wings with arched entrances. Despite declaring 'it is not our wish to play the critic and make embarrassing objections', judgement was delivered.² Among the writer's complaints was that the proposed building's cramped and low appearance was better suited to a bright-skied Grecian plain rather than the smoke-filled environment of inner-city London. Of primary concern, however, was that the architect and government would 'waste immense sums of money, and have nothing suitable to show for it!'³

In London during the 1830s a wave of metropolitan improvements and civic buildings was set in motion by the combination of economic forces and growing professional expertise. Public buildings were constructed to house the programmes of the modern capital city, including museums, libraries, art galleries, markets (money, livestock, coal), and law courts. Also at this very moment there emerged an urban public with a desire for democratic participation. This included critiquing the design of civic buildings of national and international significance. Following the 1832 Reform Act, which increased the size of the male electorate by around sixty per cent, public opinion as expressed in the increasingly influential press was seen as a feature

1	The extent of the newspaper's power was described by the early twentieth-century critic Denys Thompson in: Denys Thompson, 'A Hundred Years of The Higher Journalism', *Scrutiny* 4, no.1 (June 1935), 25–34.
2	'The National Gallery', *Literary Gazette* (23 February 1833), 122.
3	'The National Gallery', 122.

of a 'strong society'.[4] It was therefore expected that a wider public should be kept up to date with the design of prominent civic buildings located at the heart of the city – and it was therefore not uncommon for criticism of those buildings to be included in the popular press. Unlike previous generations, where architectural publications were the sole preserve of the elite, the integration of words, images, and buildings in architectural journals and the mainstream press contributed to a new public discourse, enabling both individual voices and collective identities.[5] At the heart of these discussions were the architectural models that presented the designs to the public and which were debated in newspapers, private correspondence, and in Parliament. Within the architectural profession different theoretical positions about models were contested as practitioners sought to establish themselves, in the eyes of the public, as the best-placed specialists for understanding the design, procurement, and construction of buildings.

On this particular occasion, the new building under discussion – the recipient of the *Literary Gazette*'s 'embarrassing objections' – was the National Gallery. Having rapidly outgrown its original site on Pall Mall, various solutions for the expansion of the original premises or the construction of a new building were proposed by both the Gallery's trustees and governmental committees.[6] The elevation reproduced in the *Literary Gazette* was based on a model exhibited by the architect William Wilkins to a select group of journalists at a government department, the Office of Woods and Forests, in early February 1833. Responding to the publication of the elevation and its criticism, Wilkins wrote a letter to another periodical, the *Athenaeum*, alleging that the *Gazette*'s editor, William Jerdan, had requested a drawing of the proposed National Gallery for publication, which the architect had refused on the grounds that an engraving was too expensive to produce.[7] Instead, Wilkins invited Jerdan to visit the model. Jerdan, it seems, was busy and gained permission from the Office of Woods and Forests for a 'friend' to go on his behalf. That friend, it transpired, was an artist who was later caught making an illicit drawing of the model and warned not to pursue its publication. Jerdan had the elevation engraved and published it anyway, but according to Wilkins, the reproduction wholly misrepresented the scale of certain elements and the overall building, which in turn affected other aspects of the engraving. He questioned how Jerdan could have understood the height of the proposed building since 'No scale is added to the model, and his artist could only make a *rough estimate* of its height.'[8]

[4] The impact of 1832 on the shape and size of the British electorate remained ambiguous, and a narrative of social change in the wake of the Act is complicated. In my consideration I have drawn on the work of many important scholars on the subject including: Eric Hobsbawm, *Nations and Nationalism since 1780: Programme, Myth, Reality* (Cambridge: Cambridge University Press, 1990); Jürgen Habermas, *The Structural Transformation of the Public Sphere: An Inquiry into a Category of Bourgeois Society*, trans. Thomas Burger with Frederick Lawrence (Oxford: Polity, 1992); Donald Read, *The Age of Urban Democracy: England 1868–1914* (London: Longman, 1994); Asa Briggs, *England in the Age of Improvement* (London: Folio Society, 1999), 228–60; Richard Price, *British Society, 1680–1880: Dynamism, Containment, and Change* (Cambridge: Cambridge University Press, 1999); Pam Morris, *Imagining Inclusive Society in Nineteenth-Century Novels: The Code of Sincerity in the Public Sphere* (Baltimore: Johns Hopkins University Press, 2004); Craig Calhoun, *The Roots of Radicalism: Tradition, the Public Sphere, and Early Nineteenth-Century Social Movements* (Chicago: University of Chicago Press, 2012).

[5] Briggs, *England in the Age of Improvement*, 388; Mari Hvattum and Anne Hultzsch, 'Introduction: A Storehouse of Ideas', in Mari Hvattum and Anne Hultzsch, eds., *The Printed and the Built: Architecture, Print Culture and Public Debate in the Nineteenth Century* (London: Bloomsbury, 2018), 7.

[6] For a synopsis of these solutions see: Gregory Martin, 'Wilkins and the National Gallery', *The Burlington Magazine* 113, no. 819 (June 1971), 318–26, 329; J. Mordaunt Crook and Michael Port. *The History of the King's Works: Volume VI 1782–1851* (London: HMSO, 1973), 461–63; Rhodri Windsor Liscombe, *William Wilkins 1778–1839* (Cambridge: Cambridge University Press, 1980), 180–3.

[7] William Wilkins, 'The National Gallery', *Athenaeum* (2 March 1833), 135.

[8] Wilkins, 'The National Gallery', 135.

during the many centuries they had been submerged: they appeared to be coins of Victorinus, one of the tyrants of Rome in the third century. Some pieces were said to have been found embedded in a concrete petrified mass of the surrounding matter. Mr. C. E. Gwilt presented drawings of the ground-plan and details of the Crypt lately discovered at St. Olave's, Southwark, on the site of the hostelry of the Prior of Lewes. A further portion of Mr. Borrell's catalogue of Greek coins was read.

FINE ARTS.
ANCIENT STATUE.

[We are indebted to a friend for the annexed account of one of the noblest remains of ancient art, recently found at Athens, which has been discovered for centuries.—*Ed. L. G.*]

THEY have just found, in one of the sewers of ancient Athens, a splendid statue, supposed to be of Theseus: it is naked, and of the heroic size, about that of the Belvidere Apollo, of the finest marble, and best style of sculpture, and perfect, excepting the head and feet. The former was discovered a short distance from the statue, and, from the fracture corresponding with the neck, may be easily replaced. A temple, with three columns erect, has likewise made its appearance from below what was supposed the ancient town : to secure the treasures buried there, the whole of that part of the site should be excavated to the depth of about eighty feet; but there is so little money to lay out, and the people are so impatient to build on the spot, that the whole will shortly be covered in and locked up for ever.

THE NATIONAL GALLERY.

THE proposed National Gallery is a design of so much importance, that we have long intended to bring it under the cognizance of the readers of the *Literary Gazette*, but have been deferred by various considerations. First, alterations of several kinds were being suggested, discussed, rejected, or adopted; so that we could not, at any precise moment, say, this is the plan of the building which is to be erected on such a site. Then, our information was derived from private society; the intercourse of which we have ever made it a rule to hold sacred. However, as the space for the Gallery is now boarded in, preparatory to digging the foundations, as the model is visible at the office of Woods and Forests, as the line of frontage has, it is said, been finally determined, we can see no objection to our availing ourselves of a drawing of the Elevation, which we have this day engraved for public inspection.

In laying this print before the scientific and professional world, it is not our wish to play the critic and make embarrassing objections; but we cannot help offering a few remarks for the consideration of government, to the committee to whom the execution of the design is intrusted, and to every enlightened member of the community, before it may be too late to suggest any improvement, or prevent the perpetration of any absurdity.

In our populous and crowded metropolis it is difficult to find any spot adequate to the erection of a (worthy to be so called) National Gallery. The site assigned is most eligible; with every local capability, central, convenient, and obvious to view. But when we speak of a *National* and lasting monument, suited to meet the circumstances which are likely to arise for ages to come, we are surprised to find that this project is cramped even for present use, and incapable of future extension. Should any patriotic and public-spirited individual hereafter present a noble collection of art to the country, we may indeed have, what we call, "The National Gallery," but we shall not have a place wherein to receive and preserve such a donation. There will not only be no room, but there will be no possibility of making any addition to the building, for the ground is occupied and closed in to the last available foot. Barracks, and soldiers drilling, must be associated with the receptacle of works of genius and the studies of the emulous; the parish workhouse is in the rear; and the Royal Academy divides the premises! The latter conjunction appears to us to be a great error; because the immediate contrast of the *chefs d'œuvre* of the ancient masters must be overwhelming to the miscellaneous efforts of any modern school; and because the people who can see the former for nothing, will not be in haste to pay their shillings and sixpences (catalogue) to visit the other end of the exhibition. In our opinion the National Gallery ought to stand alone; and whatever its first capacity may be, it ought to have the means of extensions to a very considerable degree, as may be required. It is true that only 50,000l. have been voted for this object; but this is a farce; thrice that amount will not complete the plan, and the first rough estimated contract will nearly double it.

What it is to be, our engraving will shew. A low and beautiful Greek structure; for the architect, Mr. Wilkins, is an idolater of the pure Greek. Now, with all our admiration of the pure Greek, we are not sure that we consider it to be the best style for a large city, like the capital, or that it will be particularly effective in this situation. On the contrary, we are of opinion that, however excellent *per se*, it will be misplaced and anomalous by the side of such an edifice as St. Martin's church, and in the midst of five-story-high houses. The difference between a Grecian plain and Charing Cross; between an ever-bright sky and our smoky atmosphere; between insulation and architectural confusion; does not seem to have been considered in a theory which would bend every thing to an idea of abstract grace. Mr. Wilkins' other buildings, Downing College, Cambridge, the London University, and St. George's Hospital, are samples — the new work will be the least elevated of them all.

Such is the architect's devotedness to the Greek architecture, that he maintains the expediency of making every thing else yield to its exemplification in this instance. Thus he contends that the much-admired portico of St. Martin's Church is an ugly, irregular, and stupid violation of the just rules of proportion; and as it is little matter what becomes of it, his line will cut it in two, and the spectator looking from Pall Mall East will see but half a portico and half a church. Vitruvius, whom, by the by, he translated, and so propagated his errors, knew, he assures us, little more than a goose about building; and, in short, that there is nothing good but the pure Greek, according to which he is resolved to frame our British Gallery.

We confess that we entertain strong apprehensions respecting this structure. Surely we are not going to perpetuate another national folly like Buckingham Palace. Waste immense sums of money, and have nothing suitable to the purpose to shew for it! But as far as we can now ascertain the fact, it appears that a fine *low* Grecian range is to hold the national pictures, and the Royal Academy offices and annual exhibitions — that it will bear neither resemblance nor relation to the buildings by which it is surrounded — that it will destroy the view of St. Martin's Church — that it never can be enlarged for the reception of any splendid gifts, and will consequently discourage their offer — that it will be infested with soldiery, and cooped in by barracks — and that it will cost thrice as much as the estimates.

We trust we are in time to prevent some of these mistakes; and obtain for this national object a more mature and deliberate consideration than it seems to have received. The talents of Mr. Wilkins we have frequently acknowledged; but when the ablest men adopt particular fancies, and excite their imagination so much as to hold that there is nothing else right or tolerable, we would advise a measure of watchfulness over the blinding enthusiasm.

SKETCHES OF SOCIETY.
MOHAMMED ALI.
[Conclusion of the Extract from the *Bulletin de la Société de Géographie.*]

THE government of Mohammed Ali is loudly censured by those who pretend that he is ruining his country by depriving it of money and men. Those who knew Egypt before he possessed himself of it are satisfied that the Arabs were never richer nor better clothed. If the revenue of Egypt is at present considerably increased, it is not by any additional burden on the people, but by increasing the extent of his possessions, in consequence of the conquest of Sennar and Cordofar; by cultivating a much larger quantity of land, by the introduction of new products, such as indigo, &c.

If the actual commercial exportation and importation of Egypt be compared with its former amount, it will be found to be at least plan to a certain extent, we trust it will afford a pretty general gratification to be enabled to mark the difference between what was originally proposed and what is at present executing — though we cannot be sure that further variations and alterations may not be made before the Gallery reach its cornice.

When Mr. Wilkins first thought it expedient to sound the trumpet of his own fame, and display his eminent literary talents in writing epistles to the newspapers in praise of his own works and depreciation of all other edifices, ancient and modern, we humbly ventured to question his assumed superiority; and, having obtained a drawing from his model for the National Gallery, as exhibited at the office of Woods and Forests, we gave the annexed engraving of it in the *Literary Gazette*, accompanied by such remarks as appeared to us to be justly applicable to its inherent defects, to its inconsistency with, and to its encroachment on other long-esteemed buildings. The wings being covered, for a reason we cannot divine, at the period the model was partially shewn, Mr. Wilkins took occasion to find furious fault with our imperfect representation of his design; and to defend it from all the objections we had suggested to its being considered *Perfection*. Now, however, that the model as it is really to be, is fairly before us in the Adelaide Street Gallery of Practical Science, we rejoice to see, not only that we were not materially wrong in our first print (though Mr. W. boldly declared it to be "*a libellous representation*"),* but that the architect has had the good sense to adopt some of the hints for improvement, which, in truth, with no other view but that of contributing to the actual embellishment, instead of deformity, of the capital, and the ad-

* We should be obliged by our readers' comparing the two, and trying to find out the libel. For our own parts, we are almost ready to fancy that, though not to the business bred, we are the better architect of the two.— Ed. L. G.

vantage of our native school of Fine Arts, we took the liberty to throw out.

Below the repetition of our first elevation will be found a correct drawing of the front of the second and amended model as it at present appears.

Having candidly stated the motives which guided us throughout the progress of this affair, it will readily be believed that we can entertain no hostility towards the architect, nor any desire to renew a controversy which he contrived to divest of public interest by making it personal. We shall be happy to see a structure finished which will do honour to Mr. Wilkins's talents, and prove an ornament to London; and in the meantime, whatever may be our misgivings, will simply notice some of the principal alterations.

In Mr. Day's excellent exhibition of architectural models, the Gallery is seen in relation to St. Martin's Church, and the two sides of Trafalgar Square. From this we observe, that according to the new line of frontage, the whole of the Portico of St. Martin's Church will be visible from the Opera Colonnade, though on advancing up Pall Mall East it will be almost obscured by the portico of the National Gallery.

On one point we think Mr. W. is much to be commended; and we wish he had been more so. We held that his elevation was too low, especially with reference to the surrounding buildings; and though he stoutly denied our position, we are glad to see that he has added several (we believe exactly seven) feet to its height, so that his cornice ranges with the cornice of the adjacent church. It is true that our original cut is still higher—which at any rate proves the fallacy of one of Mr. W.'s assertions, that we had represented his model of lower proportions than it really was.

The centre dome has also been (as we think) advantageously raised; and *door-ways* substituted for the *arch-ways*, against which we so strenuously raised our voice as grossly incongrous in the Greek style.

We request it to be observed, that the parts of the two ends of the Gallery which we have caused to be shaded in the cut, are now thrown back in the building; which contributes somewhat to the opening of the portico of St. Martin's to the view. What they were at first we cannot tell, as, when our first drawing was taken, they were, as we have noticed, concealed with paper. Our smaller domes were also misplaced, at least differ from their present disposition; but as they were movable, they had probably been shifted on the model by some ingenious amateur. We now take leave of the matter, begging room for only a few additional notes touching Mr. Wilkins's promises and theories, and Mr. Wilkins's actual practice.

March 4, 1833, Mr. Wilkins tells the editor of the *Morning Herald*, that an accurate model is in preparation, to which he will invite the attention of gentlemen connected with the press, in three weeks.—(Twelve months have elapsed!)

In his Essay on Porticos, he says of St. Martin's, that, as a principal defect, " it is not the entire width of the building; it affects to be the end of the building, but is not: every portico, whether at the end *or in the centre of a range of building*, should be, or appear to be, the ornamental termination of two flank walls. . . . . . . Our porticoes, generally speaking, appear to be mere *appliquées* stuck against a range of wall."

How does this dogma agree with the centre of the National Gallery, as he is absolutely constructing it? The clumsy extension of the centre in two divisions on either side of his portico, proves at least that it does not form the termination of two flank walls.

In the first woodcut we had given him the extension in one division only; in this we had unknowingly followed the front of St. Martin's Church, which may, perhaps, be the reason why he does not adopt it: nevertheless it is infinitely preferable to his own blank-looking design in this respect.

If our porticoes in general are mere *appliquées*, what has he to say to the four columns stuck against the wall at his two side-entrances? And let us ask, if the intercolumniation of the *grand* portico be correct, what is to be said of these two little detached affairs?—they are more *straggling* than the much-abused St. Martin's.

No good Grecian authority is to be found for a dome on a two-storied building. Our first cut gave the appearance of a principal story on a low basement—his is divided in two by equal stories.

As now erecting.

As it appeared in the L. G. No. 840.

NEW PUBLICATIONS.

Illustrations of the Pilgrims of the Rhine. Saunders and Otley.

A COLLECTION of twenty-six as elegant, charming, and highly finished little works of art as ever came under our notice. As we turned them over, we could not help continually exclaiming, in humble imitation of Cassio's ecstatic admiration of Iago's songs, " 'Fore Heaven, why this is a more exquisite print than the other!" The artist who has chiefly contributed the designs for this rich treat is Mr. David Roberts; but there are also a few beautiful productions from the pencils of Messrs. M'Clise, Parris, and Holst. The engravers are Messrs. Bacon, Carter, Deeble, Floyd, Goodall,

Wilkins's criticism of the published engraving resonated with contemporary concerns that without a scale an architectural model could potentially deceive viewers. In a series of articles published between 1835 and 1850, the critic and journalist William Henry Leeds examined the methodological issues surrounding the correct use of models in contemporary architectural practice. One essay considered how architectural models were tools to assist architects in comprehending the appearance of their proposed buildings prior to construction. According to Leeds, one benefit to their use was their legibility for viewers 'who are not conversant with geometrical designs'.[9] This advice, however, came with a warning. Despite appearing to be 'the most certain guide of all', models had the potential to mislead:

> [The model is] an exact representation of the building, but nothing more: there is no positive scale for the eye, so that either fancy or inclination may exaggerate its dimensions, and bestow upon it an importance the building itself will not possess.[10]

Evidently Wilkins was not the only one concerned about the limitations of models. At the same time, his had an altogether different purpose. Jerdan had noted in the *Literary Gazette* that the artist who visited the model had described how certain portions were covered with sheets of paper. These sheets may have concealed the ends of the model to help Wilkins focus on the design of the central portion of the building, or they may have been used to hide a now-obsolete element of the design from public view.[11] What the article neglects mentioning – and what other descriptions include – is that the model was made with movable components that enabled the testing of different formal arrangements. In a subsequent editorial Jerdan claimed that one of the discrepancies between the illicitly published engraving and the model was due to the variable nature of the object itself. Small domes on the roof of the model were movable, and at several stages 'they had probably been shifted on the model by some ingenious amateur'.[12] FIG. 5

While the feud between Wilkins and Jerdan was initially sparked by the potential (and potential problems) of an architectural model, it soon grew into a more public discussion of issues regarding the authority of the architect. On 4 March 1833, in a letter to yet another newspaper, the *Morning Herald*, Wilkins confronted the claims made by the *Literary Gazette*. Prefiguring Leeds's later suggestions about the reliability of architectural models, Wilkins wrote that the lack of scale or surrounding context in his model made it impossible to judge the proposed building in relation to Trafalgar Square. A site model was therefore commissioned in order to test the situation and to provide an accurate representation of the square for the government and King, who would make the final decision on the project. 'Highly finished', with the existing surrounding buildings depicted, the proposed portion of the model showed the National Gallery 'under all the varieties of position'. Wilkins requested in his *Morning Herald* letter that the press, and particularly Jerdan, wait until this new model was completed ('about three weeks'), 'suspend[ing]

9	William Henry Leeds, 'Modes of Architectural Representation', *Architectural Magazine* 2 (October 1835), 452–59, here: 453.	
10	Leeds, 'Modes of Architectural Representation', 453.	
11	'Happening to look in when the whole of the model was disclosed, I objected to the ends [of the proposed National Gallery] as unnecessarily weak and flimsy. After some discussion, I was informed that those ends were not decided on; that in consequence of various remarks, Mr Wilkins had consented to alter them; and further, that sheets of blotting paper, *(which somehow were then removed,)* had been placed over those ends *by Mr Wilkins himself*. To prevent further criticism on that point, and to tally with Mr. Wilkins' intention, the papers were immediately *(in my presence)* replaced.' 'Fine Arts: The National Gallery', *Literary Gazette* (16 March 1833), 171, n.*.	
12	'Fine Arts: The National Gallery', 176.	

your judgement on this point, which is a simple question of taste'.[13] Wilkins was referring to the descriptions of his 'low and beautiful Greek structure', a design that had been deemed inappropriate for the constraints and prominence of the site, the environmental conditions of London, and aesthetically inconsistent alongside the neighbouring eighteenth-century church of St Martin-in-the-Fields, already a significant monument in the city. With this plea, the architect was making the distinction between moral authority and technical authority. Unlike aesthetic judgements around taste, open to interpretation across the wider public, Wilkins argued that his authority was derived from professional expertise in the application of knowledge – in this case how to use an architectural model to design a building.

Unlike the first model, displayed to a select audience in a government building, this second model, made by Richard Day, was first exhibited to the public in February and March 1834 at the popular National Gallery of Practical Science (or Adelaide Gallery), not far from the actual site at Trafalgar Square.[14] The exhibition included a selection of other scientific and mechanical models by Day in the gallery's Long Room.[15] FIG. 6 While the National Gallery site model no longer survives, a plan accompanying Wilkins's letter in the *Athenaeum* shows two options for the alignment of the facade: one, Wilkins's proposal, angled to reveal the portico of St Martin-in-the-Fields; the other parallel to the square. FIG. 7

FIG. 6   Thomas Kearnan, Gallery of Practical Science, Adelaide Street, Strand, engraving, 1834

13   'New National Gallery and St. Martin's Church', *Morning Herald* (4 March 1833), 3.
14   The National Gallery of Practical Science was housed on the north side of the Lowther Arcade, a shopping passage built by John Nash on the north side of the western end of the Strand in 1831. Popularly known as the Adelaide Gallery (or Royal Adelaide Gallery), the Long Room (the main hall) was primarily used for the display of various scientific and mechanical models. Altick, *The Shows of London,* 375–89
15   The second model was prepared in February 1833 and exhibited in August 1833 when Wilkins wrote to one of his supporters, the politician Thomas Spring Rice, to invite him to inspect the second model. William Wilkins, letter to Board of Trustees, 10 September 1833, National Gallery [NG], 5/18/4.

THE ATHENÆUM.

from Pall Mall he will not see it at all. Surely, Mr. Jerdan, half a portico is better than no portico, as half a loaf is said to be better than no bread—a maxim, the truth of which you may live to verify, if your journal be not conducted with more regard to candour, honesty, and veracity.

"Vitruvius, whom, by-the-bye, he translated, and *so propagated his errors,* knew, *he assures us,* little more than a *goose* about building." This expression is not mine, but yours. If I had said that he knew little more about building than you, Mr. *Jerdan,* your expression and mine would have been much more easily reconcileable. Far from propagating the errors of Vitruvius, the aim of my translation is to separate them from such parts of his system as are in conformity with Grecian principles; but Mr. Jerdan, consistent in his practice of looking at nothing, has never looked into the work he mentions.

"Such is the architect's devotedness to the Greek architecture, that he maintains the expediency of making everything else yield to it ....and, in short, that there is nothing good but the pure Greek, according to which he is resolved to frame our British Gallery." If Mr. Jerdan had understood anything of Greek architecture, and had inspected the model, he would have observed some departures, and important ones, from the pure Greek: amongst others, he would have seen archways which are not of Grecian origin; but circumstances call for their introduction, and I have *yielded* to the demand. He would have observed that the building has so much resemblance with all those in the neighbourhood as to be surmounted by a parapet and ballusters; a termination that is certainly not pure Greek. He would have seen that it has a dome, which, in fact, is not Greek at all!!!

I shall end with Mr. Jerdan by recommending him to abstain from the mention of all such subjects as he is ignorant of: but, as this advice might confine his remarks within narrow limits, let him indulge in that portion of his pursuits where his ready praise of the publications of his bookselling patrons brings him certain emolument without risk; there is no danger in puffing or praising, if he steers clear of comparisons; but he will run great hazard when, as on the present occasion, he writes in ignorance of his subject: silence here is good policy; and I dismiss him with a golden rule, couched in homely language—"Eat your pudding, Sir, and hold your tongue!"

I have to entreat your indulgence, Mr. Editor, for the length to which these replies have led me. It is rather hard that I, who have abused nobody but a man who has been dead these thousand years, should be the object of personal attack. I had, indeed, expected to be assailed by the small fry of criticism, and I had made up my mind not to notice anonymous attacks; but if I had suffered the uncandid assertions of one who has erected himself into the championship of the Fine Arts, to pass unheeded, especially as the editor of a journal has the weapons in his own hands, and the power of relating the conflict in his own way, they might have been received as unanswerable.

Secure of the grounds on which I stand, I should feel no hesitation in answering the candid criticisms of any acknowledged writer, if I considered his reasoning or his arguments of sufficient force to attract attention, and to influence the hesitating portion of mankind; but I do not court controversy, and when I feel myself called upon to reply, it is with extreme repugnance. Anonymous criticism affords to the cowardly and the base the opportunity of uttering calumnies with impunity: to answer such would be to debase myself to the level of the calumniator. When attacks are personal, and conducted in a spirit of overweening assurance, I feel myself sufficiently strong to measure weapons with my antagonists, without fear of the result. As to the vanity I displayed in the letter I first addressed to you, I acknowledge myself to be guilty of the charge to any extent it may please anonymous writers to assume or assert.

I remain, Sir, your obedient servant,
WILLIAM WILKINS.
Weymouth Street, Feb. 26, 1833.

SITE OF THE PROPOSED NATIONAL GALLERY.

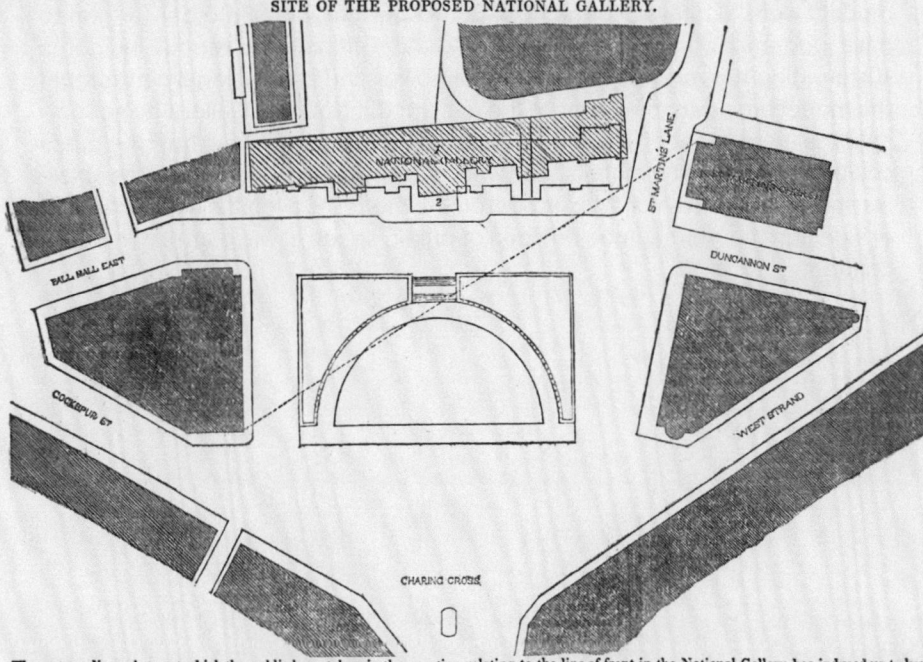

The extraordinary interest which the public have taken in the question relating to the line of front in the National Gallery, has induced us to have an engraving made of the site and neighbourhood. The ground plan, No. 1, marked in shadow, shows the *original* line of front, which extends obliquely from the east end of Pall Mall to the *northern* extremity of the portico of St. Martin's Church: that marked No. 2, in outline, shows the *proposed* line, which extends from the same point to the *southern* extremity of the portico. Whoever shall attentively consider these plans in reference merely to the general effect of the buildings, must, we think, agree with us, that the *proposed* line would be a great improvement. At the same time, it must be admitted, that other and important circumstances ought to be considered before the question is finally determined. We are of opinion, that many of the objections urged against the proposed line are founded on a mistaken feeling of personal interests; still, the interests of individuals ought not to be lost sight of. For ourselves, we are decided, that, whether the north or south pillar of the portico be determined on as the limit to the east end of the Gallery, the building must be *parallel to the proposed line*: if the architect cannot be permitted to advance beyond the north column of the portico, then the western extremity of the building *must be thrown back*, in a proportionate degree. There can be no serious objection to this change, and it would, we believe, conciliate all parties. It might, indeed, be necessary to remove a small portion of the Barrack, which, at the western end, abuts upon the site; but, the expense of this would be so trifling, as to be wholly unworthy a second thought.

Built with adjustable or alternative parts to demonstrate these two possible alignments, this model, unlike the inaccurate elevation reproduced in the *Literary Gazette*, was the instrument through which accurate assessment could be made regarding 'the proportionate magnitude' of a proposal for one of the most prominent urban spaces in London, emphasized by the fact that Trafalgar Square was also a key site of mass demonstration in the nineteenth century.[16] Despite the importance of popular politics the ultimate decision for the building's design required royal endorsement. Following their public debut, Wilkins's models and plans were presented at St James's Palace to King William IV, who approved the original and first alignment, indicated by his signature on the ground plan drawing.[17]

What these public and formal presentations highlight are the numerous levels at which an architectural model operates in the process of judgement.[18] Initially the two architectural models with their adjustable portions allowed Wilkins to examine the composition of the facade and the position of the building line in relation to the context. But the architect was not the only viewer. Unlike 'flat' drawings, which are less legible to non-specialists, the two models allowed the press to publicly weigh in prior to the building's construction. Second, in chorus with a series of orthogonal drawings, the models were displayed to the King in two permutations in order for him to pass judgement on the designs. Finally, underpinning the various incidents surrounding the models is the political power and professional control that the model provided to Wilkins. In the case of the National Gallery, he not only held the instrument of judgement but also dictated when and how the press could interact with the models. And when seeking the support of figures above his socio-political ranks, Wilkins offered the model as a legible demonstration of a design that reimagined the idea of public space at the centre of modern London.

---

16 Dennis, *Cities in Modernity*, 163–5.
17 'Our Weekly Gossip on Literature and Art', *Athenaeum*, (14 September 1833), 619.
18 National Gallery, principal floor plans, September 1833, National Archives [TNA], WORK 33/910.

COMPETITIONS AND THE PURSUIT OF TRUTH

While Royal patronage was never completely removed as a source of architectural commissions it was slowly replaced by open or limited competitions, which became the main mode of procurement for public buildings in Britain.[19] From public fountains to church altars, museums to law courts, the competition system was ad hoc, informal, and the favoured solution for new buildings and monuments in British cities. Despite its contingent nature, a competition was also the general public's preference for civic buildings because it appeared to be the fairest (and often cheapest) way of obtaining the best possible design.[20] During this time competitions were almost daily affairs, with modern historians estimating the announcement of at least one per week from the 1840s, a rate which would double by the end of the nineteenth century.[21]

The exact nature and form of the competition process was documented and debated by the architectural and building press. One attempt to institute a system came in the form of a report by an investigative committee on competitions, established by the RIBA in 1838. The report proposed that in the process of selecting an architect by competition, a 'correctly made' perspective drawing from pre-determined viewpoints, rather than a model, could depict the effects of proposed designs and therefore held primacy in the judgement of an architectural scheme.[22] By restricting the perspective drawing to specific points of view, the committee was trying to establish a framework for making objective assessments. In the eyes of the committee, architectural models came with a caution: they were not 'unexceptional tests' of the quality of a proposed design. Many architects reflected on this issue. One, Henry Austin, proposed a series of measures to regulate competitions that included standardised rules, the public exhibition of entries, and the employment of RIBA members as impartial judges.[23] In addition to these regulations, Austin noted that rendered perspective views would be prohibited and 'models would be[come] unnecessary' as 'all useful information' would be provided to the judges more directly.[24] A different article questioned whether drawings *or* models could ever communicate the merits of a design before construction, and if their 'prettiness' distracted from the 'truth' of the design itself.[25]

In the Victorian era, there was a wide-held belief that truth existed and that the mind could discover it.[26] Through a commitment to the concept of absolutism, it was thought that this truth – whether in politics, ethics, history,

---

19 For the best synopsis of this see: Barry Bergdoll, 'Competing in the Academy and the Marketplace: European Architecture Competitions, 1401–1927', in Helene Lipstadt and Barry Bergdoll, eds., *The Experimental Tradition: Essays on Competitions in Architecture* (New York: Princeton Architectural Press, 1989), 21–52, here: 38–44.

20 Geoffrey Tyack, *Sir James Pennethorne and the Making of Victorian London* (Cambridge: Cambridge University Press, 1992); Michael Port, *Imperial London: Civil Government Buildings in London 1851–1915* (New Haven: Yale University Press, 1995), 161–5.

21 Roger Harper, *Victorian Architectural Competitions: An Index to British and Irish Architectural Competitions in The Builder 1843–1900* (London: Mansell, 1983).

22 'Extract from a Report of the Committee appointed to consider the subject of Public Competitions for Architectural Designs. Laid before the Special General Meeting, held 24th January 1839', *Civil Engineer and Architect's Journal* [*CEAJ*] 2 (May 1839), 183.

23 Henry Austin, *Thoughts on the Abuses of the Present System of Competition in Architecture* (London: John Weale, 1839), 14–17.

24 Austin, *Thoughts on the Abuses of the Present System*, 22.

25 'On the Modern Practice of Competitions', *CEAJ* 6 (December 1843), 433.

26 Walter E. Houghton, *The Victorian Frame of Mind: 1830–1870* (New Haven: Yale University Press, 1985), 14–19.

economics, or art – was governed by universal laws or principles. Regarding a collected edition of Alfred Tennyson's poems published in 1855, one writer describes the mid-nineteenth century as a moment when 'the whole life of the individual, and the collective life of humanity [were] traceable to the orderly operation of fixed principles'.[27] In reality these principles were more complicated and changeable than they seemed. Historical studies of the British legal system, for instance, suggest a complex relationship with the construction of truth within society where, within the courtroom, following a series of amendments to the law of evidence, the final step towards the pursuit of legal and moral truth was the adoption of a single engine of truth in the form of cross-examination.[28]

From the viewpoint of various scientific disciplines, the veracity of truth was less clear. At the heart of nineteenth-century science was a disjuncture between the appearance and reality of the material world.[29] In a similar manner to their legal colleagues, many scientists tried to bridge this gap through standardized practices. The development of reliable common standards of measurement held the key to advances in economic, political, and scientific knowledge and were one of several instruments used to examine and uncover scientific truth.[30] The struggle for truth was greater in emerging branches, such as photography. On the occasion of solar eclipses of 1836, 1842, and 1851, the medium was termed a 'process by which natural phenomena registered their own images, and therefore its fundamental validity seemed to be beyond question'.[31] However, the authentication of claims for truth and knowledge did not end with the production of a photograph. When applied to meteorology, the interpretation of a photograph still required an experienced eye to make a series of judgements. Despite technical advances, authority, it seemed, lay in the observation and interpretation of principles.[32]

These contemporary discussions were echoed in the fine arts, not least by John Ruskin, who in the first volume of *Modern Painters* (1843) defined truth as separate from imitation. Where imitation could only be material, he wrote, 'truth has reference to statements both of the qualities of material things and of emotions, impressions, and thoughts'.[33] Ruskin proposed that the greatest distinction between the ideas of truth and imitation lay in the transmission of these concepts to the mind. Truth, he believed, was communicated through objects that allowed the mind to consider its own conception of facts, forms, and feelings while simultaneously being able to disregard 'the signs or symbols by which the notion of it has been conveyed'. The medium through which messages were transferred was vital, as 'it is that message which the mind takes from them and dwells upon, regardless of the language in which it is delivered'.

27 George Brimley, 'Tennyson's Poems', *Essays* (London: Macmillan, 1858), 85–95.
28 John Kucich, *The Power of Lies: Transgression in Victorian Fiction* (Ithaca, NY: Cornell University Press, 1994); Wendie Ellen Schneider, *Engines of Truth: Producing Veracity in the Victorian Courtroom* (New Haven: Yale University Press, 2015), here: 48–53.
29 George Levine, 'Defining Knowledge: An Introduction', in Bernard Lightman, ed., *Victorian Science in Context* (Chicago: University of Chicago Press, 1997), 15–23, here: 18.
30 Simon Schaffer, 'Metrology, Metrication, and Victorian Values', in Lightman, ed., *Victorian Science in Context*, 438–74, here: 440.
31 Jan Golinski, *Making Natural Knowledge: Constructivism and the History of Science*, 2nd ed. (Cambridge: Cambridge University Press, 2005), 134.
32 Jennifer Tucker, 'Photography as Witness, Detective, and Imposter. Visual Representation in Victorian Science', in Lightman, ed., *Victorian Science in Context*, 378–408, here: 388.
33 John Ruskin, *Modern Painters*, vol. 1 (1843), 24–5, quoted in Charles Harrison, Paul Wood, and Jason Gaiger, eds., *Art in Theory, 1815–1900: An Anthology of Changing Ideas* (Oxford: Wiley-Blackwell, 2001), 200–1.

By 1840 issues around truth were manifesting more concretely in the competition for a new building at the heart of the City of London. The 3 June 1840 edition of the *Globe*, a mainstream newspaper, carried an anonymous letter that described the benefits of the uses of models in design as proposed by important European architectural theorists such as Leon Battista Alberti and Antoine-Chrysostôme Quatremère de Quincy, and the practice of historical architects including Michelangelo, Christopher Wren, and Claude Perrault. The letter concluded by declaring:

> In truth the model is a troublesome and expensive preliminary that exposes those architects to impertinent criticisms, and puts an end to that suspense and curiosity in which it is in their interest to keep the public mind – till it is too late to alter and amend, and the percentage is duly received.[34]

Absent is any mention of aesthetic judgement, often the main subject of public debate in the construction of new building. In its place is the invocation of methodological precedent, from the great architects of Renaissance and Enlightenment Europe to a domestic tradition represented by Wren. For the author a model clearly acts as a means to police the power placed on architects when designing buildings in the public sphere.

The letter was published in response to the result of a now infamous competition for a new Royal Exchange in the City of London – the previous building had been destroyed by fire in January 1838. One twentieth-century historian has described the competition as 'a fiasco which probably did more than anything else to discredit the system of public competitions for the rest of the nineteenth century'.[35] With the loss of the original building seen as potentially catastrophic for trade in the city, a building committee was formed with members from the local government and the Worshipful Company of Mercers, the livery company (trade association) historically responsible for the import of fabric. Despite the potential complexity caused by involving two different parties in the selection process, the chairman of the building committee resolved that the design of the new Royal Exchange would be procured by an open competition.[36] The new building was to be located on the site of the previous one, to the east of the Bank of England at the heart of the City of London.[37] Whereas the previous building had entrance porticos on both north and south elevations to face the two main thoroughfares of Threadneedle Street and Cornhill, the facade of the new Royal Exchange would look to the west. Through compulsory purchases of various properties to the east and the demolition of old bank buildings to the west, the site was extended to form an irregular oblong of 302 × 168 feet, with the streets on either side widened to account for the increase in road traffic in central London. FIG. 8

---

34   'New Royal Exchange', *Globe* (3 June 1840) in John Eastly Goodchild, 'Reminiscences of my Twenty-six Years Association with the late Professor C. R. Cockerell, with a supplement of the late F. P. Cockerell Esq., to 1879' [Reminiscences], VOL/77, f. 53, Royal Institute of British Architects [RIBA].

35   Barrington Kaye, *The Development of the Architectural Profession in England: A Sociological Study* (London: George Allen & Unwin, 1960), 111.

36   Minute of meeting, 4 January 1839, Gresham Committee [GC], Mercers' Company [MC], London.

37   Important histories on the destruction and rebuilding of the Royal Exchange include: David Watkin, *The Life and Work of C. R. Cockerell* (London: Zwemmer, 1974), 207–10; Joan Bassin, *Architectural Competitions in Nineteenth-Century England* (Ann Arbor: UMI Research Press, 1984), 42–7; Michael Port, 'Destruction, Competition and Rebuilding: The Royal Exchange, 1838–1884', in Ann Saunders, ed., *The Royal Exchange* (London: London Topographical Society, 1997), 286–93; Salmon, *Building on Ruins*, 189–209; Matthew Wells, 'Architectural Models and the Rebuilding of the Royal Exchange, 1839–1844', *Architectural History* 60 (2017), 219–41.

By the end of March 1839, the building committee had decided the rules of the competition. Each entry had to submit a set of orthographic drawings alongside two perspectives: an exterior view from the west and a courtyard interior. The competition particulars went on to state that entrants should not submit a 'model, sketch, perspective, or coloured drawing', and a deadline was set for 1 August 1839.[38] Various individuals and institutions raised concerns about the timeframe of the competition process.[39] Thomas Hopper, an architect who had been narrowly defeated in earlier competitions for public works, used the occasion to publish a pamphlet on the competition process that called for all shortlisted entries to be modelled.[40] Several architectural writers agreed and suggested that in a design competition all models should be made to the same scale and accompanied with a perspective view in order to show the appearance of the building in relation to the site.[41]

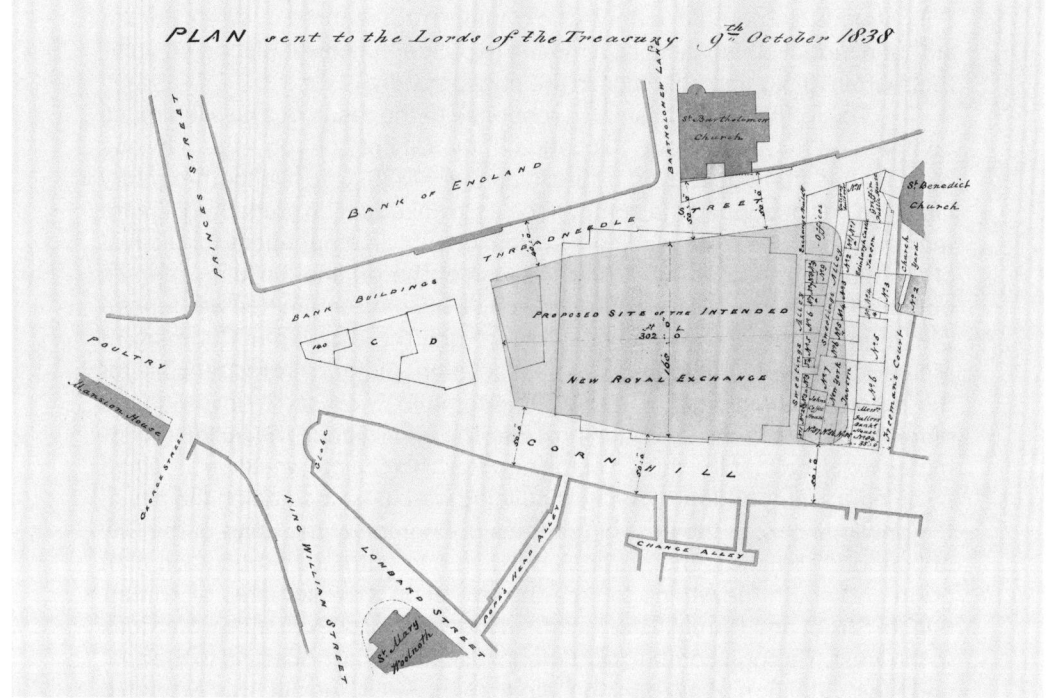

FIG. 8 George Smith, Site plan for the Royal Exchange Competition, 9 October 1838

38   Minute of meeting, 26 March 1839, GC, MC.
39   Minute of meeting, 24 April 1839, GC, MC; 'Paper Read by W. Tite, Esq., President of the Architectural Society, at the Last Soiree of the Season, 1839', *CEAJ* 2 (July 1839), 242–3.
40   Thomas Hopper, *A Letter to Lord Viscount Melbourne on the Rebuilding of the Royal Exchange* (London: John Weale, 1839).
41   'Reviews: A Letter to Lord Viscount Melbourne on the Rebuilding of the Royal Exchange. By Thomas Hopper, Architect', *CEAJ* 2 (April 1839), 143.

FIG. 9   Charles Robert Cockerell, View of courtyard, Competition entry for the Royal Exchange, lithograph by G. Moore, 1838

After the first stage of the competition, when prizes were awarded for two classes of winners but no overall recommendation for the commission was given, the committee asked six architects to submit a new design.[42] Confusingly the shortlist for the second attempt at a competition consisted of three of the original judges, Robert Smirke, Philip Hardwick, and Joseph Gwilt, alongside one of the original entrants, Charles Robert Cockerell, and two new architects, William Tite and Charles Barry. All declined the invitation except Tite, who suggested to Cockerell that they should collaborate as they had done in 1837 at the nearby London and Westminster Bank building.[43] Cockerell rejected the offer but Tite was not dissuaded, and in early 1840 the committee set a limited competition between the two architects.[44] According to his assistant John Eastly Goodchild, Cockerell accepted the challenge on the understanding that a new design would not be required. Instead he would prepare a 'model to a good scale' to supplement his proposed drawings.[45]

FIG. 9 On 28 April 1840 the Joint Gresham Committee received drawings and accompanying reports from both architects. Cockerell had sent eleven drawings to the committee and invited its members to inspect his model, 'explanatory of my design', at his office located close to the Mercers' Hall, at 20 Old Jewry in the City of London.[46] During the same meeting a letter from Tite was

42   Minute of meeting, 3 February 1840, GC, MC.
43   Goodchild, 'Reminiscences', f. 42.
44   *Royal Exchange: Extracts and Reports*, 'Proceedings', minute of a meeting, 11 February 1840, CLA/062/04/019, London Metropolitan Archives [LMA].
45   Examining the minutes of the committee meetings, it is less clear that Cockerell's intention to demonstrate the merits of his competition design through a model was as clear as Goodchild indicated. Goodchild, 'Reminiscences', ff. 42–3.
46   Minute of meeting, letter from C. R. Cockerell, 28 April 1840, GC, MC.

read, which questioned the validity of models as an accurate form of representation in a competition for a public building:

> The mode, sometimes adopted, of exhibiting an architect's intentions by a model was prohibited in this instance by the instructions of the committee. I do not complain of this, for models are said to raise expectations that are rarely realised.[47]

In response the committee allowed Tite and Cockerell to attend the next meeting, on 4 May 1840, to present their designs in person. Cockerell's report, which he read at the meeting, provides a clear indication of his belief in the model as a valid mode of representation:

> I am sorry that it is not convenient to offer these explanations with the model before us ... during the interval allowed, I thought myself best employed upon that model, because it is certain that no drawings however complete or numerous could convey all those relations and reflections which a model at once presents to the eye and understanding.[48]

These comments reveal the extent to which Cockerell relied on the model as a design tool for himself and as a method of communication to others. Significantly he argued that the model conveyed more information than a complete body of drawings, as the different parts of the proposed design can be shown relative to one another as a whole.

Unfortunately, the model itself did not survive. However, reports describe that it was fabricated in timber at a scale of half an inch to one foot (1:24), stood at over 8.5 metres in length, and cost £400 in total – £24,000 in 2021.[49] Raised on a stage at eye level, the internal floor of the courtyard could be removed in order for a viewer to place their head inside and 'walk about it from end to end'.[50] The ornamental parts were cast in plaster by the sculptor W.H.G. Nicholl, a collaborator of Cockerell's on other projects including St George's Hall in Liverpool, who added little wax figures in the niches to represent the free-standing sculptural decoration. Alongside Cockerell's own design, the existing streets and buildings of the city had been modelled, enabling not only 'the spectator to judge of its relation to all the surrounding buildings',[51] but also the architect to respond to criticism in the architectural press about the lack of representative information.[52] The model was also in line with the theoretical position advanced by W.H. Leeds in 1835, which advocated modelling a proposal's surrounding buildings as well as positioning the model at eye level in order to offer viewers the opportunity for accurate visual judgement.[53]

Again, in early May, Cockerell requested that the committee members come to view the model, and it subsequently came to light that most had carried out their inspections on unofficial visits to his office. After a protracted discussion and heated debate Tite was declared the winner of the run-off competition. Cockerell wrote several letters contesting the result and later that same month petitioned the committee in person.[54] In order to test the relative merits of the two designs, he argued that the committee should

---

47 Minute of meeting, letter from William Tite, 28 April 1840, GC, MC.
48 Charles Robert Cockerell, 'Report to the Committee of the Gresham Trustees for carrying into execution the rebuilding of the Royal Exchange in London, 4 May 1840', CoC/3/16, RIBA.
49 Goodchild, 'Reminiscences', f.43.
50 Goodchild, 'Reminiscences', f.43.
51 William Henry Leeds, 'Article III: The New Royal Exchange', *Westminster Review* 35 (January 1841), 58–88, here: 66.
52 'Royal Exchange', *CEAJ* 2 (May 1839), 173.
53 Leeds, 'Modes of Architectural Representation', 453.
54 Minute of meeting, 14 May 1840; 10 June 1840, GC, MC.

instruct Tite to prepare a model at the same scale as his own. Two members spoke in support of Cockerell, advising that 'a model was the best test, as it displayed defects as well as perfections', while another denied the necessity of a model in either situation, arguing that Tite's drawings 'most fully described the merits of the designs'.[55] Seeing as the committee could not agree on the potential benefits of architectural models, it was unlikely that the public would either, but the disagreement was far from finished.

FIG. 10 William Tite, 'New Royal Exchange – View of the western front', lithograph, May 1840

FIG. 11 'Birds eye view of the Royal Exchange & Bank', anonymous cartoon, lithograph, June 1840, published by J. T. Wood

55   'New Royal Exchange', *Morning Chronicle* (22 May 1840), 4.

During the summer of 1840 the debate about the validity of architectural models progressed from the Royal Exchange building committee room to the popular press with letters and editorials in the *Globe,* the *Morning Chronicle*, and *The Times* assessing the issues at hand. According to W. H. Leeds the chairman of the committee had described how 'all the best authorities [were] opposed to models', and that a builder – a friend whose experience he trusted – had seen the model and assured him 'it was a complete deception'.[56] Despite Cockerell's appeals to various committees and groups, at the end of September 1840 Tite was formally awarded the commission for the new Royal Exchange. His winning perspective of the portico was engraved and published throughout the professional and popular press, eliciting more outrage over the result of the competition. FIG. 10 Cartoonists ridiculed the supposed defects of the design, making drawings with contrived viewpoints that exaggerated the shallowness of the portico. FIG. 11 The portico was also a contentious subject for Leeds, whose long-form essay explained how the perspective was constructed with a vanishing point that provided a flat-on view of the portico and which concealed its lack of depth.[57] Where models had been criticized for potentially misleading viewers, it was in fact a drawing technique that had been deliberately used to deceive. He went on to suggest that future competitions for public buildings be judged solely by architects and based only on drawings. If judges had difficulty choosing between two designs of equal merit, competitors should be asked to produce a model, for which they would be paid, whether successful or not. Leeds proposed that despite the expensive and time-consuming nature of model-making, there was an objective truth to models that was often absent in drawings, which in themselves could conceal unsuccessful elements by the careful selection of vanishing points.

At precisely the same time that Leeds's essay was circulating, Tite was instructed by the building committee to consider alterations in response to criticism regarding the shallowness of the portico. The possibility for these revisions arose when the committee decided to divide the construction work into two separate contracts: one for the excavation and foundations, and the other for the rest of the building.[58] To save on construction costs the area underneath the proposed portico was excluded from the excavations. This allowed time, while the ground workers were on site, for the portico design to be more fully considered. Tite responded, returning to the committee in January 1841 with an architectural model of his design. Now the portico was deeper and included an additional row of columns in order to improve 'the effect of the building ... with reference to the surrounding objects'.[59] In the process of revising the design Tite seems to have experienced a change of heart. Six months earlier, he had asserted that models created unrealistic expectations of an architect's design, but now he saw a role for the model in the communication of a design and its effects to others. Unlike the perspectival drawings submitted in competition, the model offered an opportunity for a building to be examined at an urban scale.

In the following months the new model was examined in different areas of the public sphere. First, it was exhibited at a *conversazione* of the Architectural Society, an organization dedicated to promoting the profession through public meetings, where it received 'considerable praise and

56 Leeds, 'Article III', 67.
57 Leeds, 'Article III', 80.
58 *Royal Exchange*, 'Proceedings', 16 October 1840.
59 *Royal Exchange*, 'Proceedings', 15 January 1840.

attraction'.⁶⁰ Made at the same scale as Cockerell's model, half an inch to the foot, Tite's included carved details of the proposed capitals of the columns and pilasters, the depth and form of niches, and the shaping of various ornamental mouldings on the facade. Produced in plaster by Richard Day, the same model-maker who worked on the site model for the National Gallery, Tite's model shows the portico with an extra column, the corner arrangement, and one bay of the building's southern flank.⁶¹ FIG. 12 At the *conversazione*, the physical, textual, and visual products of the architectural profession were presented as evidence of architectural and cultural achievement and sophistication – and, equally, the capacity of architecture itself to cultivate. For an urban public these events were moments when London reflected on both the present condition of its built environment and the possibilities for change. Tite's model of the portico, removed from the context of the committee meeting, ceased to be a revision of a past design and instead acted as a mediator between present and future, a rhetorical device capable of moving between notions of idea and building, or of decision and form.

FIG. 12   Richard Day (model-maker), William Tite (architect), model of the portico of the Royal Exchange, c. 1840

60   The aim of the Architectural Society, founded in 1831, was to advance architectural knowledge, and it held the long-term ambition of establishing a school of architecture. Several members donated models and casts to the society, where Tite held the presidency from 1838 until its union with the RIBA in 1842. 'Architectural Society', *CEAJ* 4 (4 June 1841), 237.

61   Day probably met Tite through his association with the Architectural Society where, in January 1834, he exhibited 'numerous models'. 'Architectural Society', *The Gentleman's Magazine* 1 (February 1834), 209.

FIG. 13   Thomas Allom, *Prince Albert Laying the Foundation Stone of the Third Royal Exchange*, lithograph, 1842

FIG. 14   'The Queen's Drawing Room – Her Majesty Inspecting Mr Tite's Models of the New Royal Exchange', *Illustrated London News* (9 November 1844), 292

In addition to professional interest there was also public curiosity about the model that had come to represent a significant new monument for London. Several writers and journalists observed its absence from the Royal Academy Exhibition, the premier artistic exhibition in British society.[62] However, the model took on a significant ceremonial role before construction was complete. On 17 January 1842, beneath a large fabric canopy designed by Tite and illuminated by candlelight, Prince Albert laid the foundation stone for the new Royal Exchange. Prior to the ceremony, Tite had presented him with two models of the new building.[63] It is clear from a lithograph of the event that one of these was the portico model, while the other appears to have been a model of the east-facing elevation with its two towers. FIG. 13 According to newspaper reports, the exhibition of both models 'excited general admiration', albeit an admiration that was generated by a very particular public dynamic: ceremonies such as the laying of a foundation stone were part of a broader range of large-scale urban events involving crowds, which helped construct ideas of social unity.[64] Models signalled this construction in their performative role as proxies for the building under construction. In turn the witnessing of the model, blessed by the prince, was further acknowledged by the gathering crowd.

Tite's models appeared once more when Queen Victoria officially opened the new Royal Exchange at a large-scale public ceremony and banquet in October 1844.[65] Following a procession across London from Buckingham Palace to the new building, the Queen and Prince Albert were received by the Lord Mayor of London and various dignitaries in a reception room. In this space, positioned on either side of the room's mantelpiece, were two further models given by Tite to the Queen: one of the east end of the Exchange and the other of the quadrangle.[66] Neither appears to have survived, but they are visible in a lithograph of the event published in the *Illustrated London News*.[67] FIG. 14 Judging from the image, they were similar in scale to the portico model. There is no mention of any additional models commissioned by the client or architect, nor do accounts of the opening ceremony note any specific payment for models. With no evidence that the models were connected to the design or construction process, it seems reasonable to presume that they were produced only after the building was finished (at least externally). Unlike the portico model, which survives, these two models do not allow the viewer to comprehend something previously unknown. They are instead performative objects for display, allowing the building to be consumed all at once by an audience of those in the room and those of the newspaper's readership.

The medium of public opinion – the press – was expanding the public sphere beyond the physical environs of London itself, enabling architectural models and their content to move from one place to another, one situation to another, one context to another. Discussions surrounding the present and future of the built environment of Victorian London continued. A second, highly significant competition was the one held for the new Law Courts in early 1866. Due to an expansion of both paperwork and road traffic,

---

62 'Architectural Drawings, Royal Academy', *CEAJ* 4 (4 July 1841), 232.
63 'New Royal Exchange', *Observer* (17 January 1842), 3.
64 'The Ceremony of Laying the First Stone of the New Royal Exchange by Prince Albert', *The Ipswich Journal* (22 January 1842), 1; Mark Harrison, *Crowds and History: Mass Phenomena in English Towns, 1790–1835* (Cambridge: Cambridge University Press, 2002), 170–1.
65 There are various accounts of the occasion. See, for example: 'Opening of the New Royal Exchange', *Illustrated London News* (2 November 1844), 276–85.
66 'Opening of the New Royal Exchange by Her Majesty', *Chelmsford Chronicle* (1 November 1844), 2.
67 'The New Royal Exchange', *Illustrated London News* (9 November 1844), 291–3, here: 292.

the physical separation of courts and counsel between Westminster and the Inns of Court became highly inconvenient for the legal community. By the 1860s a new building was required to provide a vast central complex of courts close to the heart of London's legal profession. In February 1866 a limited competition was organized by the Office of Works for a new court complex at a site on Carey Street to the north of the Strand. In Spring 1867 eleven architects were shortlisted to display models of their designs alongside plans, sections, perspectives, and 'birdseye views' at 33 Lincoln's Inn Fields, a townhouse owned by the Office of Works and conveniently situated near the proposed site.[68] At the competition stage only two architects used models to describe their proposals. One, Henry Bayley Garling, provided a model of unknown size, scope, and material (although it must have been useful as it was referred to several times in his report).[69] A second architect, John Pollard Seddon, submitted an architectural model alongside his drawings for the competition.[70] FIG. 15 Similar to events with the National Gallery, the majority of the architectural press used the model to critique Seddon's design. However, one journal felt differently. After declaring the new Law Courts to be the most important public building in London since the Palace of Westminster competition (1835), the *Building News* described the significance of Seddon's choice to produce a model alongside the competition drawings of his proposal.[71] A week later the same journal considered whether all competitors should submit models:

> To the uninitiated public a model is always attractive, because it affords them an opportunity of forming some sort of judgement, without having to undergo the horrible task of trying to make out the relation of the several plans, elevations, and sections.[72]

But this time around the display of models was not just for the benefit of the uninitiated public; it would afford all the competitors an 'equal chance with the public and non-professional judges'.[73] This can be seen in contemporary photographs of Seddon's model, which enabled the building to be judged in relation to the competition brief. These photographs show an irregular Neo-Gothic complex with a sawtooth range of offices around the perimeter and a series of vast pitched towers containing various juridical departments and bureaucracies. Carved from white plaster and dramatically lit, the model depicted the current urban situation while offering a striking formal response to the complex demands of the programme. Its base, for instance, was carved to show the topography of the site as it sloped down to the Thames, and a colonnade wrapped around the building at street level to address the pedestrian traffic. However, the report of the surveyors appointed by the Office of Works judged that Seddon's scheme unquestionably would not fit on the extent of the site – a fact evident in the block plan that accompanied the competition entry.

---

68 'Courts of Justice Commission: Instructions for the Competing Architects', WORK 12/33/1, 12 (no. 119), TNA.
69 In his report, however, Garling made reference to the model and its purpose: 'The Detail arrangements of the Courts will be best understood from the Plans and Model.' Henry B. Garling, 'Palace of Justice: Description of Design by H. B. Garling', *New Courts of Justice* (London, 1867), 6.
70 Photographs of this model survive in the RIBA Collection, presumably because of their public display as a part of the Architectural Exhibition in the summer of 1867. 'Four General Views of Model of Building (photographs of designs sent in competition for the New Law Courts)', *Architectural Exhibition Society – Seventeenth Exhibition 1867* (London, 1867), 25, no. 320.
71 'The Designs for the New Courts of Law', *Building News* 14 (18 January 1867), 52.
72 'Courts of Justice Competition', *Building News* 14 (25 January 1867), 57.
73 'Courts of Justice Competition', 57.

THE PUBLIC SPHERE

Following the conclusion of the exhibition and blinded by public scrutiny, in July 1867 the judges announced they were unable to select a winning architect. Instead they decided that Edward Middleton Barry's plan and George Edmund Street's elevation were best. Much like the Royal Exchange fiasco twenty-five years earlier, the judges recommended that the two architects work on the commission together. The government, aware of the potential complexity of this proposal, argued that the decision was not in accord with the rules of the original competition. Architects and newspaper critics attacked the whole competition process, questioning the legality of the award; an independent surveyor evaluated the cost of each architect's design in an attempt to find a point of difference between the two proposals; and the Attorney General was brought in to untangle the legal situation. Ultimately, however, it was another competition that brought an end to the impasse: no winner had been awarded for a contemporary competition to extend the National Gallery with a suite of new exhibition spaces behind Wilkins's original building. With governmental pressure, Barry was appointed the architect of the National Gallery, thereby leaving the new Law Courts commission open for Street.

FIG. 15   John Pollard Seddon, competition entry for the new Law Courts, 1867

A NEW MODEL FOR LONDON

With two key competitions for public buildings at either end of the Strand underway, Parliament debated how to comprehend this rapidly changing portion of London. Throughout Westminster at the end of the 1860s, members of parliament (MPs) and civil servants discussed how architectural models could assist the government and the department responsible, the Office of Works, in the procurement of public buildings. One decade earlier, a new, precisely measured map of London, the 'Ordnance Survey of London and its Environs' (1851), had been a vital technical instrument for studying the city and planning improvements to its sanitation infrastructure.[74] By the 1860s, however, there was a sense that this cartographic view needed to be supplemented by something three-dimensional, a view that combined the accuracy of the Ordnance Survey with aspects of the panorama, enabling detailed representations of individual buildings and thus offering an unfolding narrative of the city's development. In March 1869 a confidential report described the production of a new architectural model of London at a moment when it was believed by Austin Layard, then head of the Office of Works, that 'The Government had to decide upon the erection of a large number of important public buildings than had ever been raised in any capital at one time.'[75] Although now lost, the report's significance is clear in both private documents and parliamentary discussions describing how the model allowed the government and the wider public to examine the many proposed public buildings during this crucial moment of urban expansion. In Parliament, at the first reading of the bill for the land purchase of the proposed Law Courts site, Layard explained he was 'strongly of opinion that no great public building ought to be erected without a model upon a large scale, having first been submitted to the public'.[76] A model, he continued, was the best means to openly display the chosen design to the government, opposition members of parliament, and the broader tax-paying public, 'in order that it might be seen and criticized'.[77]

This idea was emphasized one month later with the display of a drawing of the proposed design by Street in the Library of the House of Commons. When Layard was asked in Parliament whether he approved of the drawing, he reminded the House, 'that the elevation was a mere sketch, and is so called by Mr Street'.[78] Echoing his earlier comments, Layard noted:

> If the House should approve of the erection of the Law Courts on the [Victoria] Embankment he should think it his duty to have a model placed in the Library, or some other part of the House to which Members might have access, and so be able to form an opinion.[79]

Such a model was made and then exhibited in the Library of the House of Commons between May and November 1869. Even after Layard's dismissal from office the model continued to be an important issue for government consideration. In a parting memo Layard again outlined his intention that before 'authorising an architect to proceed with the erection of any important public building … a complete model of such a building' should be submitted to 'public criticism'.[80] This approach would avoid repeating many of

---

74   Lynda Nead, *Victorian Babylon: People, Streets and Images in Nineteenth-Century London* (New Haven: Yale University Press, 2000), 19–22.
75   Austen Henry Layard, 'Confidential Memorandum', 4 November 1869, [1], WORK 22/2/18, TNA.
76   *Hansard's Parliamentary Debates*, House of Commons, 10 May 1869, vol. 196, cc. 538–61.
77   *Hansard's Parliamentary Debates*, House of Commons, 10 May 1869, vol. 196, 538–61.
78   *Hansard's Parliamentary Debates*, House of Commons, 3 June 1869, vol. 196, 1209.
79   *Hansard's Parliamentary Debates*, House of Commons, 3 June 1869, vol. 196, c1210.
80   Layard, 'Confidential Memorandum', [9].

the 'architectural failures that are now seen in the Metropolis'.[81] True to his word, Layard offered 'to give the public a just notion of the effect and position of a new public building, and of any intended Metropolitan improvement' with an urban model of the Embankment from Blackfriars Bridge to the Palace of Westminster. Covering such a large portion of the city, this model could present both the Carey Street site for the new Law Courts and an alternative site, next to Somerset House on the Victoria Embankment, which was proposed by Layard in 1868 and endorsed by sections of the popular press. The model would be 'on a considerable scale' and required consent from the Chancellor of the Exchequer due to its expense.[82] It was later disclosed in Parliament that £2,421 16s. 3d. (some £150,000 in 2021) was spent on the preparation of the plan and model, which Layard himself described:[83]

> This model has been completed under the very able superintendence of Lieutenant Cole, RE. Upon it, nearly every building now standing is represented, and each building can be removed, and can be replaced on the model of any intended new building. I consider this model of permanent use and interest.[84]

That interest was not only reserved for the government or Parliament. A report in the *Building News* explained that the model would be exhibited in the South Kensington Museum, 'to aid in properly disposing of sites for public works'.[85] As a result the model displayed both possible sites for the new Law Courts: Carey Street and the Embankment, with the Embankment site 'occupied by a model of the experimental design of Mr Street'.[86] An entry in the museum catalogue from 1876 notes how the model was made from wood and at a scale of one inch to twenty feet (modern scale 1:240).[87] What goes unmentioned is that the model was displayed in Bethnal Green at the East End branch of the South Kensington Museum, a building which had only opened in 1872 in the working-class district, and which kept evening opening hours to suit the work shifts of its main audience. Accommodating as this was for 'those who desire to make use of it as a ready means of forming a judgement on the proposals made', by the following year sections of the architectural press were frustrated by the model's lack of detail, which Street had offered only in an elevation drawing.[88] In particular the *Builder* claimed the front facade was still unsatisfactory and should have been presented to the public in a larger model.[89] The journal repeated these grievances in March 1872 and May 1873, suggesting further expectation from within the profession for additional models and for Street to present his design for 'public scrutiny' through that very medium.[90] The situation soon became a source of amusement for portions of the profession. A poster for an event at the Architectural Association in 1872 caricatured a number of prominent figures, including James Fergusson and Edward Welby Pugin, spraying a model of Street's design in acid before a blindfolded crowd of architects as Street sits in its shadow. FIG. 16

81 Layard, 'Confidential Memorandum', [9].
82 Layard, 'Confidential Memorandum', [9].
83 *Hansard's Parliamentary Debates*, House of Commons, 20 March 1871, vol. 205, c308.
84 Layard, 'Confidential Memorandum', [9].
85 'Chips', *Building News* 18 (4 February 1870), 100.
86 'Chips', 100.
87 Henry Sandham, *Catalogue of the Collection Illustrating Construction and Building Materials* (London, 1876), 134 Y. Transferred to the Art Division of the Museum in 1873, the model appears to have disappeared when the Structural Collections were disbanded in 1882.
88 'The Model of the Thames Embankment', *Building News* 24 (14 March 1873), 321.
89 'The Proposed Courts of Justice', *Builder* 29 (2 December 1871), 949.
90 'The Designs for the Law Courts', *Builder* 30 (30 March 1872), 237; 'The New Courts of Justice', *Builder* 31 (31 May 1873), 431.

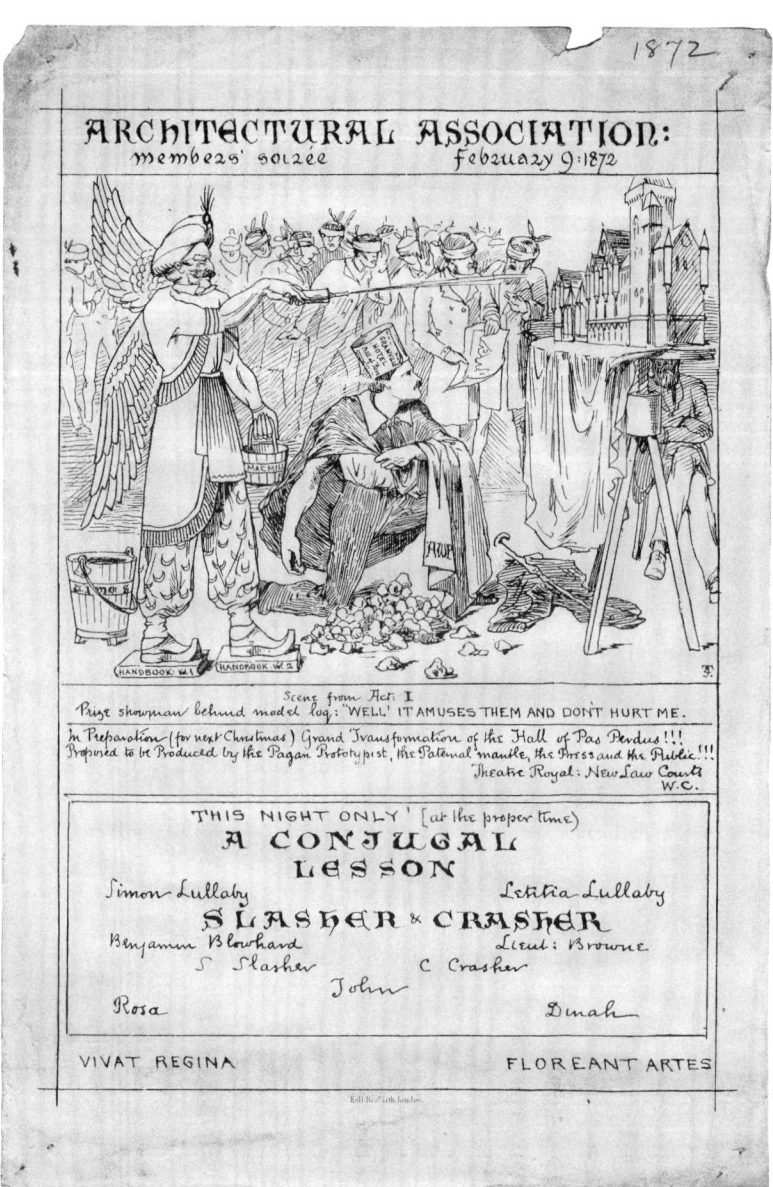

FIG.16 Edward John Tarver, 'A Conjugal Lesson', poster for the Architectural Association Members Soirée, 1872

Street himself saw architectural models as a crucial part of his practice. When designing decorative sculpture and working with stonemasons, he believed that the architect should model all the sculpture or carving in a building.[91] In addition to the urban model produced by the Office of Works, there were also discussions of a second model related to Street's design for the new Law Courts. One review of the building praised the complicated programmatic arrangement of the courts with various intertwined routes of circulation for judges, administrators, lawyers, plaintiffs, and public alongside the integration of modern building services for heating and ventilation. In particular the article described how the vertical and horizontal layout and circulation of the building ('aggroupment and arrangement') should be appreciated by visitors.[92] Earlier, during the competition stage the arrangement of the building's programme was addressed through orthographic drawings and diagrams. FIG. 17 Once Street was awarded the commission the complex hierarchy of various users (judges, barristers, clerks, witnesses, juries, defendants) was designed through models. The government even ordered that 'a specimen court was selected for trial by means of a model' constructed at 'a small scale' alongside 'the adjoining rooms, stairs, corridors, etc'.[93] Though Street explained the model, the press also found that it was

> fully competent to explain itself, was minutely examined by some members of the Government, and particularly by the Chancellor of the Exchequer, by some of the judges, and by other official personages; and in the working of each of its component parts, as also in the combined action of all its parts, the model was unanimously declared to fulfil every requirement in the happiest and most satisfactory manner.[94]

There are several significant aspects to underline here. First, Street used the model to explain his scheme in a manner that orthographic drawings, bound by particular conventions, could not. While other types of drawing, such as axonometric projection, have the ability to demonstrate both the horizontal *and* vertical distribution of various rooms, corridors, and staircases, these forms of drawing appear to have been used in a very limited capacity by architects in nineteenth-century Britain. Developed by civil engineers in the late nineteenth century, the axonometric is a form of representation that allows for multiple components to come together (or be separated) in a single drawing. Presumably the specimen court model fulfilled a similar mechanistic role, as 'the working of each of its component parts' – 'the adjoining rooms, stairs, corridors, etc.' – was shown to operate in 'combined action'. Additionally, while the architect explained the model, it was 'fully competent to explain itself'. In other words, the model rendered Street's arrangement of the programme clearly to an audience from a variety of backgrounds, some with and others without specialist knowledge of the legal system. Finally, the article describes how Street repeated the 'typical court' around the central hall of the courts, 'with certain slight modifications in some instances, such as might be demanded in certain positions on the general plan, and by special conditions of circumstances.'[95] Ultimately the model operated conceptually as

---

91   Street believed it was 'impossible to direct another man [...] by giving drawings [...] and you must learn to give your instructions in the round'. George Edmund Street, 'Study and Practice of Architecture', in Arthur Edmund Street, ed., *Memoir of George Edmund Street, R.A., 1824–1881* (London: John Murray, 1881), 329.

92   'The New Law Courts – II', *Building News* 21 (20 October 1871), 284.

93   'The New Law Courts – II', 285.

94   'The New Law Courts – II', 285.

95   'The New Law Courts – II', 285.

both an authoritative proof of Street's planning of the new Law Courts and a prototypical 'model' to be adapted in the other courtrooms distributed within the complex. This Janus-like possibility neatly encapsulates how models could be used. They not only enabled visual and spatial comprehension for proposed buildings but also provided the concrete means to contest political realities in society, thereby forming part of a new public discourse that shaped the urbanism and architecture of nineteenth-century London. In the public eye, the function and location of architectural models was never fixed but adapted and questioned by politicians and other figures. In many ways, the new Law Courts competition marked the end of the first era of popular politics in British society. With the subsequent expansion of the democratic franchise at the end of the 1860s, the place and potential of architectural models in the development of metropolitan London would be contested again, but on very different terms.

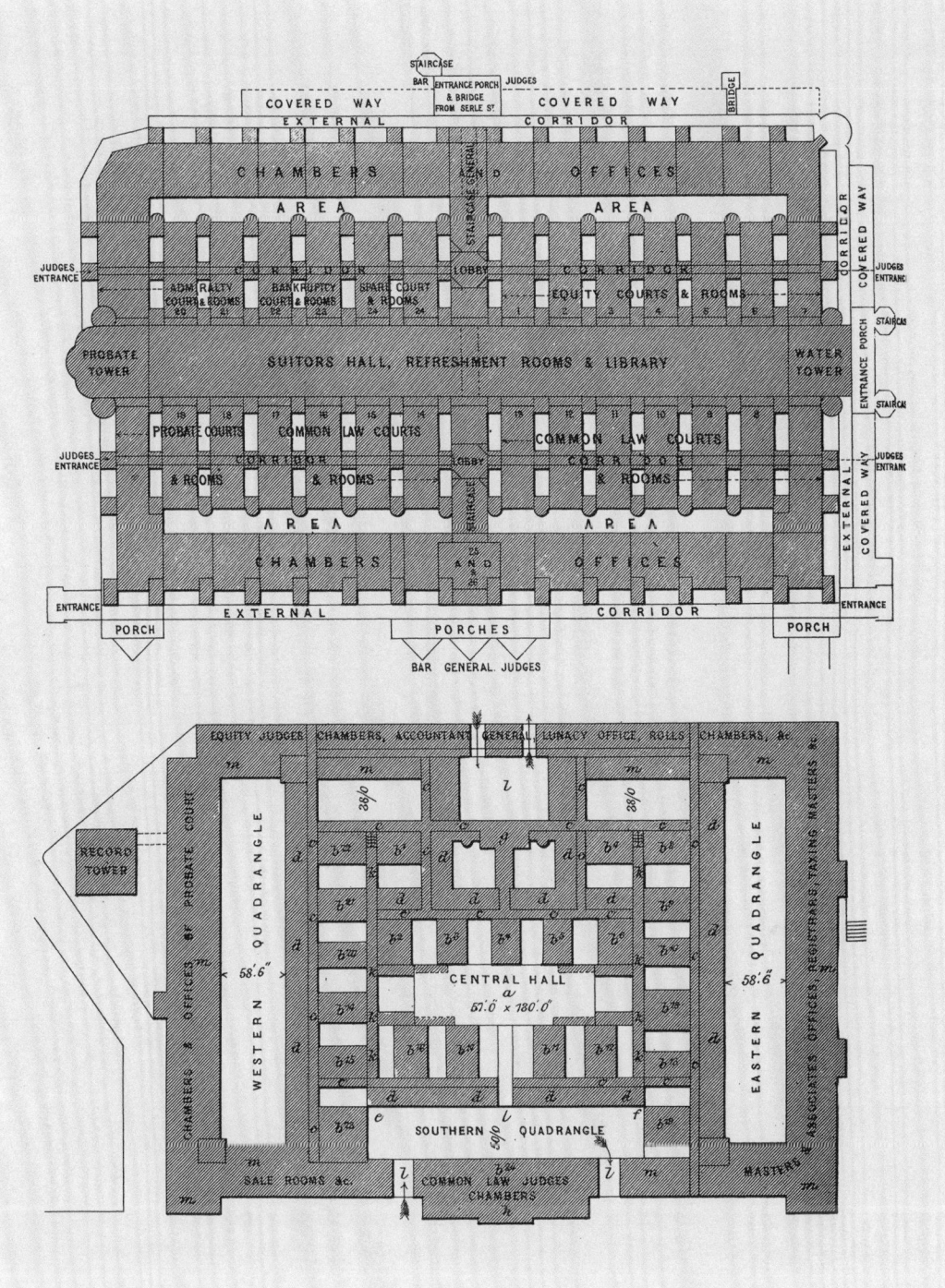

FIG. 17   'Block Plan of Mr Street's Design for the Courts of Justice', *Building News* 14 (22 February 1867), 142

THE COMMONS

> An architect cannot put up a monumental building in the hope that the public will approve of it and pay the expense. The most he can do is show a drawing or a model in public, and persuade men in power or of immense wealth that he is both capable and original, and will be able to charm the public by his work.[1]

At the end of both the nineteenth century and his three-year tenure as president of the Royal Institute of British Architects, George Aitchison argued it was the very nature of architectural practice that affected the relationship between public and profession. Architects in London, he asserted, were unable to present a civic building to the public as a fait accompli. Instead, their interaction with this wider audience was a form of negotiation. Through the presentation of models and drawings, architects worked to convince the politically powerful or wealthy of their ability to not only design but also 'charm the public'.[2] The effects of this were noted by government administrators at the time. A year earlier one senior civil servant noted that, compared to 'the splendour of continental capitals', Victorian London lacked the type of public building that contributed both to the efficient running of government as well as 'the convenience and comfort of the public at large'.[3] Again, the legislative framework of democratic politics in Victorian Britain provides a context for understanding the relationships between public, politicians, and architects in the construction of new civic buildings. Three decades after the 1832 Reform Act, which had initiated various social and legislative improvements, the 1867 Reform Act enfranchised a million new male voters, doubling the size of

---

1   'Presidential Address', *RIBA Journal* (3rd Series) 6 (1899), 4.
2   'Presidential Address', 4.
3   John Henry Briggs, *Naval Administrations 1827 to 1892,* ed. Elizabeth Briggs (London: Sampson Low & Co, 1897), 163.

the electorate, and propelling the British state into the age of mass politics.[4] Moreover by the end of 1868 all male heads of households were given the vote as a result of the termination of compounding of rents.[5] Despite this now substantial electorate the number of members of parliament (MPs) representing Greater London in Parliament expanded from eighteen to just twenty-two.[6] It is therefore no surprise that a majority of elected officials considered the support and financial wellbeing of the entire British population more important than the embellishment of nineteenth-century London.[7]

After 1867 the importance of British popular politics grew exponentially. In the second half of the nineteenth century the construction of the architect's professional authority in public life was more closely related than ever to a newly expanded democratic franchise. Concurrently, debates in the House of Commons and the House of Lords surrounding architectural models became sites for socio-political discussions about the benefits and shortcomings of London's development. In the case of the urban development and expansion of the city, architectural models and their purpose fed into these larger discussions about the public and its voice in the decision-making process. While often referring to methodological democratic and architectural precedents from Europe, much of the discussion around models took on a nationalistic tone when it came to the quality and cost of new public buildings in London. As an anonymous letter to *The Times* in May 1872 put it, 'No guarantee against a failure which is to endure for centuries and disgrace the country can be obtained except by a model.'[8] Earlier that year, the same newspaper called to parliamentary and public attention the expenditure of various proposed governmental buildings and argued that one way of preventing 'the erection of unsatisfactory buildings, would be the production of models of the buildings to be erected'.[9]

Once the government had identified the need for a major public building, the central issue was how it should be financed. Whether funded directly through government spending or bankrolled by external borrowing, the burden ultimately fell on the taxpayer. Sections of the public and various MPs raised concerns that national finances would be used, and debts incurred, for the benefit of London. This issue came to the fore in various political debates surrounding the rebuilding of government offices in Whitehall in the third quarter of the nineteenth century. Various proposals were put before Treasury select committees in 1867 and 1868 by Andrew Clarke, Admiralty Director of Works, who proposed rebuilding the entire west side of Whitehall and Parliament Street to accommodate a series of linked offices containing

---

4	Robert Saunders, *Democracy and the Vote in British Politics, 1848–1867: The Making of the Second Reform Act* (Farnham: Ashgate, 2011), 1.	
5	Chris Cook, *The Routledge Companion to Britain in the Nineteenth Century, 1815–1914* (London: Routledge, 2005); Janice Carlisle, 'On the Second Reform Act, 1867', *BRANCH: Britain, Representation and Nineteenth-Century History*, https://branchcollective.org/?ps_articles=janice-carlisle-on-the-second-reform-act-1867 (accessed 23 November 2022).	
6	Michael Port, 'Government and the Metropolitan Image: Ministers, Parliament, and the Concept of a Capital City, 1840–1915', in Dana Arnold, ed., *The Metropolis and Its Image: Constructing Identities for London, c. 1750–1950* (Oxford: Blackwell, 1999), 101–27, here: 103.	
7	Much like today, the majority of MPs were indifferent to London's local problems, fearing the creation of a powerful municipal assembly that might overshadow their own authority. See: Roland Quinault, 'From National to World Metropolis: Governing London, 1750–1850', *The London Journal* 26, no. 1 (May 2001), 38–46.	
8	'Our Public Buildings', *The Times* (27 May 1872), 7.	
9	'Modern Metropolitan Architecture', *Building News* 22 (9 February 1872), 118.	

minor government departments alongside the Admiralty and War Office.[10] The following year Clarke used two architectural models to present the scheme: one was a site-wide depiction and the other a portion of a single government building showing the three-dimensional arrangement of floors, lightwells, and corridors. The vast scale of the site model, 2.92 × 1.22 metres, was a significant moment in the development of London. FIG. 18 A concentrated sweep of buildings marked the centralization of the imperial Victorian state with Trafalgar Square at one end and Westminster at the other. Across these buildings a network of top-lit corridors would allow connections between different governmental departments, while an extension to the underground Metropolitan District Railway at a site next to Westminster Bridge united this new administrative hub with a wider public transport system.

FIG. 18   Andrew Clarke, model for the proposed rebuilding of Whitehall, 1869

10   The proposal amalgamated minor government departments, the Metropolitan Police, the Treasury, and two courtyards containing the Admiralty and War Office. Clarke argued that his proposals provided ample accommodation for civil servants, police, and military at a lower cost for the public than any of the alternatives. 'On the Arrangement of Public Offices', *Builder* 27 (13 March 1869), 200–2.

Due to opposition in the House of Commons the scheme was delayed, and in 1877 a further select committee calling for immediate expansion was curtailed by governmental budget cuts caused by the global Long Depression (1873–1879). By 1883 a fresh competition was organized for a new Admiralty and War Office. George Shaw Lefevre, incumbent First Commissioner of Works, lobbied for government and parliamentary support by announcing a two-tier competition that would be held in autumn 1883, with designs submitted in March of the following year.[11] When asked about the topic in the House of Lords, Lord Thurlow, then Paymaster General, explained that there would be time for a discussion of any selected scheme to take place, 'with the aid of plans and models', due to the required demolition of existing buildings on the site in Parliament Street.[12] A week later the Earl of Wemyss – a longtime advocate for architectural models in the presentation of public works – petitioned the government and Shaw Lefevre to locate a 'model of the buildings proposed to be erected in Parliament Street', which had been built under the supervision of the previous Office of Works director, Austin Layard.[13] On learning that Clarke's site model of Whitehall was missing, Wemyss pointed out that since 'the model cost £500, and was worth £1,500' perhaps the Office of Works should look harder.[14]

Architectural models were not present in March 1884, during the second phase of the competition submission for the Admiralty and War Office. Initially competitors were required to submit outline plans, sections, and elevations. A panel of six judges comprising four members of the Office of Works and two professional architects, Philip Hardwick and Ewan Christian, worked through 128 entries to form a shortlist.[15] Nine shortlisted architects then developed their schemes through more formalized orthographic and perspective drawings submitted in June 1884.[16] From the shortlist the judges selected the little-known Yorkshire office of John and Joseph Leeming. Despite criticism from the press regarding the brothers' handling of classical motifs and the overall massing of the project,[17] Shaw Lefevre championed the proposal and guided the architects through a series of design changes.[18] Even at this early stage the architectural press was calling for a model to help the public consider the winning submission; the *Builder* requested that this model 'be prepared to a sufficiently large scale to enable one to judge of grouping and of detail'.[19] At the time various commentators claimed the idea that a small-scale model for a public building of such importance was 'really uncomfortable to contemplate'.[20]

Following guidance from the Office of Works and departmental representatives, John and Joseph Leeming were told to change their design to reduce construction costs.[21] In a debate on 24 November 1884, Lord Sudeley

11   *Hansard's Parliamentary Debates*, House of Commons, 5 April 1883, vol. 277, 1481–2.
12   *Hansard's Parliamentary Debates*, House of Lords, 14 August 1883, vol. 283, 454.
13   *Hansard's Parliamentary Debates*, House of Lords, 20 August 1883, vol. 283, 1317–20.
14   *Hansard's Parliamentary Debates*, House of Lords, 20 August 1883, vol. 283, 1317–20.
15   Proceedings of the Committee of Judges of the designs [New War Office], WORK 12/115/4, TNA.
16   *Hansard's Parliamentary Debates*, House of Commons, 1 May 1884, vol. 287, 1033–4.
17   See: 'New Admiralty and War Offices', *Architect* (6 October 1883), 201; 'New Admiralty and War Offices', *Saturday Review* (9 August 1884), 173; 'Utility', *Building News* (15 August 1884), 280–1; *Builder* (6 September 1884), 320; *Builder* (4 October 1884), 454.
18   *Report from the Select Committee on Admiralty and War Office (Sites)*, vol. 184 (London: Hansard, 1887); various departmental memos, WORK 12/88/1, TNA.
19   'The War Office and Admiralty Competition Designs', *Builder* (16 August 1844), 218.
20   'The War Office and Admiralty Competition Designs', 218.
21   These changes included reducing the ornamentation of the building, relocating a tower to the St. James' Park facade from the Whitehall elevation, and thereby altering the attic portion of the Whitehall elevation. Proceedings of the Committee of Judges, minute of a meeting, 21 April 1885, WORK 12/115/4, TNA.

explained that two models of the revised design for the Admiralty and War Offices were being prepared, ready for inspection early in the following year: one model at the same scale as the competition drawings to explain the plan of the complex, and another model of a smaller section of the proposed building, constructed at a much larger scale 'to show all the details of the architectural workings'.[22] In response Wemyss suggested that the new models should be large enough to 'show how far the new buildings would harmonize with the general character of the surroundings and neighbouring buildings'.[23] Sudeley reminded Wemyss about the original model that depicted Whitehall and Parliament Street, and reported that the Office of Works was considering how to alter the now-located site model to show the new proposals to both Parliament and the public.

By spring 1885 John and Joseph Leeming had started the detailed design of the basement portion of the project as the first works commenced on site.[24] At a House of Lords debate that May, the Earl of Rosebery, who had replaced Shaw Lefevre as First Commissioner of Works, explained that a series of entirely new models of the proposed Admiralty and War Office were in the process of being made but had not yet been completed.[25] Three months later another MP, the Earl of Iddesleigh, reported that he had spoken with Rosebery about moving three new models from the Victoria Gallery in the Palace of Westminster to a public venue in the city where they could be 'inspected by architects and others interested in the matter'.[26] By the third week of August 1885 three models were displayed in an Admiralty office at 18 Spring Gardens, at the northern end of Whitehall adjacent to Trafalgar Square, where they were exhibited to the general public for three weeks.[27] The first model depicted the building at a scale of one inch to sixteen feet (1:192), the same scale as the plans submitted at the second stage of the competition. The next model showed 'the buildings and all the surrounding district' at a scale of one inch to twenty feet (1:240). A third model represented the southwest tower for the building at a scale of one inch to four feet (1:48).[28]

22 *Hansard's Parliamentary Debates*, House of Lords, 24 November 1884, vol. 294, 222; *Hansard's Parliamentary Debates*, House of Commons, 24 November 1884, vol. 294, 270.
23 *Hansard's Parliamentary Debates*, House of Lords, 24 November 1884, vol. 294, 222.
24 *Report from the Select Committee on Admiralty and War Office (Sites)*, 184 (London: Henry Hansard, 1887), iii.
25 *Hansard's Parliamentary Debates*, House of Lords, 4 May 1885, vol. 297, 1478.
26 *Hansard's Parliamentary Debates*, House of Lords, 4 August 1885, vol. 300, 1032.
27 'Notes on Current Events', *British Architect* 26 (21 August 1885), 82.
28 The first and third model survive in the Parliamentary Collections and were shown at the Victoria & Albert Museum's 'Marble Halls' exhibition in 1973. My thanks to Mark Collins for facilitating a visit to the two models. See also: Physick and Darby, *Marble Halls*, 46–7.

FIG. 19 John and Joseph Leeming (architects), Charles Henry Mabey (model-maker), model of the Southwest Tower of the Admiralty and War Office, 1885

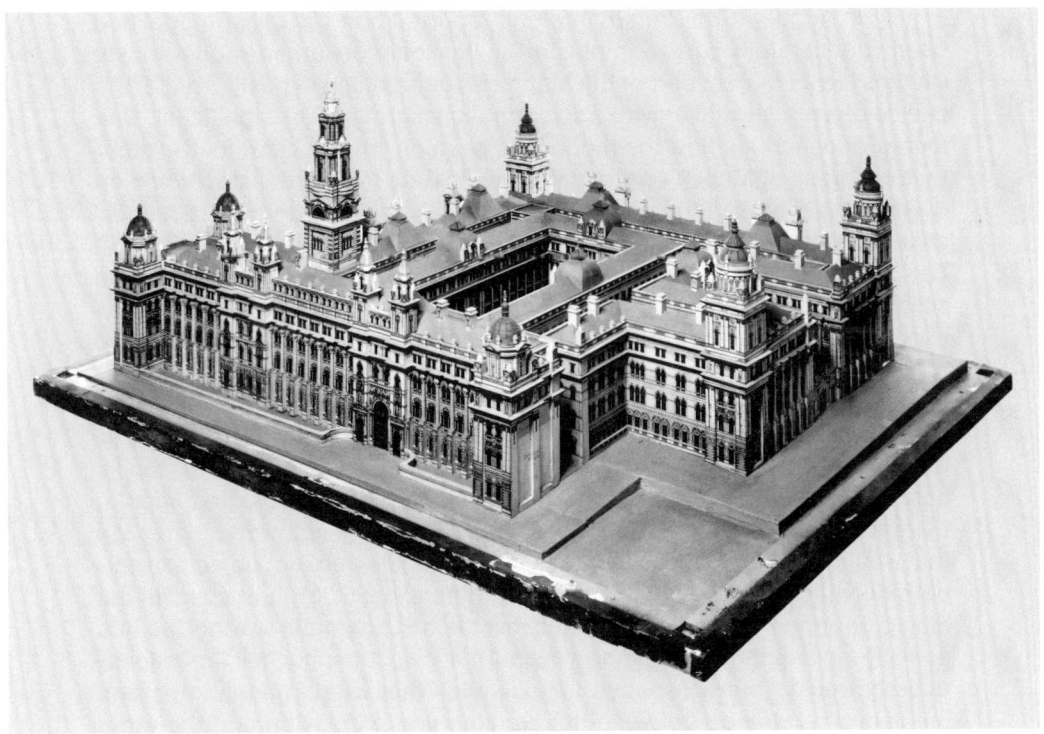

FIG. 20 John and Joseph Leeming, model of the Admiralty and War Office, 1885

In August 1885 *British Architect* reported how the tower model had been very carefully carved in plaster by the sculptor-turned-model-maker Charles Henry Mabey, part of the Mabey model-making dynasty.[29] FIG. 19 The choice of a model-maker with a sculptural background was significant. One journalist described how the model had been on 'private view' for the architectural press at Mabey's studio at Storey's Gate in Westminster. When on display, 'the merits of the design, judged as a specimen of monumental architecture', the writer noted, were 'brought out by this "study in the round"'.[30] The two other models were made by pasting lithographed elevations onto solid blocks, with certain portions, such as circular columns and vases, modelled in wood. FIG. 20 This approach to model-making, whereby flat graphic renderings are adhered to a three-dimensional form, resonates with other models of public buildings from the period, although many have not survived. In 1871 while designing the Natural History Museum, Alfred Waterhouse informed the Office of Works that if a model of the proposed design was required by the House of Commons, plans and elevations would first need to be prepared and given to the model-maker to commence work, a process that would take two to three months.[31] Such models were not objects of spatial exploration. Instead, they were three-dimensional drawings, solid timber blocks wrapped with elevations to show the arrangement of windows and openings in relation to a building's overall massing. Despite their limitations – they showed no internal spaces, for example – they were a hugely important medium of exchange between the architectural profession and the wider public. In the case of large public works this type of model 'can hardly be over-estimated', explained *British Architect*, as an illustration of British miserliness in the funding of major buildings or infrastructure.[32]

In the case of the Leeming brothers' models, these points were proven in the debate that arose during their exhibition. An anonymous article published in *Architect* criticized the proposal's 'Anglo-Italian' rationale and appearance, 'a sort of Pimlico palatialised in real stone', which it claimed no politician would support financially.[33] Situating the comment in a wider context, in the previous year the Third Reform Act extended the same voting qualifications as existed in Britain's cities and towns to the countryside. This further expansion of the electorate put more pressure on politicians from constituencies outside the metropolitan area to ensure that the rebuilding of London did not place an unjustifiable financial burden on the rest of the country. Metropolitan improvements such as roads, sewers, and other networks of infrastructure were funded directly by the city's own authorities, and there was a growing sense that the capital should also pay for its own public buildings.

29   'Notes on Current Events', 82.
30   'Admiralty and War Office', *Building News* 48 (3 April 1885), 547.
31   Office of Works, letter to Alfred Waterhouse, 15 June 1871, WORK 12/115/4, f. 209, TNA; Alfred Waterhouse, letter to First Commissioner of Works, 15 June 1871, WORK 12/115/4, f. 210, TNA.
32   'Notes on Current Events', 82.
33   'A Letter to the Right Hon J.G. Shaw Lefevre, MP On the Models for the New Public Offices', *Architect* 30 (4 September 1885), 141. A nineteenth-century area of development in marshy land to the southwest of the West End, the architecture of Pimlico was characterized by terraced houses with their principal facade constructed from brick with classical embellishments, the cheap construction method would then be hidden by a layer of white-painted lime render.

A second anonymous article in the same issue of *Architect* took a different stance, complaining about the extents and detail of the models exhibited at Spring Gardens. This time the criticism was about the model's lack of surroundings, meaning that comparisons between the internal courtyards of the proposed Admiralty and War Office with those of neighbouring buildings, such as Somerset House or George Gilbert Scott's Foreign Office, were 'rendered impossible'.[34] Without these comparative elements, the author asserted that for all practical purposes the model was useless. In fact, the author proposed that for anyone trying to 'form a correct judgement of the facts', the model was worse than useless: it was deceptive in its presentation of the Leeming brothers' proposals. Consequently, the model would 'deceive those with whom the rude privilege rests of foisting on the British nation a fatuous and shameful piece of work'. Others went beyond the press, seeking intervention from formal professional bodies. Lawrence Harvey, a British architect educated in Europe who had lectured at the Architectural Association, wrote to the RIBA council alleging that the recently installed Conservative minority government had exhibited the Admiralty and War Office models in order to drum up enough public backlash to reject the proposed design. He urged the council to call a meeting for all members to view the models and petition the government to hold a new competition for the building, one open to '*British architects only*' and which proposed a new urban plan and buildings for the whole governmental complex in Whitehall from Downing Street to Spring Gardens.[35]

34   'A Letter to the Right Hon. J. G. Shaw Lefevre', 142.
35   Lawrence Harvey, letter to RIBA Council, 11 September 1885, LC/23/8/8, 1.2.3, RIBA.

MODELS AS A MODE OF INQUIRY

During the following year these protests and complaints were formalized through a select committee inquiry – a cross-party parliamentary mechanism called upon to investigate a particular issue. Alongside the popular criticism of the new Admiralty and War Office was the government's concern about the costs of construction in the light of rising national expenditure. In March 1887 a select committee of the House of Commons was formed to consider the merit of the new building's location and design. Its seventeen members, chaired by David Plunkett, the latest First Commissioner for Works, and including Shaw Lefevre, sat for ten sessions throughout the spring and summer of 1887, calling on a host of witnesses: the architects who judged the competition (Phillip Hardwick and Ewan Christian), professional experts from the RIBA, employees of the Office of Works, and John and Joseph Leeming. The architectural models were at the forefront of the committee's cross-examination, often used as rhetorical devices to help illustrate and illuminate speeches by committee members [36] and as descriptive aids in the course of the inquiry. On several occasions one committee member asked Shaw Lefevre, 'Can you show it on the model?' [37]

In other instances the models were used to support the testimony of witnesses called before the committee. At one stage John Taylor, the long-standing surveyor for the Office of Works, was called to give evidence. Responding to a series of questions from Shaw Lefevre regarding the proposed building's ornament in relation to the surrounding context of Whitehall, Taylor described how the larger 1:48 scale model made by C. H. Mabey offered a better impression of the ornament than either of the other two models. Shaw Lefevre's final question to Taylor – on the quality of light in the building's internal courtyards – also raised experiential concerns, including whether the 'smallness of the model' gave an inaccurate sense of available daylight in the building's courtyards. With a light cast from various positions, Taylor showed that when viewed from a certain angle the model gave a 'very false impression'. [38] A model of this type, he explained, should be lit from above, which he then demonstrated to the committee.

Witnesses also used the models to help clarify matters when interrogated about certain aspects of the design. At one stage a committee member used the windows of a nearby government building as a point of reference when posing a question to Taylor, comparing the *real* windows outside the committee room with the *miniature* windows of the model. Later in the exchange, Taylor was asked about the ability of the model to simulate the visual experience of a proposed building, an experience, it was argued, that related to how the model was viewed at scale versus the 'real' experience of encountering the constructed building. Taylor answered by referring to the model, its scale, and his own body to show how a person would have the same view of the completed building from nearby St James's Park as he had in the committee room where the model was shown. He concluded by stating he believed

---

36 For instance: 'Surely that would be an impossibility; just look at the model behind you.' *Report from the Select Committee on Admiralty and War Office (Sites)*, 101, minute of a Select Committee meeting held on 10 May 1887, para. 1751.
37 *Report from the Select Committee*, 50, 29 April 1887, para. 829; 71, 6 May 1887, para. 1231.
38 *Report from the Select Committee*, 34, 26 April 1887, para. 462.

the proportions and detail of the building were rendered at scale on the model 'without damage'.[39]

The models were used in two ways when John and Joseph Leeming were called before the committee in May 1887. First, they communicated potential changes to the design, especially those for which at that moment there were no drawings or model to illustrate. Second, when questioned by the committee about the estimated cost of construction in relation to the then low price of building materials, the architectural model of the proposed Admiralty and War Offices deputized for the building to come. The approach, however, did not exactly work in the brothers' favour, since the committee proposed reducing costs by constructing a 'building on the lines suggested in that model, but with less architectural pretensions'.[40] The solution was analogous to stripping the lithographed elevations from the model and revealing its modest wooden superstructure underneath, with the effect of reducing its sculptural ornamentation and associated costs. Despite acknowledging the praise the plans had received from within the architectural profession, the select committee proposed that John and Joseph Leeming's scheme should be abandoned. Instead of a new building, members recommended that the existing Admiralty complex be reconfigured for the current needs of the department at a more moderate cost.[41] Later, in February 1888, John and Joseph Leeming prepared new plans for a western extension to the existing building, which were exhibited in the House of Commons.[42]

As a result of the inquiry, the models of Admiralty and War Office subsequently became part of a much broader debate on how new buildings and infrastructure in London should be designed, procured, and constructed. This effort was led primarily by the Earl of Wemyss who favoured the use of models in public competitions and had demanded a search in the House of Lords for the missing model of Westminster. During the various internal and public arguments over the appropriate style for the New Foreign Office (1857–60), he attempted to mediate between the two opponents – the 'Goths' and the 'Classicists' – by displaying a model of George Gilbert Scott's Gothic design in the Library of the Palace of Westminster for both parties to view. FIG. 21 An article in *Builder* described how this act of diplomacy enabled 'non-professional judges … a better means of arriving at [their] decision' than plans, elevations, or working drawings.[43]

Throughout his political career Wemyss was firm in his belief that the production of models could allow for public debate. His campaign to display architectural models for proposed public works continued into the 1890s and 1900s, going so far as to demand the practice be made a legal requirement for all publicly funded buildings in Britain.

39	*Report from the Select Committee*, 40, 26 April 1887, para. 614.
40	*Report from the Select Committee*, p. 81, 6 May 1887, para. 1444.
41	*Report from the Select Committee*, viii. This moderate cost was estimated by the committee to be more than £500,000, without even including the value of the Spring Gardens site that could be used for further additions to the Admiralty and the opening of the Mall in Charing Cross. *Report from the Select Committee*, viii, 15 June 1887.
42	Port, *Imperial London*, 242–3.
43	'The New Foreign Office', *Builder* 17 (26 February 1859), 158; 'Lord Palmerston on Architecture: The New Foreign Office', *Builder* 17 (6 August 1859), 515.

Oct. 6, 1866 — THE ILLUSTRATED LONDON NEWS — 341

THE NEW FOREIGN AND INDIA OFFICES: THE PARK FRONT.

The stately pile of buildings which has for several years past been under construction at Westminster, adjoining the Government offices in Downing-street, and situated between King-street, which is to be merged in an enlargement of Parliament-street, and St. James's Park, near Storey's-gate, is now so far approaching completion that it will probably be ready for the accommodation of the Secretary of State for Foreign Affairs and the Secretary of State for India early in the next Session. The buildings as yet erected compose three sides of a quadrangle, open on the side towards Parliament-street; but it is proposed ultimately to complete the quadrangle with a range of apartments on the fourth side for the Secretary of State for the Colonies.

We now present two Views of the new edifice as it will soon appear; one view representing the quadrangle, with the sculptured figures which are to adorn the outside of the topmost story; the other showing the park front, as seen on approaching it from the parade behind the Horse Guards; the principal features on this side being the lofty tower of the India Office and the grand semicircular sweep which rounds off the angle of the building towards the park. The niches on this side will also be adorned with statues of Indian statesmen. The tower on the Foreign Office side is not so lofty, but more massive than that of the India Office.

The exterior of the whole group of buildings was designed by Mr. George Gilbert Scott, R.A., who is the architect of the Foreign Office throughout; while the interior of the India Office, with the external work of the inner court belonging to that range of buildings, is in the hands of Mr. D. Wyatt. The contractors for the whole are Messrs. Smith and Taylor. The facing material employed is Portland stone, of the brown, hard sort; granite for the columns in windows; and granite, marble, and glass, mostly red and green, in the shape of bosses and otherwise, in the friezes. The carving for the Foreign Office, both inside and out, is executed by Mr. Farmer; while for the India Office Mr. Earp is intrusted with it for the inside, and Mr. Philip for the outside. The series of sculptured figures on the Foreign Office front are emblematical of countries, such as Italy, France, and America; those on the India Office represent the Indian tribes, an Afghan, a Ghoorka, a Malay, a Mahratta, and so on. These statues are in course of execution by four sculptors, Mr. Protat, Mr. Philip, Mr. Armstead, and Mr. Raymond Smith. In the inner court of the India Office where the most elaborate ornamentation externally is displayed, some of the panels in relief are being carved by Mr. Phyffers. In this court the friezes of the three orders that mainly form the elevations are of majolica and mosaic work; the columns are of granite, grey and red; and the ceilings of the corridors surrounding it are of coloured tiles, with patterns in relief, highly enamelled, from the works of Messrs. Maw, of Broseley. Some of the ceilings of rooms on this side will show handsome work in plaster, partly modelled from Indian fruit and flowers. The inner court of the Foreign Office, on the contrary, is quite plain.

The principal apartments in the Foreign Office are on the one-pair floor, and include the Cabinet-room, 70ft. long and 35ft. wide; and two conference-rooms, 108 ft. long together and 30 ft. wide. These all communicate with each other,

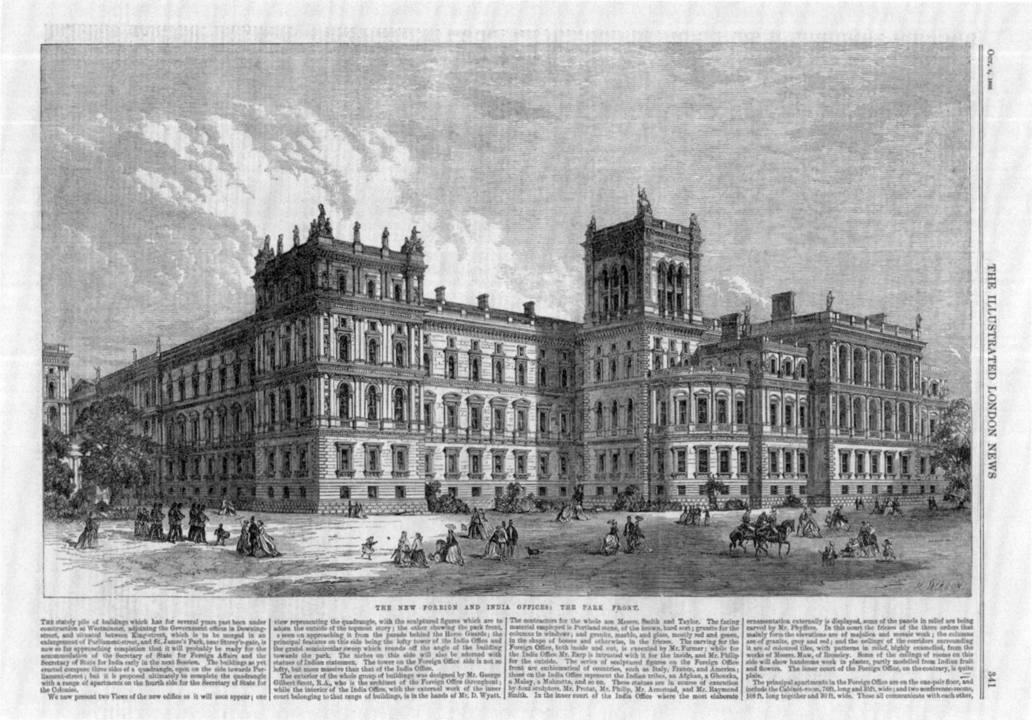

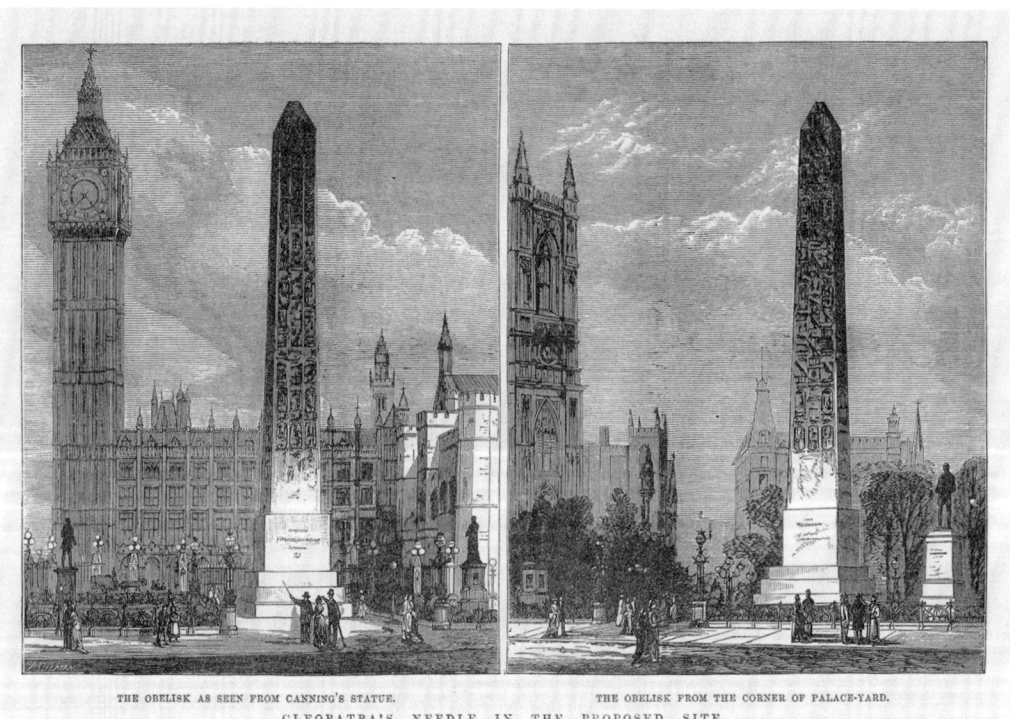

FIG. 21 'The New Foreign and India Offices: The Park Front', *Illustrated London News* (6 October 1866)

FIG. 22 'Cleopatra's Needle in its Proposed Position at Westminster', *Illustrated London News* (26 January 1878)

Wemyss launched the campaign at a meeting of the RIBA meeting in May 1899 where he forcefully argued that the public exhibition of architectural models was 'a necessity' that the 'Institute should take action upon'.[44] Based on his experience, 'architects' drawings were the most deceptive things in the world' and 'the only safe course was to see everything in model'. Once an architect had a 'satisfactory design', he explained, they should first model it in plaster and afterwards produce a part of the building in its proposed materials at one-third scale, as was standard practice in Continental Europe, especially France. Offering examples of freestanding sculptures tested first in models at the Houses of Parliament and the Tate Gallery, he encouraged the Institute to petition the government that 'all public works paid for with public money should be put up in model first'.[45] As for the proposals for the next generation of governmental buildings in Whitehall, he issued a warning: they 'were to be put up without any model, and someday [the government] would regret it.'

In reply, George Aitchison recalled a discussion with the current First Commissioner of Works on 'the importance of having models made, and understood they were going to be made'. Robert Kerr spoke to indicate his agreement with Wemyss. He noted that while a full-sized mock-up of a new building was overly ambitious, if, as Wemyss described, the government did not understand architectural drawings, there was no harm in making a model. In Europe, Kerr added, 'it was a rule to present a model of a public monument of a reasonable size before the public committed to it', and to not follow European precedent would be a 'great mistake' on behalf of Britain and its architects.[46] There was, in fact, precedent of this method in Britain: twenty years earlier, in 1878, a full-sized wooden model of Cleopatra's Needle was placed outside the Palace of Westminster to judge its appearance. FIG. 22 The site was rejected by politicians and engineers due to the additional groundworks required to reinforce the District Line train tunnel below, and the wooden mock-up was relocated to the Victoria Embankment, the final site for the monument.

With the support of RIBA members, Wemyss remained on the offensive, launching the second part of his campaign a few months later. In May 1899 following criticism from various peers and ministers in both chambers of the Houses of Parliament on the lack of architectural models made for the new War Office, improvements to Parliament Street, and the refurbishment of Westminster Hall, Wemyss published a memorandum calling on the government to take action.[47] In the Lords on 4 August 1899 he opened a debate on the topic by announcing:

> It is desirable that models of all public buildings of importance that are about to be erected at the public cost should be made and publicly exhibited, and that this is more especially to be desired at the present time.[48]

This method, Wemyss told the packed chamber, was 'an almost universal custom' in Continental Europe. He described how in Europe 'a *plébiscite* [is held] on public intended improvements and art decorations', a contrast with Britain where, if models happened to be made, they would be displayed only

---

44   'The Architectural Element of Engineering Works', *RIBA Journal* (3rd Series), 6 (1899), 396.
45   'The Architectural Element of Engineering Works', 396.
46   'The Architectural Element of Engineering Works', 396.
47   Francis Charteris [Earl of Wemyss], 'The New War Office Building', *British Architect* 40 (28 July 1899), 55. The majority of the 140 signatories were peers in the House of Lords.
48   *Hansard's Parliamentary Debates*, House of Lords, 4 August 1899, vol. 75, 1430–46.

in the Palace of Westminster and therefore only accessible to politicians and not the public. However the European system, he argued, was not simply a 'private or foreign practice' but also one that had been 'successfully adopted in our own country' in 1869 when Austin Layard was First Commissioner and the large-scale model of Westminster was produced by Andrew Clarke. As discussed earlier, Wemyss described how when used as a part of the public judgement of designs for the Admiralty and War Office, the model 'so shocked the public who saw it that the plan was knocked on the head'. He continued to read from his memo:

> By the public exhibition of models, as proposed, successful precedents established in the case of designs for public buildings by Her Majesty's Office of Works, should now be followed.[49]

The House of Lords then debated the topic. Opening remarks were given by the Marquess of Lansdowne, who claimed that 'a model on a table never by any chance presents the appearance of the actual building' due to its elevated position.[50] And while a model would allow the government to regulate the size and proportion of buildings on its property, the same did not apply to neighbouring plots of privately owned land. One effect of this was that the new War Office could be designed in proportion to the height of the surrounding government buildings, but any adjacent private development 'might put out the whole scale of proportion'. Lord Stanmore rejected Lansdowne's observation that a viewer's position in relation to a model affected both the worth and the value of the model in presenting the actual appearance of the proposed building. Instead, he argued, this depended on the viewpoint of the observer and the relative height of a model's base or stand. Wemyss advised that when studying a model there was 'a possibility of raising the model to the level of your eye' in order to examine the object from preferential viewpoints. Other peers supported Wemyss and Stanmore. The Duke of Norfolk, the Paymaster General, described how 'Personal experience has taught me that models of intended buildings are of great use' and encouraged the government to provide models in future. After having also raised this issue the Marquess of Lothian demanded that models of all proposed public buildings should be exhibited:

> I do not think it is at all fair that the taxpayers should be called upon to pay for buildings, which might be very bad, and which they have no opportunity of saying beforehand whether they like [the proposals] or not.[51]

As a result of the support, Wemyss, who was partially deaf, withdrew his own motion, thereby ending the debate. Later in a letter to the newspapers he would write that he had incorrectly interpreted the comments of Duke of Norfolk and Marquess of Lothian as a firm promise to change government policy, rather than an empty one.[52]

Nevertheless this was not the end of the discussion. In October 1899, during a debate in the Lords on new sites for governmental buildings near to Parliament, Wemyss again spoke about architectural models in relation to public expenditure. He reported that the government had consulted the RIBA and George Aitchison on the topic ahead of a debate in the Lords, and that during consultation Lansdowne (who had opposed Wemyss's earlier campaign efforts) had implied that Aitchison 'thought [models] were neither

---

49 *Hansard's Parliamentary Debates*, House of Lords, 4 August 1899, vol. 75, 1430–46.
50 *Hansard's Parliamentary Debates*, House of Lords, 4 August 1899, vol. 75, 1430–46.
51 *Hansard's Parliamentary Debates*, House of Lords, 4 August 1899, vol. 75, 1430–46.
52 'The New War Office', *Daily Graphic*, 4 August 1899.

necessary nor desirable'.[53] In recent months Wemyss, however, had exchanged letters on the topic with Aitchison that contradicted Lansdowne's claims. Standing again in the House of Lords, Wemyss recalled Aitchison's letter: 'I certainly think that, even now, there ought to be models made of the new War Office ... The expense would be a mere fleabite.'[54]

When designs were prepared for the new Admiralty and War Office sites in July 1901 another round of debates in the Lords on the production and public display of models followed.[55] Subsequently Aitchison himself wrote to *The Times* to criticize the government for the absence of models of the project: 'I believe that all the principal buildings of the world, since Justinian's time, were built from models.'[56] And yet even with all the support Wemyss had garnered – from Aitchison, the RIBA, and the majority of peers in House of Lords – the Office of Works denied the request to have models made for public display. Writing in a letter to *Architects' Magazine*, the denial was 'an official slap in the face to professional architectural authority and public opinion'.[57]

[53] *Hansard's Parliamentary Debates*, House of Lords, 27 October 1899, vol. 77, 749–760.
[54] *Hansard's Parliamentary Debates*, House of Lords, 27 October 1899, vol. 77, c749–760.
[55] *Hansard's Parliamentary Debates*, House of Lords, 16 July 1901, vol. 97, 551–69; *Hansard's Parliamentary Debates*, House of Lords, 22 July 1901, vol. 97, 1082–1105.
[56] 'The New Government Offices', *The Times*, 8 June 1901, 9.
[57] 'A Question of Models', *Architects' Magazine* 1 (September 1901), 203.

THE COURTROOM

Despite the rejection of Wemyss's proposed legislation in 1899 to include models for all proposals for public buildings in London, there were other ways in which models were a central part of the interaction between architects and society in the construction of the metropolis. In addition to these public projects, as described during the debate in the House of Lords, private individuals and companies led much of London's reconfiguration and expansion during the nineteenth century. This development was aided by a new role for the architect and their expert knowledge of building litigation as architectural models started to appear in the capital's courtrooms.

The legal cases held in these courtrooms show how debates surrounding London's appearance and the experiences of its inhabitants pivoted around the use of architectural models. A genre of model-making in its own right, legal models – architectural models deployed in a legal setting – were used as rhetorical aids. In court they were deployed by architects to persuade a specific perspective of a case to non-experts, and in turn these objects broadened the understanding of architectural practice – new textbooks were even required to support the architects undertaking this particular activity. At both an urban and a socio-political scale, models were a mechanism through which the conduct of private interests was mediated, regulated, and governed in the contested development of Victorian London. At the same time the emergence of the architect as an expert witness introduced a new role for the model as a medium for professional knowledge in the British courtroom, a space which in itself became shaped by the requirement to display legal models.

Against this background in 1886 Robert Kerr, one of the founders of the Architectural Association and recently appointed professor at the University of London, published a new book, *The Consulting Architect: Practical Notes on Administrative Difficulties and Disputes*. A prolific author, Kerr had written books on domestic architecture (*The Gentleman's House*, 1864) and regulations related to planning (*On Ancient Lights,* 1865) alongside running his own private practice. In *The Consulting Architect* Kerr offered everyday advice to other architects, covering the principles of consultation and evidence in the situations where their professional viewpoint might be brought to bear. Among other things these included cases of property disputes, structural damage caused to neighbouring buildings during construction, and rights of light – a quirk of English civil law that entitles the long-standing owner of a building the legal right to maintain a set level of illumination within their property. FIG. 23 One particular issue that Kerr addressed was how architects should present themselves and their evidence when called into a courtroom. Lawyers, he advised, 'always prefer models to drawings'.[1] For one, models could 'afford a better illustration of the facts [in a case] because their language is more intelligible'. In certain types of legal cases, architectural models are 'almost invariably produced in court' and as a result 'a great deal turns upon the impression of the facts thus created'. A model therefore should be highly finished, he continued, as 'the representation of detail assists identification in a most important degree' with judges and juries 'who are not well acquainted with the subject'. Kerr also issued a caution: beyond a certain point in legal proceedings a model is 'necessarily fallacious, because of its small scale'. The medium should therefore not be used in the courtroom for any purpose other 'than to aid a verbal description of the buildings in question'. In any case, Kerr advised, a model could never replace 'a personal view of the buildings themselves, and especially their interior' as provided directly by an architect. Questioning perception and ideas of truth, Kerr's book sharply summarized the debates surrounding the use of models by architects in nineteenth-century London.

The legal model has been almost completely ignored in secondary literature by historians. This new aspect of professional practice, in which the architect, serving as an expert witness and accompanied by a model, is called upon by lawyers in cases connected to property or construction disputes, emerged due to new legislation related to the built environment.[2] There was no active framework of development for the world's biggest city, only a mixture of passive constraints accumulated over the nineteenth century. The Prescription Act of 1832 protected building owners' rights to daylight in the face of new development in Britain's rapidly expanding cities, while the London Building Acts (1840) and Metropolis Management Act (1855) sought to improve drainage and sanitation, regulate demolition, and establish standards for urban design. Taken together, these codifications were designed to improve the city by curtailing its risks and stimulating more congenial conditions for social coexistence in all parts of London.

1 Robert Kerr, *The Consulting Architect: Practical Notes on Administrative Difficulties and Disputes* (London: John Murray, 1886), 15.
2 The only example I can find reference to was by John Soane in 1812 over disputes regarding the projecting bay to his property at Lincoln's Inn Fields. See Timothy Hyde, *Ugliness and Judgement: On Architecture in the Public Eye* (Princeton: Princeton University Press, 2019), 113–4.

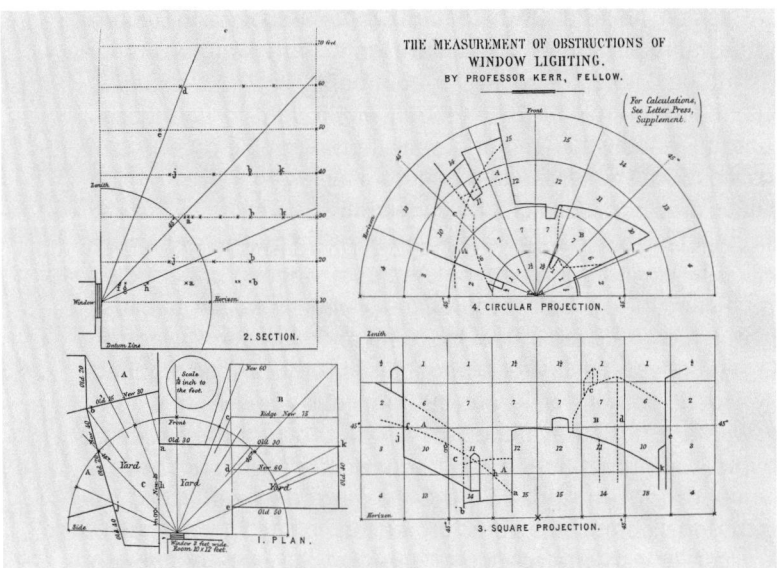

FIG. 23 Supplementary diagram to Robert Kerr, 'Remarks on the Evidence of Architects Concerning the Obstruction of Ancient Lights', *RIBA Proceedings* 1st Series (30 April 1866), 159

Throughout the second half of the nineteenth century at the RIBA and other architectural societies around the country, speakers delivered papers on these legal acts and how professional practice should respond. Similarly, the architectural press covered all the major legal cases related to construction and property law (even if the reported instances of models in a courtroom offer only a glimpse of the actual number), from the first case in 1851 to the majority that were heard after 1879. The use of models in legal disputes even affected the architecture of the courtroom itself. For instance, the competition instructions for the new Law Courts in London (discussed in the chapter 'The Public Sphere') specified that lifts were required 'for large models to be produced in Court', and once inside the courtroom the models required a place and position to be viewed by all parties.[3] Discussing the internal arrangement of a proposed courtroom, one prominent barrister stated that the central part of the floor should be 'kept clear for the exhibition of models and plans', in which 'in their introduction and exhibition, great inconvenience is frequently experienced'.[4] This approach was not purely confined to hypothetical reflection. When the Assize Courts in Durham were refurbished in 1870, at the front of each courtroom was a large table, 'having in it a moveable circular disc, so constructed as to be raised at pleasure, to enable models to be shown and described'. FIG. 24 Solicitors seated around this table could then direct architects and models as cases were presented to the sitting judges.[5]

Whether discussed in Parliament or reported in the press, much of the contemporary discourse surrounding the benefits of architectural models in all forms of practice related to the ability of a model to be understood by a lay audience who was not conversant in orthographic drawings or might be swayed by the beauty of a coloured perspective. This viewpoint was held by many other

3   'Courts of Justice Commission: Instructions for the Competing Architects', 10, WORK 12/33/1, ff.113–121, TNA.
4   'The Proposed Palace of Justice', *Builder* 23 (9 December 1865), 867.
5   'The Assize Courts, Durham', *Builder* 28 (22 January 1870), 64.

quarters of the profession: an article from the *Architects' Magazine* in December 1900 noted, 'the value of models in Ancient Lights, Party Wall, and other similar cases ... is too obvious to need further comment'.[6] In *The Consulting Architect*, Kerr examined the role of the architect within right-to-light cases, noting that the untrained individual might prepare orthographic drawings of the properties in question. These visual aids were useless, in Kerr's opinion, as plans and elevation drawings could only be understood by architects. Instead the task for the architect as expert witness was to represent the facts of a case in the 'most intelligible' way through either a sectional diagram or a model.[7] On the latter, Kerr claimed that models favoured the plaintiff in a case 'because of the impression which is produced by looking down on [the model]'. Here, he identified a recurring conceptual issue: how one uses (or views) an architectural model relates to the content, tone, and authority of its message.[8]

These views were not always consistent with those of the judiciary, however, and despite their prominence architectural models did not have a monopoly on the courtroom. In April 1879 the *Building News* published an article explaining the legal components that formed the right to light in English civil law, making reference to one particular case at a brewery in London where the judge returned a negative verdict citing the need for the 'direct evidence of injury' rather than 'the mere exhibition of models'.[9] This ruling led the journal to advise architects to make a distinction between different types of legal cases: those that dealt with the obstructions caused by newly constructed buildings, and legal cases that contested the potential obstruction that might be caused by proposed buildings. The article proposed that the former should not use architectural models, as the testimony of affected parties would have 'far greater weight [in court] than any scientific theoretical evidence'.[10] In the case of proposed buildings, models were to be exhibited to the court and 'scientific theoretical evidence given as to the result which would follow from the erection of the proposed buildings'.[11] In reality, though, for architects the question of how best to visually represent the case – in a model or a drawing – was not quite so clear-cut.

FIG. 24   'The Assize Courts, Durham', *Builder* 28 (22 January 1870), 67

6   'Some Uses of Architectural Models', *The Architects' Magazine* 1, no. 2 (December 1900), 32–4, here: 33.
7   Kerr, *The Consulting Architect*, 94.
8   Kerr, *The Consulting Architect*, 95–6.
9   'Light and Air', *Building News* 37 (18 April 1879), 425.
10   'Light and Air', 426.
11   'Light and Air', 426.

PRODUCING LEGAL MODELS

Unfortunately, no legal models have survived, and the only visual evidence of their existence comes from photographs published by the architectural and popular press. Many feature the work of the model-maker John Thorp, who operated for most of his career from a workshop at 98 Gray's Inn Road, near the four Inns of Court that form the legal community in London. (His specialization in this service was almost certainly a result of his location.) A profile on Thorp from a popular magazine described how it was only when he had been engaged as a witness in court that he came to understand the importance of models in legal cases: 'no evidence, [Thorp] realized, had such weight and influence with a jury'.[12] On several occasions Thorp made the distinction between models 'to show what a building will be like when completed' and 'diagram models', for legal cases.[13] In early twentieth-century London the demand for legal models appears to have been high. As Thorp himself reflected, 'the majority of the models I make are for legal purposes'.[14]

FIG. 25   Andrew Soutar, 'Produced in Court', *The Strand Magazine* 39 (January to June 1910), 615

The genre itself took on a variety of disputes and grievances. A published photograph shows one of Thorp's legal models, made to explain a dispute between two building owners in London's West End regarding who had right of way across an alley.[15] FIG. 25 The popular *Strand Magazine* reported that the model had been made to show 'how drastically the way had been barred' by one of the owners.[16] It is not possible to identify further details of the case, but the photograph provides some clues to the rationale behind the model. First, the model was performative, with elements that could be removed and added to demonstrate the changes to the alley. Second, the image makes clear what the model was intended to show: the elevation of the houses behind is treated as a backdrop while the building (including the outbuilding that 'obstructed the right of way') in the foreground is shown in

12   Andrew Soutar, 'Produced in Court', *The Strand Magazine* 39 (January to June 1910), 613–19, here: 614.
13   'Some Uses of Architectural Models', 33.
14   Soutar, 'Produced in Court', 618.
15   All the legal cases discussed in this section are easements, a branch of common law where one party holds the right to use, enter, or enjoy access to another party's land without possession.
16   Soutar, 'Produced in Court', 618.

section, thereby allowing the court to understand how the plaintiff's everyday life and 'enjoyment' of their property was affected. Despite the lack of available information, what we can make out from the photograph corroborates with Thorp's comments that models were 'akin to diagrams', enabling lawyers to 'readily grasp the fundamental facts of a case'. Once inside the courtroom, models were capable of describing the legal and technical issues at hand in a direct and clear manner. As Thorp explained, 'The production of a well-made model has on many occasions quashed opposition in a few minutes.'[17]

Models also played an important role in right-to-light cases, since they had the ability to illustrate the two types of evidence given in this type of legal situation. On the one hand there was witness testimony that described 'the actual effect that has been, or will be, produced by the defendant's wrongful action'.[18] On the other hand, there was evidence provided to demonstrate, 'the amount of sky area of which the plaintiff will be deprived'. According to one advisory article in the *Building News* it was typical to produce a model that synthesized both these aspects in order for lawyers or architects 'to show the changes that have been, or are to be made' to a disputed property. An example of this is found in a legal case heard in 1904 regarding two properties on the corner of Dover and Stafford streets in Mayfair.[19] FIG. 26 The plaintiffs filed an injunction to restrain the defendants from erecting any building on the site that would obstruct light from entering into their property. A report in the *Builder* described how technical evidence was given by two architects: Ravencroft Elsey Smith, then Professor of Architecture at King's College, supported the plaintiffs, and Henry John Treadwell, one-half of the Treadwell Martin partnership, was called in for the defendants.[20] The defendants lost the case and there was no mention in the press of the model. The photograph that accompanied the article shows a model with alternative options: on the far left of the photograph, a plain model showing only the massing; the other, at the centre of the image, a more detailed model made in the same realistic manner as the surrounding streets of central London. However, this photograph was first published in December 1900, just over three years before the case was first heard in court. It is therefore probable that the model was first made by Thorp for Treadwell and Martin to show their client the scheme to enlarge the property on Dover Street. Subsequently the model was then appropriated for use in the legal case with the simpler massing model produced to show the existing condition on the site. This hypothesis is supported by closer study of Thorp's model-making techniques. A piece in an American magazine noted that when made for legal purposes, 'an artistic finish is not desirable' and that models were often simply coloured with distemper paint.[21] Contrary to this approach, Thorp explained that making a model for an exhibition entailed a more elaborate treatment: the wooden base of the model would be lined with paper onto which the details of stonework and brickwork were reproduced with watercolours.

17	Percy Collins, 'Practical Modelling', *The World's Work* 17 (1911), 85–7, here: 85. '[Models in legal cases] are in their nature, akin to diagrams, and elaborate adornment would tend to detract from their value by confusing the points at issue.'
18	'Ancient Lights – II', *Building News* 39 (1 October 1880), 377.
19	'Legal: West End Ancient Lights Dispute', *Builder* 88 (30 January 1904), 118. For a further discussion on this case see: 'Easement – Ancient Lights – Light and Air – Obstruction by Building – Claim for Injunction – Damages', *The Estates Gazette Digest of Land and Property Cases* (London, 1905), 39–40.
20	The partnership was active in the late-nineteenth century designing of commercial buildings and public houses in Westminster. For an outline of their lives see: Alison Felstead, Jonathan Franklin, and Leslie Pinfield, *Directory of British Architects 1834–1900*, vol. 2 (London: Mansell, 1993), 604 (Martin) and 924 (Treadwell).
21	Collins, 'Practical Modelling', 87.

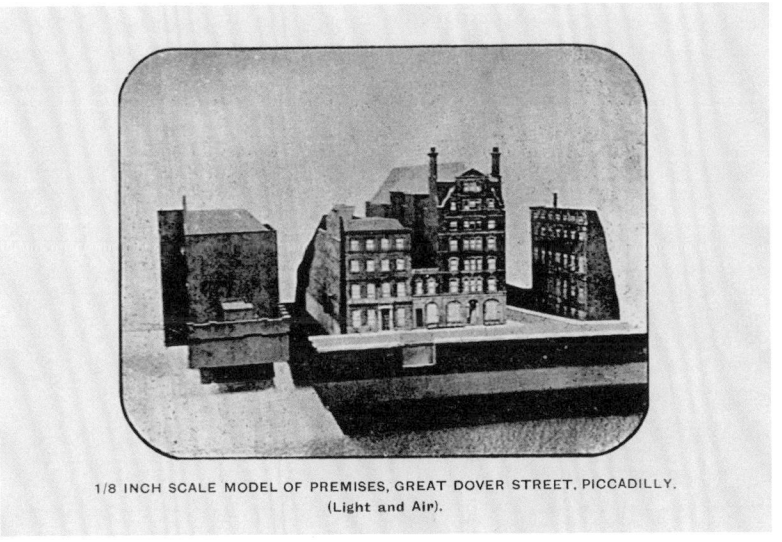

FIG. 26　'Some Uses of Architectural Models', *Architects' Magazine* 1, no. 2 (December 1900), 33

FIG. 27　Robert Randoll, 'Crosby Hall Aug 1899 Showing General View', ink on paper

FIG. 28 '¼ Inch Scale Model of Crosby Hall', in John Thorp, *Concerning Models of Buildings, Estates, Works, etc. for Exhibitions or Law Cases* (London: n. p., 1913), 16

There were still occasions when a certain level of material depiction in a model was vital to a legal case. For instance, in January 1899 at the City of London Court, Horatio Davies MP, brought action against a company intending to demolish an adjoining property to his own in order to construct a much taller building.[22] The dispute was over who owned which part of a boundary wall, but the situation was complicated: Davies's property was no ordinary building but in fact Crosby Hall, the surviving portion of a fifteenth-century mansion built in the City of London in 1466.[23] A sketch by the artist Robert Randoll from August 1899 shows the situation in question with Crosby Hall to the left, a disputed wall covered in scaffolding, and to the right, the empty site where the adjoining building previously stood. FIG. 27 Before the case entered the courtroom, both plaintiff and defendant had appointed architects, respectively T. H. Smith and Donald Campbell, and a legal agreement was drawn up by an independent party and third architect, Edward I'Anson. Included within the initial agreement was a drawing of the boundary wall that indicated, in blue, the portions that could be demolished.[24] When the matter reached court, most of the independent legal agreement was no longer disputed. Rather, the issue was which parts of the structure were shared and which were solely the property of Crosby Hall. Press reports reveal that Davies and his architect, T. H. Smith, had appealed to the commissioner assigned to the case that the designated 'party structure' was in fact the property of Crosby Hall and not a shared wall at a legal boundary.[25] Plaintiff and architect claimed that a new party wall was required to shore up the existing structure of Crosby Hall. This new boundary wall is evident in the model that Thorp produced for the courtroom, which showed the prominent facade of Crosby Hall and the exposed wall structure with each timber stud carefully depicted. FIG. 28 To the right of the model are additional pieces, perhaps the structure that Smith and Davies proposed should be constructed (and paid for) by the defendant in order to support the existing wall. Although they were not awarded legal costs, Smith and Davies won the case. The judge's ruling settled several common disputes and established a precedent that limited the changes to existing party walls for several years.[26] In a complicated legal situation involving disputed boundaries to existing buildings, contractual obligations, and the three-dimensional party wall structure, an architectural model provided the judge with a clear depiction of the existing building alongside a representation of the intricacies of the dispute. Mediating between past and present, or existing and proposed, the legal model could affect not only individual rulings, but wider legal codes, and in turn the scope of London's development.

22   My information on the case is based on three reports published in journals by the Royal Institution of Chartered Surveyors: 'The London Building Act, 1894: A Note on Two Recent Party Wall Cases', *RICS Professional Notes* 9 (1899), 349–51; 'City of London Court: Davies v. Lewis and Marks', *RICS Professional Notes* 9 (1899), 428–31; 'Ordinary General Meeting, Held on Monday December 11th, 1899', *RICS Transactions* 32 (1899), 93.

23   Crosby Hall was adapted for various uses until the early twentieth century when, faced with demolition, it was moved stone by stone to a site on Cheyne Walk in Chelsea where it was re-erected in 1909. Charles Knight, 'Crosby Place', in *London*, vol.1 (London: Charles Knight, 1841), 317–32; Norman, Philip, and William Douglas Caröe, *Survey of London*. Monograph 9: *Crosby Place* (London: Guild & School of Handicraft, 1908); Philip Norman, 'Crosby Place', *London Topographical Record* 6 (1909), 1–22; Andrew Saint, 'Ashbee, Geddes, Lethaby and the Rebuilding of Crosby Hall', *Architectural History* 34 (1991), 206–23.

24   'City of London Court', 429.

25   'Alterations at Crosby Hall', *City Press* (18 January 1899), 6.

26   'Ordinary General Meeting', *RICS Transactions* 32 (1899), 93.

THE EXHIBITION

Every summer dating back to 1769, the Royal Academy held the most prominent artistic exhibition in Britain, regarded as the official showcase for the achievements of contemporary painters, sculptors, and architects.[1] Initially based at Somerset House, the academy relocated to the east wing of the National Gallery (1837–66) before establishing itself at Burlington House, its home from 1867 and which featured a dedicated Architecture Gallery. Discussions in the popular press from this period indicate an expectation that architects should participate in the exhibition and engage with a varied audience drawn from across society: wealthy urban dandies, provincial clergymen, groups of young women escorted by chaperones, the Royal Family, journalists, and critics. FIG. 29 A leading art magazine, the *Athenaeum*, proposed that although it might be unreasonable to expect exhibits from exceptionally busy architects, the public would expect that those 'occupied on important works… would let us see what they are doing, or about to do'.[2] Alongside more established figures, other architects used the exhibition to place their designs in the public eye. Emerging designers keen to present themselves on the public stage regarded models as an effective means of promotion to gain future clients.[3] Others used the exhibition as an opportunity to display failed competition entries as portfolio pieces to a wider audience.

With 332,365 visitors to the 1874 exhibition, the architecture contingent did not go unnoticed, and two models in particular sparked significant controversy. These were exhibited by the architect William Burges and showed

---

1   David Solkin, 'Preface: The Exhibition', in David Solkin, ed., *Art on the Line: The Royal Academy Exhibitions at Somerset House 1780–1836* (New Haven: Yale University Press, 2002), xi.
2   'Architectural Drawings', *Athenaeum* (22 May 1847), 553.
3   Matthew Wells, '1847: J. B. Bunning and the Coal Exchange Model', in Mark Hallett, Sarah Victoria Turner, and Jessica Feather, eds., *The Royal Academy of Arts Summer Exhibition: A Chronicle, 1769–2018*, https://chronicle250.com/1847 (accessed 1 December 2022).

his proposal for the interior redecoration of St Paul's Cathedral. But their details – a set of paper decorations pasted onto the interiors – created debate. Heavy outlines and flat colouring gave the models 'a certain appearance of crudeness', reported the *Architect* in a page-long editorial in its 16 May edition. The central question was whether the combination of these issues affected the success of the models, which 'are not meant to be more than a sort of conventional representation of the designer's purpose while we have been rather looking at them as constituting a realistic presentment of the actual edifice'.[4] The problem, in other words, was the models' depiction of the 'real experience' of the proposed decoration. To start, the interiors were not completely true to scale. There were also elements such as windows where 'opaque pictures' representing the painted-glass clerestory provided effects that were nothing like that of translucent glass. Burges responded to the criticism with an eighteen-page pamphlet explaining that the models were for the wider public 'with the view of facilitating their examination, and of explaining the principles on which they are constructed'.[5] Moreover, they were merely a representation of an interior and not a simulation of reality. Anyone examining the models, he argued, must not forget that they are viewed 'under very different conditions from those of the Cathedral itself'. This explanation came as no surprise. Burges had already spent three years at work on a project that had become increasingly difficult for both professional and political reasons.

FIG. 29   William Payne (attributed), 'Private View of the Royal Academy', watercolour, 1858

4   'Draughtsmanship in the Architectural Room of the Royal Academy', *Architect* 11 (16 May 1874), 273.
5   *A Description of Mr. Burges' Models for the Adornment of St Paul's Now Exhibited at the Royal Academy* (London: E. Stanford, 1874), 3.

Following his appointment Burges would make three models that showed how the existing stone interior of the cathedral would be overlaid in marble. The first model, representing one bay of the nave, was produced at Burges's office in May 1873 by Horatio Walter Lonsdale.⁶ FIG. 30 At the end of May an artist recorded only as 'Pembury' came to the office to help Lonsdale paint the model. One month later, at the end of June, Burges was due to present his designs to the executive committee, which denied his request to show the model. Two committee members requested drawings, but Burges 'refused and stuck to models'. A resolution was agreed: if Burges would not make drawings of the work, he would instead produce a second model, this time 'a coloured model of apse – to be ready by November'.⁷ Three days later, in an attempt to mediate between Burges and the committee members who wanted to examine drawings, the Dean of St Paul's wrote to Burges suggesting that he supplement the model with drawings. Burges, it seems, refused to entertain the idea, replying 'drawings would be useless for those parts not studied in model'.⁸ Subsequently the committee authorized a budget of £100 for a model of the apse (around £6,250 today).⁹ FIG. 31 According to the receipts in Burges's journal, it is likely that John Walden – a Covent Garden-based craftsman who had worked with Burges at Cardiff Castle and the Tower House in Kensington, and made many pieces of furniture for the architect's designs – built the timber structures of both the nave and apse models.¹⁰ Lonsdale also continued to work on the model during the summer of 1873, decorating and painting the plain timber base. Work continued during the autumn (three committee members – the supportive William Longman, Alexander Beresford Hope, and Charles Eastlake – called at Burges's office to see the model), and Burges was asked to have the nave model ready 'for inspection' at the end of the November 1873.¹¹ In advance of this, Burges requested additional fees for model-making and suggested that work on a third model, a model of the dome, should commence at once. The superiority and importance that Burges placed on these models was clear. At one stage he informed a committee member that if drawings were still required, the committee would need to instruct someone else to make them from the models – and at its own expense.¹²

6	After studying at the Royal Academy Schools, Lonsdale had entered Burges's office as a pupil in the late 1860s and rose to become first an assistant and then the chief architectural artist.
7	William Burges, 'Journal for the Interior Decoration of St Paul's Cathedral, London', 27 June 1873, BuW/1, ff. 152–3, RIBA.
8	Burges, 'Journal', 30 June 1873, f. 156.
9	Burges, 'Journal', 12 July 1873, f. 160. Longman informed Burges that any excess from the £100 could be used to pay off the cost of the first model.
10	Burges, 'Journal', 14 July 1873, f. 160. For a discussion on Walden see: Adrian Tilbrook, *Truth, Beauty and Design: Victorian, Edwardian and Later Decorative Art* (London: Fischer, 1986), 26.
11	Burges, 'Journal', 8 November 1873, f. 162.
12	Burges, 'Journal', 15 November 1873, f. 166.

FIG. 30　William Burges, St Paul's, first model, one bay of the nave, 1873, in Richard Popplewell Pullan, *The Designs of William Burges, ARA* (London: Batsford, 1885), 2

FIG. 31 William Burges, St Paul's, second model, the apse, 1873, in Richard Popplewell Pullan, *The Designs of William Burges, ARA* (London: Batsford, 1885), 3

Eventually the model of the nave was shown at a meeting of the executive committee held at St Paul's in November 1873. On this occasion Burges was not allowed to present the model or explain its depiction of his proposals.[13] Instead, 'a memorandum explaining materials' was read aloud. The meeting concluded with a resolution that the presentation of the model of the apse would be deferred until March 1874. Following the meeting William Longman wrote to congratulate Burges, indicating that the Executive Committee appreciated the model, and requested his itemized bills. Beresford Hope and Longman again visited Burges's office at the start of the year to see the model in a semi-official capacity. Despite the visits and words of encouragement, when the models of the nave and apse were formally presented in March 1874, the executive committee, voting four to three, decided against recommending either 'as a basis for the decoration of S. Pauls'.[14]

The issue became a matter of public debate a few months later when Burges showed both models at the Royal Academy Summer Exhibition, and several editorials, opinion pieces, and correspondence about their display appeared in the press. One of Burges's friends, the architect Edward William Godwin, reviewed the models for a literary journal. After condemning the views of the opposition, Godwin admitted there were several difficulties affecting how the models were seen. First, because the models were sectional the colours were illuminated inaccurately – 'unless the entire west end, dome and transepts of the church, were removed and the windows barricaded on the outside'.[15] Second, in an echo of the *Architect*'s assessment, the windows were deeply problematic: the stained glass, which in reality would admit light and become illuminated with colour, was made from an opaque model-making material. As a consequence, the brightly lit spaces of the proposed building were depicted in shadow within the model, while portions of the interior that in reality would be the darkest were in fact bathed in light due to their presence at the 'front' of the models. Finally, scale was an issue. Believing that Burges had neglected many of the details of the decorative scheme because of the models' scale, Godwin proposed that the cartoons for the decoration should have been prepared at full scale, photographed, and mechanically reproduced at the correct scale for the model rather than being painted by hand.

The review drew criticism from within the architectural profession. In an article published the following week, the *Building News* declared that a model at one-half inch to the foot (modern scale 1:24) should not be deficient in 'representative power', as many architects 'seldom adopt so large a scale for their drawings'.[16] Instead the journal claimed that the model represented the decorative scheme accurately – but as a poor design: 'If the model looks confused under a glare of light, the darkened interior of the cathedral will look more so.'[17] In a letter to the *Architect*, Thomas Leverton Donaldson discussed the effect of the models on a viewer, suggesting that there was too much glare, too many gilded surfaces and colours, with 'no sufficient quantity of surface left plain for repose to the eye and mind'.[18]

In a letter to the press, T. Roger Smith wrote that the renovation scheme required careful study of both the models and the pamphlet. Smith also highlighted problems with the way the models had been produced and

---

13   Burges, 'Journal', 25 November 1873, f. 166.
14   Burges, 'Journal', transcription of Committee report, 27 March 1874, ff. 185–6.
15   Edward William Godwin, 'The Decoration of St Paul's Cathedral', *Fraser's Magazine* 90 (August 1874), 214.
16   'The Decoration of St Paul's Cathedral', *Building News* 27 (7 August 1874), 179.
17   'The Decoration of St Paul's Cathedral', 179.
18   'St Paul's Cathedral', *Architect* 11 (20 June 1874), 350.

exhibited. Members of the public, for example, could not be expected to comprehend how 'a luminous and brilliant surface like that of marble will be substituted for stone' due to the dull rendering of the model. Additionally, Smith noted, if the pamphlet had been properly consulted and Burges's plans to redecorate the existing fabric were correctly understood, then the models offered little assistance in comprehending the effect this alteration would have on the interior. Smith also criticized the Royal Academy's curation of Burges's display. The models had not been arranged to be viewed simultaneously by visitors in a single glance and therefore 'the effect of the whole building [that] might be obtained by looking through the nave-model at the choir model is lost'.[19] Despite defending the models as 'excellent in their way', Smith conceded that what was required was 'a decorated model of the whole building' rather than the two isolated fragments.[20] If a model of the entire cathedral was 'too costly or too troublesome' he proposed that Burges prepare 'a series of sections and interior perspectives embracing the entire design'.[21] The guidance provided by such drawings was not only necessary for the wider public, who Smith believed 'cannot fail to misunderstand Mr Burges's proposals', but also essential for the architectural profession when it came to ascertaining the reality of Burges's plans.

    Further public criticism over the depiction of materials and the simulation of experience shows how the models were used as vehicles for contemporary disputes and weaponized by critics of the pre-Reformation scheme. One anonymous architect, initially taking a similar line as Smith, argued that the models could not offer an adequate representation of the effects of marble that overclad the existing stone interior. The author suggested that until the decoration was seen in reality people would not 'believe in its beauty'; despite this lack of realistic depiction, the writer believed the colour of the proposed materials could be judged 'if not adequately, at least to a great extent'.[22] The author also accused the press of making 'very vague denunciations of its gaudiness and its un-Protestant quality' rather than articulating legitimate concerns in which 'critical faculty is really called into play'.

    On 19 May 1874, shortly after the models were put on display at the Royal Academy, the executive committee overruled its previous decision and accepted Burges's scheme 'as a basis' for the renovation of St Paul's. In June the four members (including James Fergusson) who had originally voted against Burges's design wrote a letter of protest, which was published in various newspapers. The letter claimed that the scope of the models did not constitute 'sufficient groundwork for a final decision': they lacked furniture and features such as an altar, and further complaints described how Burges's persistent refusal to include drawings with the models meant there was no way of judging how the other spaces of the cathedral (i.e., those that had not been modelled) would appear. There was no discussion of the models' inability to simulate the experience of the proposed interior. Instead the main objections were to Burges's aesthetic decisions, from the proposed colour scheme, which would 'absorb light in an interior already too dark', to the variety of marbles that risked producing 'an effect at once confused and gaudy'.[23] The following week, a letter from the executive committee was published announcing that 'every portion' of the models would be examined before the

---

19   'St Paul's Cathedral', 350.
20   'Correspondence: The Adornment of St Paul's Cathedral', *Architect* 11 (18 July 1874), 36.
21   'Correspondence: The Adornment of St Paul's Cathedral', 36.
22   'The Decoration at St Paul's', *Architect* 11 (11 July 1874), 21.
23   'St Paul's Cathedral', 349.

commission was formally awarded.[24] By July Burges was ordered to provide coloured perspective drawings and designs for the elements shown in the model, and for the rest of the cathedral.

The press continued to be divided over the design and models long after the close of the Summer Exhibition. In October 1874, facing mounting public pressure, the committee terminated Burges's appointment. Subsequently Burges wrote a letter to the Dean of St Paul's acknowledging the committee's actions while underlining the importance of architectural models in the conception of his design. He preferred to work with models rather than drawings, he explained, as 'the difficulties [are] better foreseen by their use than by coloured drawings, where colours can be blended, softened down, and hidden by convenient shadow'.[25] These difficulties are almost certainly a reference to the three-dimensional nature of the applied decoration to the walls, vaults, and other surfaces of the cathedral. From his experience, the colours of a 'working model' – for instance the paper decorations applied to the models at the Royal Academy – needed to be 'slightly more crude than in a picture' as 'their intensity is very considerably altered by the accidents of position' or how the model is viewed by visitors at the exhibition. The nature of the model as a working tool for Burges gave it certain qualities that in turn portrayed an unfair version of the design to visitors at the Royal Academy.

The termination of Burges's appointment did not signal the end of the saga. One year after the exhibition of the models, three perspectives of the scheme drawn by Axel Haig were exhibited at the 1875 Summer Exhibition. FIG. 32 A highly skilled draughtsman, the Swedish-born Haig was the leading architectural perspectivist in mid-Victorian London. He was a regular delineator for Burges's designs and on this occasion was paid £250 for his work.[26] Reviewing the Summer Exhibition, the *Architect* noted that Haig's drawings not only supplemented the models, but also corrected the 'erroneous impressions which the crude tinting of the model, entirely devoid of atmospheric effect, could not fail to give'.[27] Burges had arguably hired Haig to make the drawings in order to 'win back' the commission at St Paul's by ensuring that visitors to the summer show could clearly see the 'atmospheric effect' of his design. This reading aligns with the idea examined in the chapter 'The Public Sphere': did a model or a drawing offer a more realistic preview of a design? Extending these earlier debates, at St Paul's the discussion shifted to consider the atmosphere and experience of an interior – a depiction that the models were unable to replicate due to their materials and positioning in the Summer Exhibition.

---

24   'The Decoration of St Paul's', *Architect* 11 (27 June 1874), 365.
25   Burges, 'Journal', letter from Burges to Dean, 23 November 1874, f. 240.
26   Burges, 'Journal', letter from Burges to Dean, 4 August 1874, f. 222.
27   'Architecture at the Royal Academy – I', *Architect* 13 (8 May 1875), 272.

FIG. 32　Axel Haig, *St Paul's Decorated*, 1874, watercolour after William Burges

While the drawings were on display at the Royal Academy, Burges wrote to William Longman (still a member of the St Paul's executive committee) admitting that Haig's drawings 'have convinced the public that the effect of colour in the model was an erroneous one'.[28] Despite this realization, the executive committee thought otherwise and Burges remained unemployed. Following the termination of Burges's appointment the paper decorations were stripped from the models by an unknown individual and pasted into a scrapbook that remains in the cathedral's archives.[29] FIG. 33 Burges's two exhibited models show the problems between realism and abstraction in how models are both constructed and subsequently perceived. It is clear that in the renovation of St Paul's Cathedral Burges was convinced of the conceptual role of a model ahead of a perspective drawing. Nonetheless when displayed in public the models could not replicate the internal lighting, accurately depict the decorative scheme, or offer a view of the whole project in one image – something the public demanded, and which was only provided by Axel Haig's atmospheric perspectives. However, towards the end of the nineteenth century the role of the model was beginning to change, and a new generation of architects would go on to reconceptualize its use in public exhibitions.

FIG. 33 William Burges, paper decorations made for model, removed and pasted into a scrapbook at a later date, 1873

28 Burges, 'Journal', letter from Burges to Longman, entry for 16 June 1875, f. 296.
29 Subsequently the timber frames of the models were adapted and reused by William Blake Richmond in the course of designing his decorative scheme at St Paul's between 1891 and 1904.

EDWARD SCHROEDER PRIOR AND THE MODEL AS 'FEELING'

> The Architecture Room this year contains two models of buildings, in addition to the usual drawings. What may be hoped from such an innovation?[30]

Twenty years after the St Paul's controversy the Architecture Room at the Royal Academy Summer Exhibition continued to serve as a space for debate. Without doubt, the question of the model's role within the profession and the public's perception had endured. However, there had been a 21-year absence of models on display, something that was to change in 1895. Displayed in the corner of the Architecture Room at the summer show was a model of a house by Edward Schroeder Prior. It showed the external form of the building and was accompanied by small plan drawings pinned to the corners of a baseboard. Despite the house's innovative butterfly plan, the true innovation that attracted the above comment from the *Builder* was the presence and expression of the model. Although 'comparatively rough in appearance', the editorial noted that it was 'revolutionary in its tendencies'.[31] This radical potential was found not only in its formal or spatial characteristics, but its authorship. As the journal explained, 'we strongly suspect Mr Prior of having made the model with his own hands. He is quite capable of it'. Only a black-and-white photograph of the model survives. FIG. 34 Fixed to a baseboard and roughly occupying a diamond-shaped outline, the model featured rubble walls, a pan-tile roof, leaded casements, tall chimneys, and was surrounded by lawns and paths. This depiction of materiality is both descriptive and naturalistic: the rubble stone walls are coarse and irregular; the weather-boarded gable ends are rough and uneven. The cumulative effect offered a more naturalistic image of a building than any previous model-maker had been able to achieve in cardboard, plaster, or timber. Prior's model signifies an emerging shift in architectural practice at the end of the nineteenth century as architects began to see the potential of model-making through their own hands as a tactile way of simultaneously developing formal ideas and intellectual concepts.

The model of the house was seen by approximately three hundred thousand exhibition visitors over the summer of 1895. That July, some fifty individuals had written to various journals with opinions about how the architectural profession should exhibit their designs at the Summer Exhibition.[32] Almost everyone was dissatisfied with the Royal Academy and discussed topics including the purpose of architectural exhibitions, how the exhibition should be curated, the employment of external artists, and the question of authorship. Many architects called for more architectural models to be displayed. Others welcomed the exhibition of 'models of all sorts – of whole buildings or portions of them'.[33] Prior himself wrote to the *Builder's* editor and proposed that the Royal Academy should only admit submissions from architects 'which are modelled and can stand on the same basis as the sculptor's models, as the work of the artist himself'.[34]

---

30 'Architecture at the Royal Academy', *Builder* 68 (4 May 1895), 323.
31 'Architecture at the Royal Academy', 323.
32 'The Representation of Architecture at the Royal Academy', *Builder* 69 (6 July 1895), 1–3; 'The Representation of Architecture at the Royal Academy: Concluded', *Builder* 69 (13 July 1895), 21–3, 25–8.
33 'Representation of Architecture at the Royal Academy', 3.
34 'Representation of Architecture at the Royal Academy: Concluded', 27.

FIG. 34　Edward Schroeder Prior, model of a house, 1895

Prior subsequently clarified his views on model-making as a creative act in an essay titled 'Architectural Modelling', which addressed subjects such as the purposes of model-making for architects, the practical use and representational qualities of materials, and the conceptual role of the medium in comparison to other artistic disciplines. From the first line, 'The architectural model is not recommended to the profession as a new device for client-getting',[35] Prior aimed to establish a clear purpose for models in contemporary architectural practice: they were for architects, not clients, who he believed were unable to understand drawings and could, at most, be shown sketches of initial designs. According to Prior it was risky to show clients a model for two reasons. First, a model was too revealing of the architect's intentions: 'It is dangerous to show what is so near the truth.' Second, a model was an experimental tool for the architect, but because of its legibility, 'it may provoke criticism'. When used in the office, however, in the context of furthering a design, models were vital for architects as they enabled an opportunity to review work 'before the imprimatur of the builder is set upon it'.

In addition to answering the question of who models were for, Prior had extensive thoughts on how models were made, and his essay suggests a wide variety of materials. For sketch models cardboard or French putty, a type of impure soap, could readily take the form of architectural surfaces. For more elaborate models wax was indispensable due to its ability to represent both the colour and texture of real materials. Powdered pigments could suggest colours, and any required texture could be achieved by adding sand or powders to a combination of paraffin and turpentine. Wax could be applied to pasteboard and worked with modelling tools to replicate the material texture of a wall. In turn these models could be used to discuss aspects of construction with craftsmen – aspects which otherwise resisted representation in drawings, such as 'the desired texture and arrangement' of a wall. And while the specification and contract should dictate how a building should be assembled, a 'serious practitioner' should always produce a model in order for the contractor and craftsman to 'see' what the contract states: the architect 'will be loath to trust the success of the operation to drawings, plans, and specifications'.[36] This attitude was closely aligned with the Arts and Crafts idea that architects should not only understand the principles of construction, but also be trained in craft-based building techniques – an attempt to reform design against the perceived decline in standards of quality caused by wholesale industrial production. Prior's unique contribution to the field was that an architect could explore their own subjectivity towards the colour, texture, and materiality of a building through the production of models.

Another aspect of importance was the three-dimensional nature of models. Similar to the view expressed in his letter to the *Builder*, he complained: 'It is continually forgotten that an architectural design is a sculpture in the round.'[37] Prior proposed that the way that architects made drawings was largely to blame. The standardized use of technical drawing instruments such as T-squares encouraged parallel composition in plan and elevation, while drawing plans and elevations on separate pieces of paper had the effect of separating the design into abstract categories. Instead, Prior proposed, 'if modelled first, the design would have had unity of plan and elevation impressed on it from the first'. This was not the only occasion that Prior discussed

---

35   Edward Schroeder Prior, 'Architectural Modelling', *Builder* 69 (29 June 1895), 482–3, here: 482.
36   Prior, 'Architectural Modelling', 483.
37   Prior, 'Architectural Modelling', 483.

the form-making characteristic of model-making. Later, in his inaugural lecture as the Slade Professor in Fine Art at the University of Cambridge, he articulated the fundamental importance of model-making in the university education of an architect: 'He must model so as to understand how form is situated.'[38] And yet, the benefits of perspective drawing over an architectural model (and vice versa) was a recurring issue in debates over architecture. After Prior exhibited his work at the Royal Academy, the artist Dugald Sutherland MacColl proposed that in future any model on display should be covered in part by a screen, 'pierced with eyeholes at a height corresponding to the height of the spectator's eye on the scale of the model'.[39] Fixing the viewpoint of an observer would render the model into a perspective, separating the subject from the object and flattening its three-dimensional character – ironically turning a model into a form of drawing, an act that sat in complete opposition to Prior's conception of architecture as a three-dimensional art form.

For Prior, one of the biggest problems of architectural drawings was their lack of materiality, colour, or texture in representation. Much like today, the Victorian architect used written specifications to communicate the material aspects of a construction to clients and builders. But this, Prior analogized, was like a painter who would not make paintings, only a written register of pigments: 'How can the delicate inspirations, that come of personal feeling in such matters as texture and colour, be expected from such methods?' The 'present habits' of architectural practice, Prior continued, caused a separation between the architect and his work. In order to bridge this gulf, 'The model brings the architect a step nearer his work than the drawing did.'[40] The expressive nature of model-making meant the medium was a representation suited for an emotive purpose rather than a purely imitative one. In part, this was related to the choices and types of materials used. Wax models, for example, could convey 'feeling to oneself rather than facts to another ... the use of wax is but a door to experiment'.[41] And indeed, experimentation through making played an important role in Prior's ideas around the use of models. This was underlined by the fact that both the first model he exhibited at the 1895 Royal Academy Summer Exhibition and a second model, shown at the academy in 1899, were theoretical projects later used as prototypes in Prior's domestic work.[42] FIG. 35 The 1895 model appears to have been the forerunner to 'The Barn', a cottage in Exmouth built in 1897, while the 1899 model represents a period of development in Prior's domestic architecture that culminated in his celebrated work at Voewood in Norfolk, completed in 1905.

Both Prior's models and the theoretical discussion surrounding their use exerted an influence beyond Britain. The plan of 'The Barn' was reproduced in Hermann Muthesius's *Das englische Haus* (1904) and exerted a particularly strong influence on German Expressionist architecture in the early twentieth century.[43] FIG. 36 German architecture transitioned from Jugendstil through Expressionism and into Neue Sachlichkeit of the 1920s in part due to the reshaping of architecture into a plastic art form with spatially conceived structures, responsive to the modern human experience. Contemporaneously the

---

38 'In the Value of Architecture', *Building News* (7 June 1911), 804.
39 'Architecture and the Royal Academy: A Discussion V', *Architectural Review* 13 (1903), 47–51, here: 47.
40 Prior, 'Architectural Modelling', 483.
41 Prior, 'Architectural Modelling', 483.
42 As with the 1895 model, this model has not survived, but there are two black and white photographs of the model in the British Architectural Library. Additionally two other photographs were published in the *Architectural Review*: 'Supplement: Architecture and Crafts at the Royal Academy, 1899', *Architectural Review* 6 (June 1899), 81.
43 Hermann Muthesius, *Das englische Haus*, vol. 2 (Berlin: Ernst Wasmuth, 1904), 128.

clay model played an important role in the design processes of architects including Hans Poelzig, Hans and Wassili Luckhardt, Hermann Finsterlin, and Bernhard Hoetger. FIG. 37 Their use of clay models as conceptual tools emerged thanks in part to their study of Prior's two Royal Academy models and his 1895 theoretical text, mediated through Muthesius as well as Wassili Luckhardt's 1921 polemic 'Vom Entwerfen' (On Designing).[44] Luckhardt paraphrased Prior's critique on conception through parallel projection and encouraged architects to put pens and paper aside in favour of expressing a design in plasticine and clay. Dissimilar from how his predecessors had considered the medium, Prior's approach to model-making held the potential to redefine architecture an an art form more akin to sculpture, in turn raising questions of authorship, agency, and expertise; questions that can only be answered by turning to consider the model-makers themselves.

FIG. 35   Edward Schroeder Prior, model of a house, 1899

44   Prior, 'Architectural Modelling'; Wassili Luckhardt, 'Vom Entwerfen', *Stadtbaukunst alter and neuer Zeit* 11 (1 September 1921), 169–70. See also Ralf Liptau's discussion on Luckhardt: Ralf Liptau, 'Selber kneten: Modellbasiertes Entwerfen zwischen Originalität und Nachbildung', in Eva von Engelberg-Dočkal, Markus Krajewski, and Frederike Lausch, eds., *Mimetische Praktiken in der neueren Architektur Prozesse und Formen der Ähnlichkeitserzeugung*, (Heidelberg: arthistoricum. net, 2017), 131–43.

es die Bauunternehmer fabrikmäßig herstellen, hat alle Bestandteile des größeren, Halle, Drawingroom, Eßzimmer und womöglich noch Rauch- oder Frühstückszimmer, aber alle Räume sind so klein geworden und dazu in der Regel noch so mit unnützem Hausrat angefüllt, daß es schwer ist, sich in diesen Räumen überhaupt zu regen, geschweige denn darin zu wohnen. Wer in England ein Haus mit wenigen aber großen Zimmern haben will, wird finden, daß es solche Häuser heute unter den Durchschnittshäusern nicht mehr gibt; nur wer das Glück hat, ein altes Haus zu erlangen, kann seinen Wunsch erfüllt finden. Zimmer von einer annehmbaren, nach unsern Begriffen immer noch bescheidenen Größe, etwa von 5 zu 5 1/2 m, findet man erst in Häusern, die wenigstens 12 Wohn- und Schlafzimmer haben. Das kleine Haus hat nicht nur winzig kleine Zimmer, sondern diese sind auch alle fest gegeneinander abgeschlossen, wie die großen Zimmer des großen Hauses (vgl. S. 27), sie stellen also eine Reihe trostloser kleiner Käfige dar.

Bei dieser Sachlage ist es begreiflich, daß vernünftige Architekten gegen dieses zimperliche kleine Haus von heute Front machen und alles versuchen, um es durch eine bessere Lösung zu ersetzen. Wer sich aber klar macht, daß selbst in England von hundert Häusern, die gebaut werden, kaum fünf in die Hände von Architekten fallen, der weiß, wie schwer dieses Beginnen ist,

Abb. 101. Haus „The Barn" in Exmouth, Devonshire. Vorderansicht.
Erbaut von Edward S. Prior.

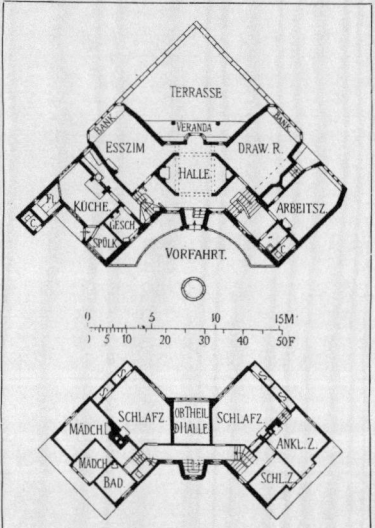

Versuche zu einer bessern Grundform.

Abb. 102 und 103.
Haus „The Barn" in Exmouth, Devonshire.
Grundrisse des Erdgeschosses und ersten Stockwerkes.
Erbaut von Edward S. Prior. 1 : 400.

FIG. 36 Edward Schroeder Prior, ' "The Barn", Exmouth, UK, 1897', in Hermann Muthesius, *Das englische Haus*, vol. 2 (Berlin: Ernst Wasmuth, 1904), 131

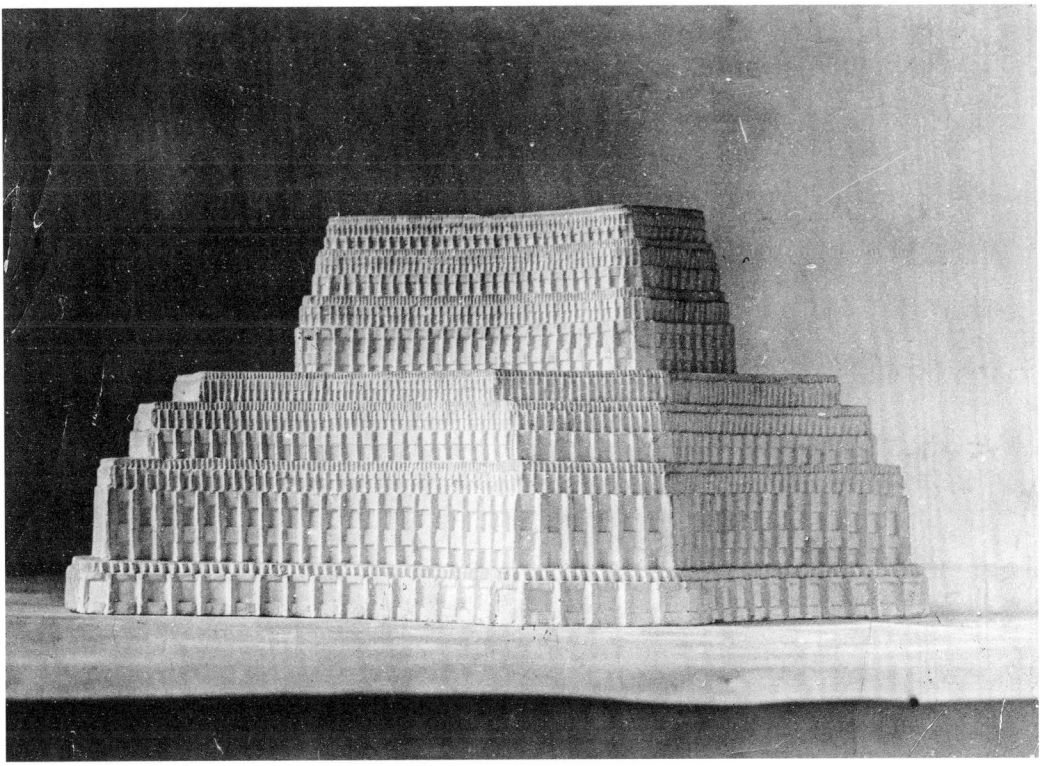

FIG. 37   Hans Poelzig, project for a town hall, Dresden, 1917

THE MODEL-MAKERS' WORKSHOP

Towards the end of September 1849 a curious letter arrived at 27 Argyll Street, the office of Lewis Vulliamy. An architect best known for his ecclesiastical work across England, Vulliamy had just begun designing an Italianate palazzo for the art and plant collector Robert Holford on Park Lane. The new building, later described as the 'most opulent of all the Park Lane palaces', was to replace an existing house, one of a number of new mansions that were rising on the easterly edge of Hyde Park as the area became the most sought-after London address of the mid-Victorian period.[1] FIGS. 38, 39 The letter explained that the model-maker Richard Day had died a few days earlier from cholera (almost certainly linked to a large-scale outbreak of the disease in London at the time). In the months leading up to his death, Day had been building a plaster model of Dorchester House for Vulliamy at his workshop in Southwark. The son of a mason, Day worked as a sculptor of funerary monuments before his involvement as a stone-carver on Buckingham Palace in 1827–28.[2] After exchanging architectural sculpture for model-making, his work was well known among Londoners as it was exhibited publicly for the display of new buildings in the capital. Despite his minor fame, the press reported that Day had been struggling for new orders ('he must either seek some other occupation or starve') and, praising the quality of his work, encouraged readers to commission him for new projects.[3] What was curious about the letter, however, was that the writer introduced himself as Richard Day Jr. He offered his services to complete the model of Dorchester House and reassured Vulliamy of his abilities. The following

1 Sheppard, Francis, ed. *Survey of London.* Volume 40: *The Grosvenor Estate in Mayfair,* Part 2: *The Buildings* (London: London County Council, 1980), 273.
2 Ingrid Roscoe, M.G. Sullivan, and Emma Hardy, *A Biographical Dictionary of Sculptors in Britain 1660–1851* (New Haven: Yale University Press, 2009), 349.
3 'Day, the Architectural Modeller', *Builder* 6 (7 October 1848), 490.

week a contract was agreed for the younger Day to complete the model started by his late father.[4]

Letters from Day Jr to Vulliamy offer a glimpse of a model-maker's working life. Day Jr reported how his father's death had affected his ability to finish the model – his mother had been moved into new apartments, his father's personal effects had to be thrown away, and, crucially, modelling apparatus needed to be removed from his father's studio, some of which was being repaired and repurposed by Day Jr in his workshop at 42 Commercial Road in Southwark. A year later Day Jr moved to a new workshop on the New Kent Road, which caused further disruption as his tools and equipment were packed away for a week, leaving him unable to continue with his work.[5]

The location of these workshops shows the complicated logistics of model-making in the rapidly expanding capital. With architects based in more upmarket locations for their clients, often in the West End, and model-makers in cheaper accommodation, often south of the river Thames, the physical distance between the office and the workshop could easily cause problems and delays. On one occasion Day felt he had to apologize to Vulliamy for not leaving a model at Dorchester House after a meeting because he was working on it in his studio. Day explained how travelling to Park Lane, 'causes such a loss of time, & I cannot work the hours there that I can at home'.[6] Day operated alone, without assistants, which reduced the speed at which he could complete projects. While Vulliamy had a team of architects engaged on the project at each stage, Day frequently worked on the model until the early hours of the morning. During a long period of work, from October 1849 until May 1857, Day made at least three major models for Dorchester House: a ¼-inch scale model of the house (begun by Day Sr in 1849), a larger model of the main facade, and a multi-tiered model of the interior with a central hall, staircase, and adjoining vestibules. These were supplemented by a series of smaller models made at various stages.

4 'Memorandum of understanding between Richard Day junior and Robert Holford', 1 October 1849, VuL 13/1/3, RIBA.
5 Richard Day, letter to Lewis Vulliamy, undated, VuL 13/1/19, RIBA.
6 Richard Day, letter to Lewis Vulliamy, undated, VuL 13/1/47, RIBA.

FIG. 38   Dorchester House, view from northeast, H. N. King (photographer), in *Round London* (London: George Newnes, 1895), 151

FIG. 39   Dorchester House, view of south facade, Cassel and Co (photographer), in *The Queen's London* (London: Cassel, 1896), 82

At the start of the project the scope and scale of the first model was undecided. A letter from Robert Holford to Vulliamy in June 1849 questioned why a larger-scale model was not being produced by Day.[7] As a client Holford was highly educated, capable of understanding orthographic conventions and making his own copies of Vulliamy's drawings in order to offer suggestions to the design. Additionally, Holford proposed that a fourth model should be made to solve a disagreement with the landowner, the Grosvenor Estate, about the leasehold of Dorchester House. Perhaps influenced by the use of models in courtrooms, Holford made a small sketch to outline to Day a rough block model to solve this dispute. Similar to Day Sr's 1834 model of Trafalgar Square and the National Gallery (discussed in the chapter 'The Public Sphere'), this model included two possible views: one showing the relation between the boundary wall and the existing house, and the other showing the relation between the boundary wall and the proposed design.[8] FIG. 40 It is unclear whether this model was ever executed by Day, but Holford's diagram shows how clients also conceived of models as explanatory aids to others, especially those with public and private interests in the contested spaces of the metropolis.

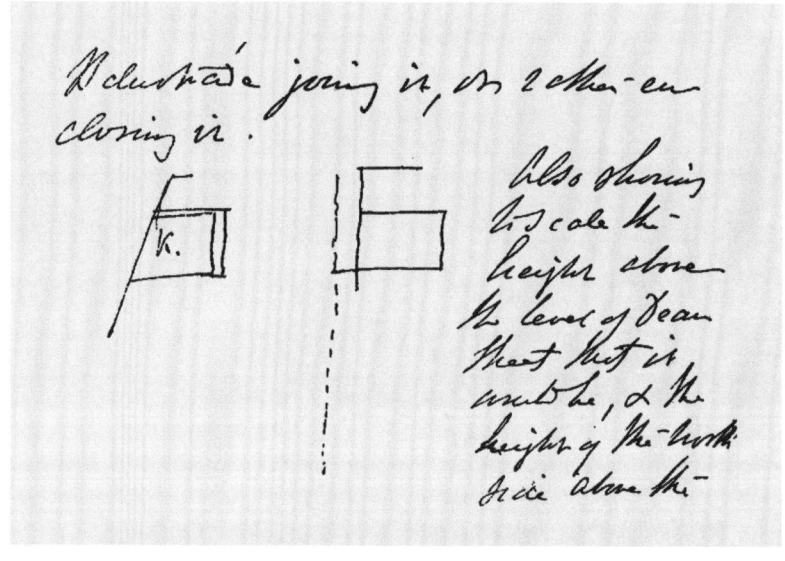

FIG. 40   Robert Holford, diagram in a letter to describe how a model should be made, 1850

7   Robert Holford, letter to Lewis Vulliamy, 14 June 1849, VuL 1/1/3, RIBA.
8   Robert Holford, letter to Lewis Vulliamy, 19 August 1850, VuL 1/2/5, RIBA.

In addition to spatial logistics, the business of model-making also included the organization of labour. Although he lacked a dedicated team of assistants like Vulliamy, Day collaborated with other skilled trades, subcontracting out portions of the work that he was unable to produce himself. Initially Day made slow progress on the first model. He was late on his promise to finish the first part by Christmas 1849 – its incompleteness, he claimed, was not his fault because the decorative figures were the responsibility of a friend, a sculptor in Liverpool working on St George's Hall.[9] It is possible that Day was working with William Grinsell Nicholl, who not only carved the pediment and free-standing sculpture at St George's but also produced the sculptural figures for C. R. Cockerell's now lost model for the Royal Exchange (discussed in the chapter 'The Public Sphere'). Day's schedule was often badly organized – no doubt a point of contention with Vulliamy's office, which kept highly detailed accounts of the work undertaken despite the small sums involved (typically £3 or less; £240 in modern money). After a year of work and several disputes with Day over money, Vulliamy's method of recording Day's work changed from a linear description to a tabular system of labour. Every single action related to the production or alteration of the model was itemized by Vulliamy's employees. By way of contrast, Day's own records for each payment were far more concise. For instance, the work undertaken in the summer of 1850 was detailed over two pages by Vulliamy's office, where Day's account describes it in just thirty words. In one invoice Day explains how he would have asked for an advance on the work completed but he knew that Vulliamy preferred 'having the exact account of the works done'.[10] These accounting practices may relate to Vulliamy's family background: Lewis Vulliamy was the son of the clockmaker Benjamin Vulliamy who also operated a tabular record keeping system. Unlike a linear system where each entry features a simple written description of the job or work to be performed (similar to Day's books), Benjamin Vulliamy's tabular system itemized the watches he was repairing into individual components (e.g., cylinder, wheel). Each listed component was detailed with a series of actions that described the specific activity happening to that portion of the watch (e.g., polishing, fitting, mending). This 'language of action' was the result of an emerging technical or operative culture within the economy of production.[11] From one type of work to another in London, wider practices of economic management affected multiple aspects of society including the production of architectural models.

Despite discrepancies over their costs, one thing is clear about Day's models: they were not produced from a complete set of drawings. Instead their fabrication was a site of exploration where the model-maker helped to adjust the object in relation to the conversations between architect and client. In the summer of 1850, the ¼-inch scale model of the house was reworked as the design progressed through discussions between Vulliamy and Holford.[12] Alterations were made to the facade, roofline, and details like the balustrade or profile of windows. Much of this work appears to have been made to the 'original' model (started by Day Sr), but other portions of the

9	Richard Day, letter to Lewis Vulliamy, 12 December 1849, VuL 13/1/6, RIBA.
10	Richard Day, letter to Lewis Vulliamy, 17 December 1853, VuL 13/1/17, RIBA.
11	I adopt the approach taken in Liliane Hilaire-Pérez's work on eighteenth-century subcontracting techniques in artisanal trades: Liliane Hilaire-Pérez, *La pièce et le geste: Artisans, marchands et savoir technique à Londres au XVIIIe siècle* (Paris: Albin Michel, 2013); Manuela Martini, Liliane Hilaire-Pérez, and Giorgio Riello, 'Practices of Fixed-Price Work: Trades, Techniques and Subcontracting in a Eurasian Perspective, Eighteenth to the Twentieth Century. An Introduction', *Revue de Synthèse* 140, nos. 1–2 (December 2019), 1–12.
12	Lewis Vulliamy, account book, entries for June 1850 and July 1850, VuL 13/2/16, RIBA.

building may have been modelled to show options. Across several days in July 1850 Day modelled two possibilities for windows on the west facade of the building, which he followed with a much larger, one inch to one foot (1:12 scale) model of part of the lower storey of the facade. Models were also used to examine proposed changes to the location of the house. In August 1851, Day lowered the roadway of the carriage porch on the model and added moveable pathways to the porch from the corners of the building's east and west fronts, colouring them to differentiate from the rest of the model. Working back and forth between different scales, Day would use the models to test different designs and then present them to Holford. This iterative approach meant that work on one model to, say, explore the design for a facade, had a chain reaction as revisions would then be required on another. Day worked in this fashion, moving from scale to scale, model to model, from September 1849 (when he first wrote to Vulliamy) to July 1852. Then in the early autumn of 1852 Day began work on a new model, cast and carved in plaster, which included the staircase and surrounding rooms of Dorchester House. FIG. 41 Over the five years it took to complete Day continued to make adjustments as new elements were examined and subsequently changed[13] The model was made in distinct sections enabling new components, such as options for the ceilings, to be applied to test different spatial possibilities.

Innovative as his methods were, the process was incredibly slow. While Day himself was often unwell – writing to Vulliamy, Jacob Wray Mould (Vulliamy's assistant) or Clement Thomas (the clerk of works) to offer his excuses – the task of model-making appears to have been delayed by the techniques he used. A letter written during the process of making the staircase model describes part of Day's working method. Day explained to Vulliamy how he had not fully assembled the staircase as his approach was to cast and carve each individual component before connecting them together.[14] As a result, progress was often delayed as Day required drawings of particular portions, from tracings of plans to more decorative details, which Vulliamy and his assistants failed to deliver in a timely fashion. Another cause of delay was Holford's irregular presence in London. Unlike the drawings, which Holford had sent to his country residence where he would copy and return them, any discussion surrounding the architectural models required the attendance of all three men. From his letters, Day is often surprised by Holford's sudden appearance in London ('I did not expect Mr Holford would have been in London so soon or [I] would have had the lower part ready for his inspection') and often had to either delay presentation of the models or work faster to finish them.[15] As the project developed Vulliamy's office became better at working with Day, writing several weeks in advance to warn him of Holford's arrival, but even when all three were in a room together there was still sometimes cause for confusion.[16] For instance, in December 1850, Day responded to a note from Vulliamy who wanted to understand why the model had only four windows with pediments, rather than the six requested in his last letter. Day explained that these written instructions were contrary to the verbal discussions between the three during their last meeting.[17] When a simple note

13   Lewis Vulliamy, copy of payment receipt issued to Richard Day, 23 May 1857, VuL 13/2/22, RIBA.
14   Richard Day, letter to Lewis Vulliamy, 23 October 1852, VuL 13/1/12, RIBA.
15   Richard Day, letter to Lewis Vulliamy, 23 October 1852, VuL 13/1/12, RIBA.
16   For instance, the warning of Holford's presence in the copy letter written by one of Vulliamy's assistants in October 1853: 'I am directed by Mr Vulliamy to say that as Mr Holford will shortly be in town, he will thank you to make all possible effort in forwarding the model of the Grand Staircase.' Mr Young, copy of letter to Richard Day, 12 October 1853, VuL 13/1/15, RIBA.
17   Richard Day, letter to Lewis Vulliamy, 31 December 1850, VuL 13/1/10, RIBA.

would not suffice, Day enclosed drawings of his own. On one occasion Day wrote to Vulliamy's office asking for a plan to be cut at a much higher level than normal drawing conventions would allow in order to represent the three-dimensional projection of a window and balcony. To illustrate exactly what he meant, he added a small sketch elevation of the stones above the window, annotated with a horizontal line ('A to B') to show the exact location where he required a plan to be drawn. FIG. 42

FIG. 41 William Hatherell, views of the staircase and hall at Dorchester House, lithograph, 1883, in Eustace Balfour, 'Dorchester House', *Magazine of Art 6* (October 1883), 398

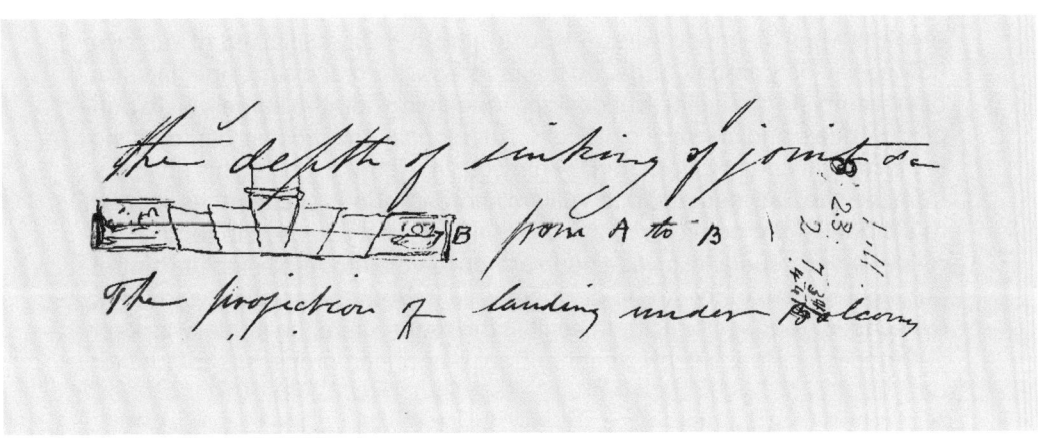

FIG. 42 Richard Day Jr, detail of letter showing diagram of measurements required for model, c. 1850–52

FROM DRAWINGS TO MODELS

Issues with the translation of scale and dimensions emerged in the drawings that Vulliamy sent to Day. Day once had to apologize to the architect for the size of the sculptural panels he had attached to the ¼-inch model and noted, 'I am not aware that they are any larger than those sketches you gave me. I perceived that they were to inch scale so I made mine ¼ size of them.'[18] On another occasion Day questioned Vulliamy on the usefulness of a drawing, a pattern for a window and the above cornice, which lacked dimensions and a scale. He requested that in the future all of the issued information 'be drawn to the scale I am at work upon & that there will be nothing of the ornament left to my taste'.[19] There were instances when without the architect's drawings Day was unable to work. At one stage he explained to Vulliamy that he needed drawings for the ornament on the main cornice and balcony in order to continue while other parts of the model were drying.

In addition to these complications, the physical attributes of plaster also factored into the making of Day's models. Even the storage of the model at Dorchester House required particular environmental conditions. In December 1850 Day wrote to Vulliamy requesting that the clerk of works not remove the model from the room where it was stored. He also specified the temperature and lighting conditions needed to protect and present the model:

> I hope you will not give orders to Thomas to remove the 1st model down to the room below during this weather as it will greatly affect the model, there should be a good Fire every day for at least a week previous; to drive off the damp. & perhaps you would arrange the sky light, so as to put the model in proper effect. Please excuse these suggestions but I know that the consequences would be ruinous to the model if placed in a damp room; it being nearly as absorbent as a sponge.[20]

Day's concerns were not unfounded. Over the course of the project there were several accidents involving the models. At one stage a portion of the parapet on a model was broken by a builder working on the new house.[21] This was the same portion, Day noted, that had already been twice smashed and repaired when the model was previously moved.[22] Day explained to Vulliamy how he had only partially repaired the model as the 'real' balustrade had now been completed to a different design, underlining how the models were part of an iterative and discursive process. Additionally, the process of modelling in plaster caused setbacks for Day himself. In a letter excusing his absence from the site, Day described to Vulliamy how a 'serious accident' happened to a model of the cornice which would take at least two days to repair.[23] Already behind schedule, he had been at work on the model all night and, after putting it in front of the fire to dry, damaged it. Both the accident and Day's subsequent request for a fire to be lit in the room where the model was kept at Dorchester House show the importance of drying processes for plaster

18 Richard Day, letter to Lewis Vulliamy, undated (c. 1850–52), VuL 13/1/39, RIBA.
19 The flattery was connected to Vulliamy's various published volumes on ornament: Lewis Vulliamy, *Examples of Ornamental Sculpture in Architecture Drawn from the Originals of Bronze, Marble and Terra Cotta in Greece Asia Minor and Italy*, 3 vols. (London: Lewis Vulliamy and Henry Moses, 1823–24, 1827). Richard Day, letter to Lewis Vulliamy, undated (c. 1850–52), VuL 13/1/33, RIBA.
20 Richard Day, letter to Lewis Vulliamy, 24 December 1850, VuL 13/1/8, RIBA.
21 Richard Day, letter to Lewis Vulliamy, undated (after 1852), VuL 13/1/53, RIBA. Day immediately repaired the model and was paid 12s by the subcontractor's clerk for the repair.
22 This is possibly the house with the skylight referred to in the letter from 24 December 1850 (see Richard Day, letter to Lewis Vulliamy, 24 December 1850, VuL 13/1/8, RIBA).
23 Richard Day, letter to Lewis Vulliamy, undated, VuL 13/1/35, RIBA.

models. Wet, recently cast plaster can be carved and worked into the required form and details can be added with tools, but this also means that the model is soft and weak. Recently cast plaster also retains the water mixed with the raw plaster and is therefore incredibly heavy until this water evaporates. At the same time, dried plaster can reabsorb moisture in the atmosphere, causing the model to soften again or even crack at particular junctions.

Following the completion of the models for Dorchester House in 1857, Day continued to work for Vulliamy and Holford between 1861 and 1868, making architectural models related to the rebuilding of Westonbirt, Holford's country house in Gloucestershire. In August 1859 the Science and Art Department of the South Kensington Museum, which was acquiring contemporary specimens for public display, wrote to Vulliamy's office requesting models of Dorchester House 'which illustrate the appliances adopted in the construction and fitting of the edifice'.[24] By 1861 a model of the staircase and corridor at Dorchester House was displayed in the museum's collection of Construction and Building Materials alongside prototypes of ventilators, lavatories, and zinc roofs.[25] It remained there until at least 1876.[26] Catalogues note the material of the model as 'marble and alabaster', suggesting that Day produced a second more decorative and final model of the staircase after March 1854, once adjustments to the design had been tested on the plaster version. It was absent from documents from 1876 to 1916, when it was named in lists of architectural models held in the store room of the Science Museum.[27] Unfortunately this was its last recorded sighting. The two other major models have also disappeared.[28]

Despite the press related to his father's lack of clients, the Dorchester House models were not Day Jr's only commissions. In December 1850, while working for Vulliamy and Holford, he was also making models for James Pennethorne and excused himself from work on Dorchester House.[29] In March 1854 he excused himself again to build a model for Decimus Burton. In April 1851 Day explained to Vulliamy that he had stopped work on the models for Dorchester House to prepare his models for display in the Great Exhibition.[30] Additional longterm relationships with institutional clients required his attention ahead of work on the models of Dorchester – for instance, a model of an unknown subject for the Corporation of London (c. 1853–54) became 'a longer job than I first thought'.[31] Even after retiring to Kent in the 1860s, Day appears to have continued making architectural models until the 1870s. The limitations of his practice, however, became clear by the 1880s when a new type of model-maker emerged in London, providing a wide range of models, and operating from a centrally located workshop staffed by a cohort of workers.

24 Science and Art Department, letter to George Vulliamy, 19 August 1859, VuL/3/5/6, RIBA.
25 Science and Art Department, *Catalogue of Building and Constructing Materials* (London, 1862), 49M.
26 Science and Art Department, *Guide to the South Kensington Museum,* 2nd ed., (London, 1866), 12; Henry Sandham, *Catalogue of the Collection Illustrating Construction and Building Materials* (London, 1876), 109-Y.
27 Science Museum, Lists of Architectural Objects in the Store Room of Southern Galleries Science Museum, '11 June 1916', MA/1/5851, Victoria & Albert Museum (V&A).
28 Science and Art Department, *Catalogue of Building and Constructing Materials* (London, 1862), 22M.
29 Richard Day, letter to Lewis Vulliamy, 30 December 1850, VuL 13/1/9, RIBA; Richard Day, letter to Lewis Vulliamy, undated (c. 1850–52), VuL 13/1/23, RIBA. The model Day was working on may have been related to Pennethorne's work as architect to the Offices of Works, perhaps his design for the Museum of Practical Geology or the Ordnance Office, both of which he was working on at the time.
30 Richard Day, letter to Lewis Vulliamy, 25 April 1851, VuL 13/1/45, RIBA. These consisted of five architectural models exhibited under his own name: the portico of the Parthenon, The Temple Church, the portico of the Pantheon at Rome, the Martyrs' Memorial at Oxford, and a window from St Paul's Church on Herne Hill. *Great Exhibition of the Works of Industry of all Nations, 1851: Official Descriptive and Illustrated Catalogue,* vol. 2, (London: William Clowes, 1851), 830, no. 161A.
31 Richard Day, letter to Lewis Vulliamy, undated (c. 1853–57), VuL 13/1/49, RIBA.

ACCIDENTS, EMPIRE, AND BEER: JOHN THORP AND HIS WORKSHOP

On their return to the office after the Christmas holiday, in January 1900 every architect in London received a surprise gift through the post: a wall calendar with monthly 'tear-off' slips from the London Drawing and Tracing Office. Prepared by the manager, John Thorp, each month of the calendar was illustrated with colour plates depicting architectural models made by the office.[32] Seven years earlier, in 1883, following his training at the Royal Academy Schools and pupillage in practice, Thorp got his start offering architectural services at Moorgate in the City of London. After 1897 he moved to new premises at 98 Gray's Inn Road. Thanks to his proximity to the surrounding community of legal chambers in Holborn, he would go on to specialize in the production of models used in legal cases, a major source of his commissions (see chapter 'The Courtroom'). Alongside this work Thorp's business provided working drawings, perspectives, surveys, photocopies and blueprints, models, and diagrams to independent or overstretched practitioners, and he regularly advertised these services in the architectural and trade press. FIG. 43

FIG. 43 'The London Drawing and Tracing Office', *Builder* 78 (6 January 1900) xxviii

32 'A Calendar', *The Surveyor* (9 February 1900), 124.

The wall calendar marked a turning point in Thorp's work as interest grew in the office's model-making. In February 1900, following the direct mailing, two models made by Thorp for the 1900 Exposition Universelle in Paris became the subjects of extensive press coverage. At a scale of 1:200, both depicted hospital complexes: Brook Hospital on Shooter's Hill in Greenwich, FIG. 44 and the North Eastern Hospital in Tottenham.[33] FIG. 45 Commissioned by the Metropolitan Asylum Board, responsible for treating infectious diseases and caring for people with learning difficulties, Thorp worked on the models for nine months. *The Builders' Journal* commented on their 'utility', observing that the 'excellent manner in which [Thorp's models] show how the buildings will look when completed well repays their cost'.[34] After Paris the models travelled to several other European exhibitions before being exhibited again at the 1909 Imperial International Exhibition at White City in Hammersmith. Perhaps as a way of promoting the value and quality of Thorp's services, the cost was widely reported: the Brook Hospital model was £300 and the North Eastern Hospital £100. Both were large-scale site models but for the more expensive Brook Hospital, Thorp made a smaller model of a portion of the interior with descriptive labels in English and in French. FIG. 46 One of five new fever hospitals constructed in London at the turn of the twentieth century, Brook Hospital consisted of forty two-storey pavilions built in terraces to separate infectious areas of the complex from the non-infectious.[35] The smaller model depicts one floor of a pavilion with a ward hall for patients suffering from fever. Following contemporary developments in medical science, a short corridor led to each ward, past a staff room on one side and storage and a bathroom on the other. Accessed directly from the ward hall itself, toilets were contained in a cruciform tower that projected from the side of the ward. Large windows and an air-warming system allowed for natural ventilation three hundred days of the year, while a perimeter balcony meant that patients could be nursed in the open air. As well as showing another aspect of Thorp's work as a model-maker, these models indicate both the further expansion of the metropolis (to the northeast and the southeast) and the refinement of the modern hospital as a building typology.

33 'Some Uses of Architectural Models', *The Architects' Magazine* 1, no. 2 (December 1900), 32–4, here: 32.
34 'Two Interesting Models', *The Builders' Journal* (21 February 1900), 6.
35 Gwendoline Margery Ayers, *England's First State Hospitals and the Metropolitan Asylums Board, 1867–1930* (London: Wellcome Institute of the History of Medicine, 1971), 95–102.

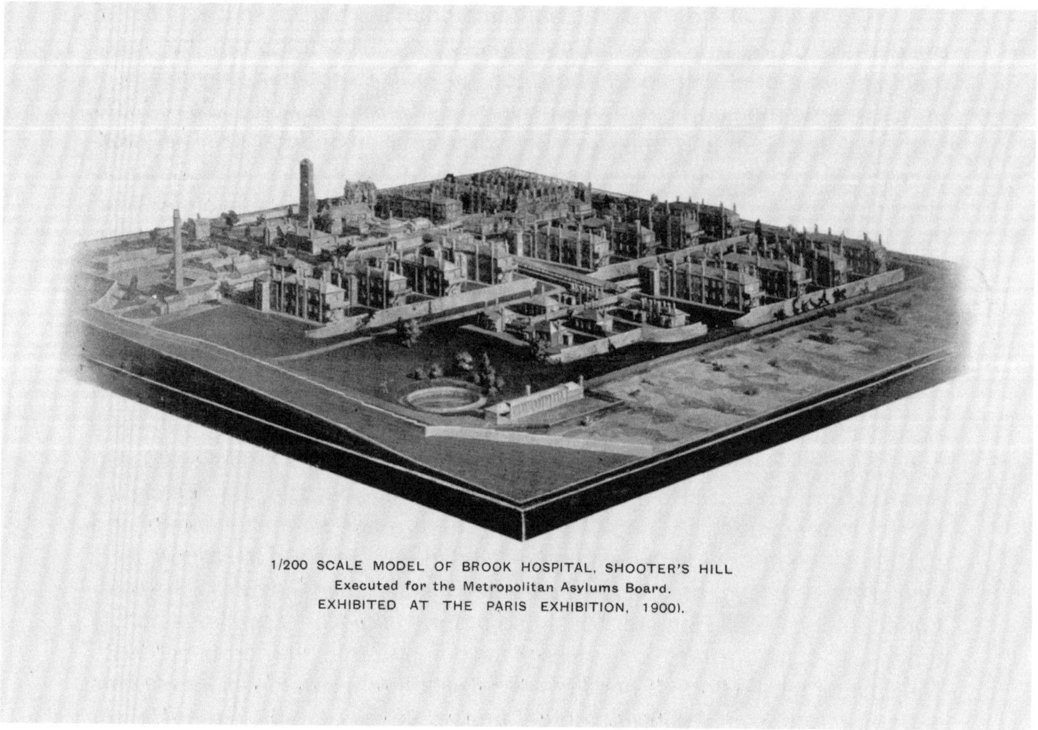

1/200 SCALE MODEL OF BROOK HOSPITAL, SHOOTER'S HILL
Executed for the Metropolitan Asylums Board.
EXHIBITED AT THE PARIS EXHIBITION, 1900).

FIG. 44　John Thorp, Model of Brook Hospital, Shooter's Hill, London, 1900, *Concerning Models of Buildings, Estates, Works, etc. for Exhibitions or Law Cases* (London: n. p., 1913), 22

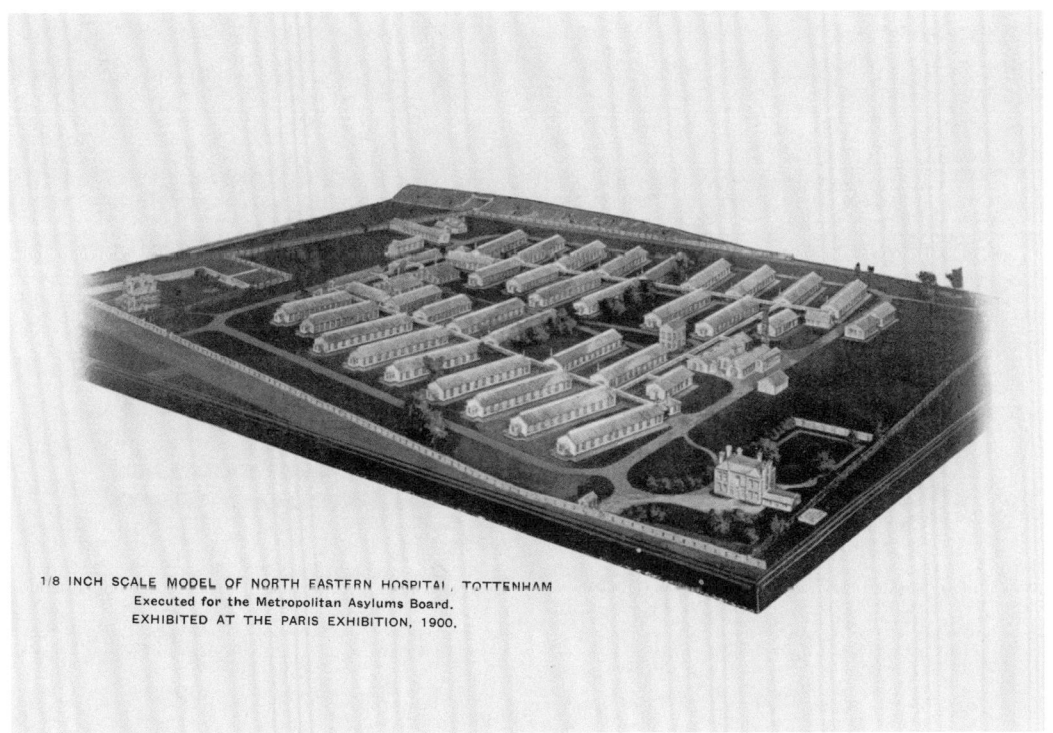

FIG. 45 John Thorp, Model of North Eastern Hospital, Tottenham, London, 1900, *Concerning Models of Buildings, Estates, Works, etc. for Exhibitions or Law Cases* (London: n. p., 1913), 24

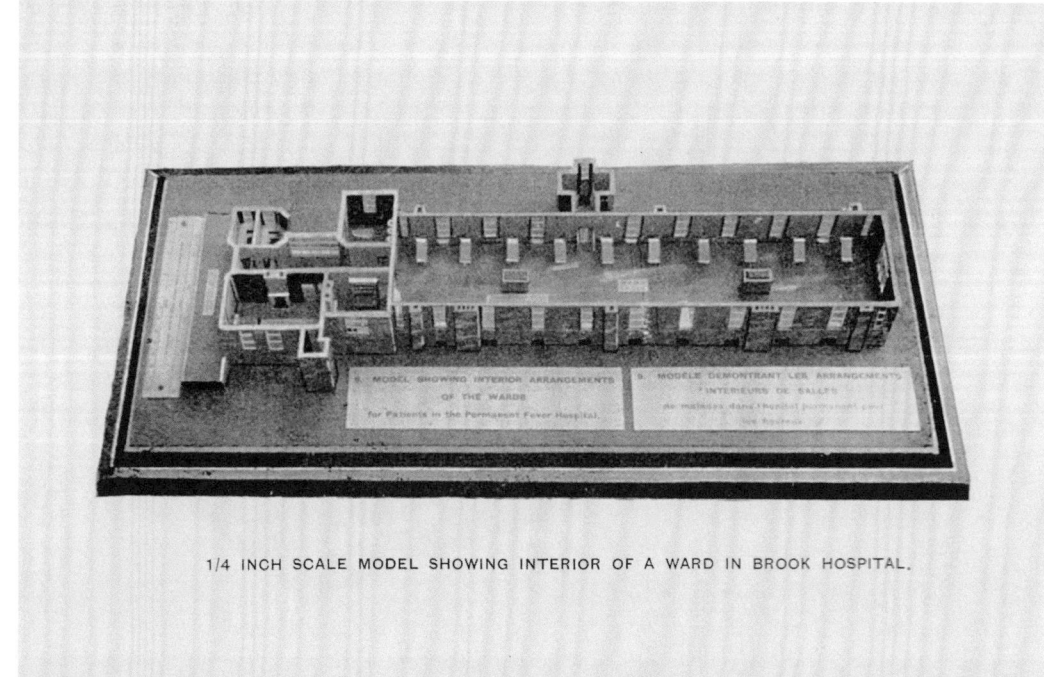

FIG. 46 John Thorp, model of the interior of a ward at Brook Hospital, Shooter's Hill, London, 1900, *Concerning Models of Buildings, Estates, Works, etc. for Exhibitions or Law Cases* (London: n. p., 1913), 23

Thorp's self-promotion did not stop at advertising. Operating as his own public relations agency, he ensured that his models were featured in the architectural press and popular magazines in both Britain and America, from *Strand Magazine* (1910), *The World's Work* (1911), and *Pall Mall Magazine* (1912), to *American Homes and Gardens* (1915). These articles almost always included a photograph of the model-maker in his workshop, accompanied by assistants. FIG. 47 Compared with Richard Day, on his own and cut off from Central London in his Southwark workshop, Thorp employed several assistants and his proximity to architects and other clients greatly increased the number of his commissions.[36] It is likely that the other figure in the published photographs is Thorp's wife Annie (née Farish). Following their marriage in 1895 it appears the couple lived at the same address as the workshop (98 Gray's Inn Road) until their relocation to Herne Hill in around 1909.[37] (While unfortunately I have found no further information on Annie Thorp her clear role in the production of celebrated architectural models must be acknowledged.) As described in magazine articles and visible in a photograph showing Annie Thorp at work, the workshop required drawings from a client in order to begin building a model. FIG. 48 Beyond aiding the model-making process there were administrative purposes for this. Thorp described in 1913 how in the instance of exhibition or legal models, 'all the drawings must be carefully studied before a price can be quoted'.[38] In practice, however, the drawn information available to Thorp varied depending on the situation. Retrospective of its construction, Thorp made a model of the Princess Mary Village Homes at Addlestone, an industrial school for the children of convicts on the periphery of London, for the Victorian Era Exhibition held at Earls Court in 1897, which was 'worked up entirely from photographs and the ground plan'.[39]

Often the models made by Thorp required more study than simply consulting given drawings. A series of models of reconstructed monuments of London, first exhibited at the 1908 Franco-British Exhibition, were historical studies of the Early Modern city based on 'books, prints, and contemporary documents of the period'.[40] Following initial research Thorp 'conceived the idea of reconstructing the most historic portions of the capital' and built a model of London Bridge (c.1630) at a ¼ inch to the foot.[41] FIG. 49 At over twenty-one feet long and encompassing both banks of the Thames, this model was available for hire to the public. FIG. 50 A painted backcloth and 'proscenium opening representing a large stone arch' would allow sixty or seventy people to view 'a large working representation' of the bridge.[42] At the time a friend advised Thorp of the potential public interest in the model and similar ones of other reconstructed monuments:

36	For a discussion on this in an American context see Fankhänel, *The Architectural Models of Theodore Conrad*, 22–6.
37	John B. Thorp remained on the electoral register for Holborn until 1906. The family does not appear on the register until the 1911 census when the address is given as '52 Winterbrooke Road, Herne Hill, S[outh]. E[ast]. London'. John Brown Thorp household, 1911 census of England, Surrey, Camberwell south, RG14, piece number 2481.
38	John Thorp, *Concerning Models of Buildings, Estates, Works, etc. for Exhibitions or Law Cases* (London: n. p., 1913), 30.
39	Andrew Soutar, 'Produced in Court', *The Strand Magazine* 39 (January to June 1910), 613–19, here: 616.
40	'Notes of the Month', *Architectural Review* 24 (November 1907), 212.
41	Soutar, 'Produced in Court', 613.
42	John Thorp, 'A Great Attraction', undated advert (c.1910), Thorp Architectural Modelmaking Archive, Arts University Bournemouth, United Kingdom.

> Why not construct the whole of the more interesting portions of London? The average Londoner's love of the capital is such that a model, when replete with panoramic equipment, would bring him from far and near to see it.[43]

A contemporary article in the *Architectural Review* reported that several notable antiquaries had praised Thorp's model of London Bridge. 'The purpose of Mr Thorpe [sic] has not been to provide a sensational toy', observed the author, 'but to build up a realistic and accurate presentation of the structures and districts of old London'.[44] Most important was the potential educational role that these models could offer to wider audiences:

> These models will have not merely an interest for the architect, artists, antiquarians, and historians, but that they should appeal to all classes of people for their educational and instructional value.[45]

At the end of their article, the author describes a more ambitious project by Thorp to make a model of the whole of 'Old London'. In addition to the probable cost attached to this task, the model would require 'a large turntable base on which it could be revolved and explained to a seated audience'. Despite the complexity and expense, the project held the potential 'to combat the growing Philistinism of the present day, and rouse the lay public to the urgent necessity of preserving those relics that still remain to us'. Thorp carefully studied 'old pictures and records' and from 1907 produced a suite of models of historic sites in London.[46] Five models covered an area of twenty-seven square metres: four showed the City of London prior to the 1666 fire and a fifth depicted the village of Charing Cross (the area adjacent to Trafalgar Square and a midpoint between the historic core of Westminster to the west and the City of London to the east). Similar to the model of London Bridge, each one had a panoramic backdrop to 'present to the observer a realistic vision of what the city looked like prior to 1666'.[47] They were exhibited as 'Old London' in a specially constructed building at the Franco-British Exhibition held in White City between 14 May and 31 October 1908. An earlier report described how the models were exhibited 'in a series of compartments under special lighting'.[48] Each one was built in solid parts and could be disassembled and displayed at different locations. Thorp later claimed the models had been seen by more than five hundred thousand people, including Queen Alexandra and other members of the Royal Family.

---

43 Soutar, 'Produced in Court', 613.
44 'Notes of the Month', 212.
45 'Notes of the Month', 212.
46 Percy Collins, 'Practical Modelling', *The World's Work* 17 (1911), 85–7, here: 87. See also: 'Models of Old London', *Tatler* 336 (4 December 1907), 232.
47 Collins, 'Practical Modelling', 87.
48 'Models of Old London', *Builder* 93 (19 October 1907), 405.

FIG. 47 Percy Collins, 'Old London: Mr Thorp and His Models', *Pall Mall Magazine* 17 (June 1912), 803

FIG. 48 'Mr John B. Thorp, Maker of Models for Law Cases in His Workroom', in Andrew Soutar, 'Produced in Court', *The Strand Magazine* 39 (January–June 1910), 616

FIG. 49   John Thorp, 'Old London Bridge in Miniature', *Illustrated London News* 790 (30 November 1907)

A GREAT ATTRACTION

CAN BE HIRED AT A FIXED SUM
OR
LENT ON SHARING TERMS

A LARGE WORKING REPRESENTATION
OF
OLD LONDON BRIDGE, A.D. 1630.

A Model, over 21 feet long, showing the west side, with the Water Works on the City Bank. The Water Wheel and Pumps are seen working. Behind these, is the Church of St. Magnus the Martyr. On the Southwark side are the Corn Mills, with the Church of St. Mary Overey, and the Tower of St. Olaves, Tooley Street, while in the background is the Tower of London, and in the distance, the Palace of Placentia, on the site of which now stands Greenwich Hospital.

A short historical account of the Old Bridge is given, which includes the Corn Mills, erected in 1588, to enable the poor people to get their corn ground cheaply, The Traitors' Gate, Nonsuch House, with the Drawbridge adjoining, the remains of St. Thomas's Chapel in the centre of the Bridge, London Square, with the Statue of St. Thomas a'Beckett, Patron Saint of the Bridge, and the Water Works, erected in 1582 by a Dutchman, named Peter Morris, to supply the city with water to deal with the many fires which occurred in the olden days.

After the description, the lights are slowly lowered by an automatic arrangement, and the whole Bridge is shown by moonlight, with the windows in the old houses lighting up one by one, giving a night effect.

This Model is to a scale of one-fiftieth full size, and is complete on wooden stand, with painted backcloth and proscenium opening representing a large stone arch, through which the Model is viewed. Sixty or seventy people, or even more, can see this Model at one time.

APPLY TO:— JOHN B. THORP, 98, Gray's Inn Road, London, W.C.1.
Maker of the Noted Models of Old London at the London Museum.

See Press Notices on back

FIG. 50   John Thorp, leaflet advertising the Old London Bridge model for hire, c.1910

An international exhibition displays the world, past and present, in a microcosm to visitors through its objects.[49] In its display and content 'Old London' represented a national past, one securely overtaken by technological progress, with the old values conserved as 'ancient' alongside 'modern'. The Franco-British Exhibition's visual presentation of the British Empire to a mass audience in the metropole was covered by the press. In particular the *Builder* elucidated the message the models communicated about the relationship between historic London and the subsequent development of the contemporary British Empire: 'It is hoped that [the models] may be interesting especially to our Colonial visitors, as illustrations of the mother-city from which all our Colonial development sprung.'[50] With this attitude in mind it is hardly surprising that the model of 'Old London' reappeared at the 1909 Imperial International Exhibition (at White City) and in 1911 at the Festival of Empire (at Crystal Palace in South London). Subsequently the five models were acquired by the London Museum in March 1912 and permanently exhibited in a specially constructed annexe to Kensington Palace, the London Museum's first home from 1912 to 1914.[51] When the museum relocated to Lancaster House in 1914, the initial five models were joined by a new 1:100 scale model made by Thorp to depict the Tower of London as it appeared in 1600. All were displayed in a series of rooms in the basement, and postcards of these versions of 'Old London' were even available to purchase.[52] FIGS. 51,52 Later moved into storage, the models remain in the possession of the museum and may form part of the displays at their new premises.

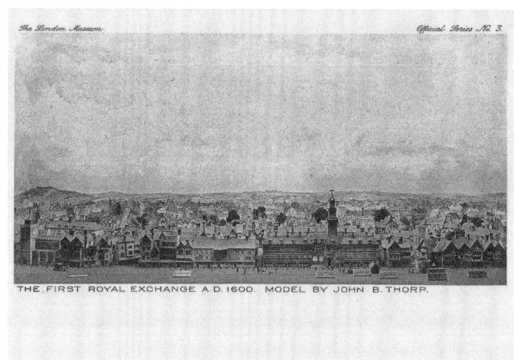

FIG. 51   Museum of London, postcard of Old London: First Royal Exchange, c.1920

49   See for instance: Tony Bennett, *The Birth of the Museum: History, Theory, Politics* (London: Routledge, 1995), 66; Itohan Osayimwese, 'Expositions in German Colonialism and German Architecture', in *Colonialism and Modern Architecture in Germany* (Pittsburgh: University of Pittsburgh Press, 2017), 21–60; Rosemary Spooner, 'Day-Tripping: Urban Excursions and the Architecture of International Exhibitions', *Architectural Theory Review* 23, no. 3 (2019), 326–44, here: 341.

50   'Models of Old London', 405.

51   'Our Own Cable', *Building News* 102 (22 March 1912), 433; Francis Sheppard, *The Treasury of London's Past: A Historical Account of the Museum of London and its Predecessors, the Guildhall Museum and the London Museum* (London: HMSO, 1991), 59 cites: Guy Laking, letter to William Edward Harcourt, 9 November 1911, DC3/2, Museum of London.

52   Findlay Muirhead, *London and Its Environs* (London: Macmillan, 1927), 356. Commissioned from Thorp and donated to the museum by John George Joicey. The *Building News* suggested that the Tower of London model was 'one of the finest pieces of work [Thorp] has executed'. 'The Tower of London AD 1600', *Builder* 98 (27 February 1914), 259. 'Notices', *Building News* 106 (6 February 1914), 209.

FIG. 52   Museum of London, postcard of Old London: Old St Paul's, c. 1920

Thorp continued to be prolific in his output, and in 1913, more than a decade after the success of the wall calendar, he produced an extensive brochure of the office's work: *Concerning Models of Buildings, Estates, Works, etc. for Exhibitions or Law Cases.* At the time a short article on the publication of the brochure noted:

> Every architect knows that sometimes a model can be of far greater use in conveying to a client an idea of the general massing of a design than any number of perspective drawings, while modifications of his own working drawings may suggest themselves to him when he sees a well-made model of his own design.[53]

Aside from being a masterful piece of self-promotion, midway through the publication, Thorp discussed a particular model made for the little-known London-based partnership of John P. Bishop and Henry Etherington-Smith.[54] Thorp's discussion offers a detailed view of the relationship between the model-maker and the architectural profession, showing how an architect's working drawing or sketch design could be examined by the production of a model and with quite different consequences to those at Dorchester House.

In 1906 Meux's Brewery Company commissioned John Bishop and Harry Etherington-Smith to design new facilities for the firm in Wandsworth.[55] Originally based on the Tottenham Court Road, the firm's potential move to Wandsworth shows the urban dispersal of industry from the centre of the metropolis to its periphery that occurred at the start of the twentieth century. The appointment of Bishop and Etherington-Smith was closely linked to the brewery's struggling performance. From 1891 to 1904 production fell by almost fifty per cent due to reduced levels of industrial efficiency.[56] In 1905 the brewery's chairman, William Harris, complained of old facilities in a poor state of maintenance, inefficiently arranged for modern methods of production.[57] 'Landlocked' in the centre of London, the current buildings caused an enormous amount of wasted labour with a wage bill per annum considerably higher

53   'Models of Buildings', *Builder* 96 (13 February 1913), 212.
54   A few minor details on Etherington-Smith can be found in: Felstead, Franklin, and Pinfield, *Directory of British Architects 1834–1900*, vol. 1 (London: Mansell, 1993), 294.
55   For a discussion of Meux's brewing history see: Lesley Richmond and Alison Turton, eds., *The Brewing Industry: A Guide to Historical Records* (Manchester: Manchester University Press, 1990), 233. For a broader history of brewing and development in the Nine Elms area see: Thom, Colin, ed. *Survey of London*. Volume 50: *Battersea: Homes and Housing* (London: Yale University Press, 2013), 322.
56   Meux Brewery Company, Report of an Extraordinary General Meeting, 28 January 1914, 4435/A/01/003, London Metropolitan Archives [LMA].
57   Meux Brewery Company, Proceedings of an Extraordinary General Meeting, 16 March 1905, 4435/A/01/003, LMA.

than their competitors.⁵⁸ Just over a year later, in January 1906, Meux's directors and shareholders met to debate the purchase of nine acres of land in Wandsworth. This proposed site would not only contain a new plant and brewing equipment but also provide improved access to logistics networks via the river Thames and nearby railway line. FIG. 53 An unnamed firm of architects had been commissioned to make 'a rough sketch' for a new brewery which would contain 'every modern labour-saving appliance'.⁵⁹ According to a directors' report, an increase in trade for Meux caused the architects' plans to be revised twice during 1906. Ultimately it was this increase in business that prompted the board to abandon plans for the new buildings at the end of 1907 (instead 'considerable sums' were spent on new equipment for the existing brewery).⁶⁰ However, earlier in 1907 John Thorp and his workshop made a model of the proposed new brewery buildings in Wandsworth from a series of the architects' 'rough plans'.⁶¹ FIG. 54 Produced in timber at the scale of ¼ inch to a foot, the model measured six square feet and cost £300 (£23,000 in today's money). Comprising fifty-two separate blocks, each made up of small components, the model could be taken apart to present the individual spaces and rooms that made up the brewery. Thorp's construction no longer survives. Photographs show it as a spatial diagram that does not follow the typical conventions of plan or section drawings. Ignoring these conventions, the partially dismantled model opens up to reveal the overall functional and structural layout of the proposed building along with the plants and machinery of a modern brewery. In addition to the separate blocks and components, a complete set of scaled horses, drays, men, and barrels were prepared to ascertain the exact amount of space that objects and actions would occupy in the complex.

A popular American magazine, *The World's Work,* described how the model 'brought to light several ambiguities in the architectural plans, the discovery of which served to effect a saving of over £10,000 in the building contract'.⁶² Photographs accompanying the article (and published in other pieces on Thorp) capture the model from a bird's eye view. In the 1913 office prospectus the model was presented in two ways. First, as a pair of photographs taken from an oblique position to demonstrate the overall composition of the various buildings that make up the brewery complex. Second, as a sequence of six images photographed from above that depict each level of the complex. FIG. 55 Set within a decorative border that frames the six abstracted images, the sequence forms a taxonomy of the model's various components, offering a serial image of construction from basement to roof.

The irregular spaces, varying levels, and different-sized equipment of the buildings, along with the architects' brief to Thorp – 'that all parts of the Model should take to pieces and be accessible' – made for a project of enormous complexity.⁶³ The architects acknowledged Thorp's achievement in a letter thanking him for his excellent work on a model that allowed simultaneous comprehension of the building, its contents, and its programme – all in a way that an orthographic drawing was incapable of visualizing. Additionally, as

58	Meux Brewery Company, Précis of an Extraordinary General Meeting, 23 January 1906, 4435/A/01/003, LMA.	
59	Meux Brewery Company, Précis, 23 January 1906.	
60	Meux Brewery Company, Directors Report and Balance Sheet to 31 December 1907, 13 March 1908, 4435/A/01/003, LMA.	
61	Soutar, 'Produced in Court', 616.	
62	Collins, 'Practical Modelling', 86. This would amount to around £785,000 in today's money.	
63	John Bishop and Harry Etherington-Smith, letter to John Thorp, 2 January 1907, Thorp Architectural Modelmaking Archive.	

several authors at the time noted, the model revealed discrepancies in the drawings, which would have cost Meux vast sums once the project was under construction. Alongside these revelations, there is a connection between the model's fabrication and the efficiency of industrial production. In light of comments about the wasted labour at the existing Meux brewery and press observations that the model was made to ascertain the exact amount of space required for the brewery, Thorp's model of the proposed complex offered a framework on which stakeholders could measure distances, volumes, and cost. For Meux, the model allowed a three-dimensional understanding of human labour in relation to the raw materials, equipment, and spaces required for producing beer. Viewing the model, with its miniature horses, men, and barrels, the directors and shareholders – owners of the means of production – saw for themselves how they could control, regulate, and direct labour to increase the efficiency of the brewery.

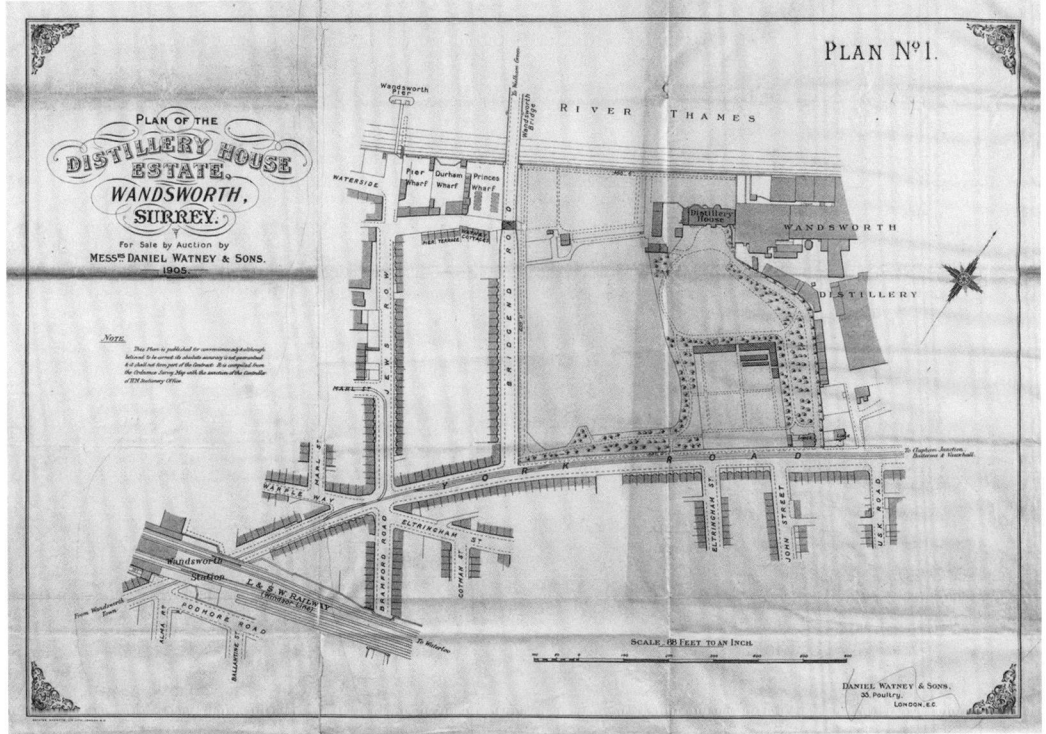

FIG. 53   Plan of new site for Meux at Wandsworth, 1905

FIG. 54 John Thorp, west elevation of model for Meux Brewery, Wandsworth, 1907, *Concerning Models of Buildings, &c*, 19

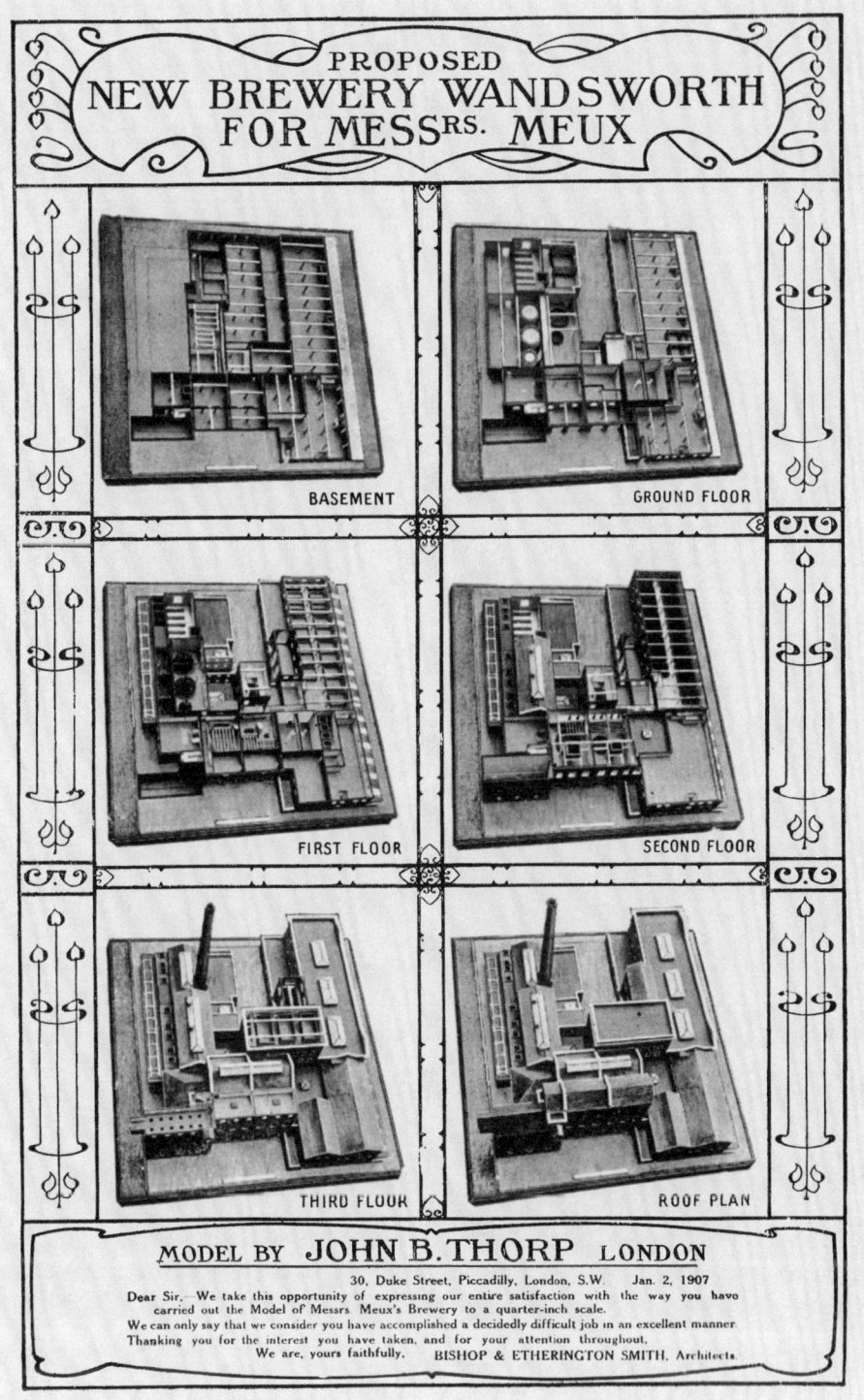

FIG. 55   John Thorp, west elevation of model for Meux Brewery, Wandsworth, 1907, *Concerning Models of Buildings, &c*, 19

THE UNIVERSITY

Speaking to a crowded room in central London at the Architectural Society in September 1834, John Blythe expressed a common opinion about the education of the nineteenth-century British architect. Unlike centralized education in France at the École Polytechnique or the *polytechnische Hochschulen* of German-speaking Europe, the British architect was educated in a 'discouraging and rambling way', Blythe believed, across a variety of organizations and modes of education including pupillage, evening classes at the Royal Academy, and self-directed study at the British Museum.[1] Until the establishment of architecture as a university subject in the mid-nineteenth century, the predominant mode of training in Britain was through pupillage, where a student was articled to an architect for three to five years (during which they were referred to as pupils or architectural assistants). Alternatively, a 'National School of Architecture', Blythe argued, would provide a student with a comprehensive understanding of architecture, its history, principles of construction, and the latest developments in material science, taught through lectures and a 'suitable museum and gallery, supplied with the best description of models, specimens, casts, and drawings'.[2]

Although a national school of architecture never fully emerged, in early Victorian London a number of new institutions offered a degree of systematic training for architects. At the University of London, parallel departments of civil engineering and architecture were established at King's College (1840) and University College London (1841), while a group of younger architects founded the Architectural Association (1847) as an independent institution.

---

[1] John Blythe, 'The Necessity of a National School of Architecture', *CEAJ* 1 (October 1837–December 1838), 158–9. For a discussion on the German situation see: Christiane Weber, 'Technical Nation Building: German Professional Organizations and Their Journals in the Nineteenth Century', *The Journal of Architecture* 25, no. 7 (October 2020), 924–47.

[2] Blythe, 'The Necessity of a National School of Architecture', 158.

Initially the courses of these three institutions were only ever considered as a supplement to pupillage; operating as a series of evening lectures they made up part of the broader spectrum of informal education that Blythe criticized. Within this spectrum there were also other environments where students learned about architecture, including drawing classes taken as a complement to pupillage, as well as handbooks and instructional articles on how and why students should make architectural models. Every evening, drawing classes were held across central London. Based around the observation of simple geometric models these classes allowed students to practice their skills in perspectival drawing for a small fee. Judging from the course titles the classes contained a mix of architectural pupils, engineers, tradesmen, and medical students.[3] Some gained more fame than others. George Maddox, a former assistant to John Soane, taught students from his apartments in Holborn, which contained a museum of architectural models and casts to study and draw.[4] Similar to the contemporary study of medicine and anatomy, these objects played a central role in supporting young architects' understanding of three-dimensional forms and how to draw them in perspective.[5]

Alongside evening drawing classes, pupillage for a select group was supplemented by instruction at the Royal Academy Schools through an annual course of six evening lectures delivered by the academy's professor of architecture.[6] These lectures often addressed how models should be used in professional practice, and on occasion the professor would refer to a model to support the didactic message of their lecture series. For instance, John Soane, Professor of Architecture at the Royal Academy from 1806 until 1837, allowed students access to the collection of drawings and models at his house in Lincoln's Inn Fields before and after each lecture.[7] The importance of models as educational aids was underlined by Soane's comments in his third lecture when he complained that an architecture student 'has no models of ancient buildings to consult'.[8] He believed that the architectural model allowed students to transcend physical and economic barriers imposed by long-term study on the Grand Tour – a crucial part of Soane's and other Regency architects' education.

---

3   In another school for the study of anatomy and perspective from models, run by J. M. Leigh at 181 Maddox Street, 'a class for modelling and a collection of architectural models is contemplated'. 'Advert: Drawing from Models', *Athenaeum* 823 (5 August 1843), 705; 'Advert: Drawing Classes for Tradesmen', *Athenaeum* 825 (19 August 1843), 746; 'Miscellanea: Practical School for Artists, Designers, and Amateurs', *Builder* 3 (29 November 1845), 579.

4   'Recollections of George Maddox by One of His Pupils', *Architect* 12 (19 Sep 1874), 143–4.

5   For studies on the contemporary use of wax anatomical models in medical education see: Alan William Bates, 'Indecent and Demoralising Representations': Public Anatomy Museums in Mid-Victorian England', *Medical History* 52, no. 1 (January 2008), 1–22; Anna Maerker, 'Between Profession and Performance: Displays of Anatomical Models in London, 1831–32', *Histoire, médecine et santé* 5 (Spring 2014), 47–59.

6   For a discussion on this see: Neil Bingham, 'Architecture at the Royal Academy Schools, 1768–1836', in Neil Bingham, ed., *The Education of the Architect: Proceedings of the 22nd Annual Symposium of the Society of Architectural Historians of Great Britain* (n. p., 1993). The sequence of professors at the Royal Academy was as follows: John Soane (1806–37), William Wilkins (1837–38), C. R. Cockerell (1839–59), Sydney Smirke (1860–65), George Gilbert Scott (1866–73) E. M. Barry (1873–80), G. E. Street (1880–81), George Aitchison (1887–1905), Reginald Blomfield (1907–11).

7   Soane only gave the lectures himself from 1806 until his eyesight failed him in 1824. From 1832 Henry Howard, Professor of Painting at the Royal Academy, read the lectures on Soane's behalf. Records at the Soane Museum and in the press indicate that the twelve lectures were presented across two years in two six-lecture cycles before the sequence started again. For a full chronology of the lectures given see: Susan Palmer, 'Chronology of the Delivery of Sir John Soane's Royal Academy Lectures', in David Watkin, ed., *Sir John Soane: Enlightenment Thought and the Royal Academy Lectures* (Cambridge: Cambridge University Press, 1996), 731–2; John Soane, 'Lecture VI', in David Watkin, ed., *Sir John Soane: The Royal Academy Lectures* (Cambridge: Cambridge University Press, 2000), 137–55, here: 155.

8   John Soane, 'Lecture III', in Watkin, ed., *Sir John Soane: The Royal Academy Lectures,* 63–88, here: 86.

THE UNIVERSITY

MODEL-MAKING HANDBOOKS

While only a select group studied at the Royal Academy Schools, many more complemented their apprenticeship through the study of handbooks and manuals. In Victorian London there were several books for pupils on how to make architectural models. In 1827 Bernhard Heinrich Blasche's *The Art of Working in Pasteboard* was translated from German for a British audience.[9] One of many European model-making handbooks, its arrival echoed the import of anatomical models to Britain from Italy, France, and Germany in the 1820s, countries where, unlike Britain, model-makers had perfected the art of anatomical modelling in paper paste or wax.[10] (Although London was an important centre for medical education, there was a shortage of cadavers available for study in Britain in the early nineteenth century, something that enterprising continental model-makers saw as a potential market.) For the architectural profession, Blasche's book featured illustrations of folded paper templates that dissected the elementary geometries of archetypal houses and agricultural buildings.[11] In addition, Blasche offered readers 'the theoretical principles of the art', with directions provided on tools, materials, and techniques, beginning with instruction on how to model simple forms. Once these forms had been mastered, the appendix provided a general outline of how to make a model of a Greek Ionic Temple.[12] FIG. 56

FIG. 56 Bernhard Heinrich Blasche, *The Art of Working in Pasteboard*, 3rd ed., trans. Daniel Boileau (London: Boosey, 1831), 1, Plate 8

9   Bernhard Heinrich Blasche, *The Art of Working in Pasteboard*, 3rd ed., trans. Daniel Boileau (London: Boosey, 1831). Blasche was a German educationalist and teacher who taught the principles and practice of handicraft at the Schnepfenthal Institution (*Salzmannschule Schnepfenthal*) in Gotha.

10 For discussions on anatomical models in nineteenth-century London see: Alan William Bates '"Indecent and Demoralising Representations": Public Anatomy Museums in Mid-Victorian England', *Medical History* 52, no. 1 (January 2008), 1–22; Anna Maerker, 'Between Profession and Performance: Displays of Anatomical Models in London, 1831–32', *Histoire, médecine et santé* 5 (Spring 2014), 47–59; Alessandro Riva, 'The Evolution of Anatomical Illustration and Wax Modelling in Italy from the 16th to Early 19th centuries', *Journal of Anatomy* 216, no. 2 (February 2010), 209–22.

11 Werner Oechslin, 'Le modèle architectural. "Idea materialis"', in Sabine Frommel and Raphaël Tassin, eds. *Les maquettes d'architecture: Fonction et évolution d'un instrument de conception et de réalisation* (Paris: Picard, 2015), 103–17, here: 108.

12 This outline advised using an accurate drawing or engraving of the temple alongside several thicknesses of Bristol board – an unfinished paperboard – to achieve a successful result.

Blasche's book, however, was limited to model-making techniques – rather than their application to contemporary situations in modern Britain. It is therefore of little surprise that in 1859, three decades after the publication of Blasche's volume, a new handbook was released to aid young British architects within working settings. *The Art of Architectural Modelling in Paper*, written by the little-known British architect T. A. Richardson, was a textbook within the publisher's 'Rudimentary' series, with a principal audience of architectural assistants – 'a large and increasing body' – who in preparation for professional practice required practical knowledge of model-making.[13] In particular Richardson believed that the instruction offered in his book held the potential to provide the architect with certainty when presenting the designs of buildings to clients. Reflecting on the role of models in Victorian London, he noted that three-dimensional representation was becoming more widespread in competitions for buildings, and that this function had consequences for architects: the short timeframes instilled by the competition system increased the importance of producing models quickly and effectively. FIG. 57

Structured around the production of a hypothetical model, Richardson's book begins by focusing on the materials for making models, the qualities of different paper stock, and the adhesives required to bond sheets together. From personal experience Richardson recommends J. Whatman's drawing paper for its uniform surface and pale cream tone resembling the colour of Bath stone. Alongside a discussion of the paper's qualities a specimen was bound into the book for readers to examine. Although paper could imitate stone, Richardson suggests using other substances to imitate particular building materials. To represent the glass in windows, students should procure mica from an ironmonger. To stick pieces of card and paper together, Richardson offers different recipes for adhesives: one based on flour and sugar; another made of a gum arabic to join the larger elements of the model. The next chapter of the book is dedicated to the required tools: a cutting board, modelling press (to help form cardboard from individual sheets of paper), T-square, adjustable straight-edge jig, modelling knives, and knife compass. FIG. 58

13   T. A. Richardson, *The Art of Architectural Modelling in Paper*, Weale's Rudimentary Series 127 (London: John Weale, 1859), 16.

FIG. 57 T. A. Richardson, *The Art of Architectural Modelling in Paper*, Weale's Rudimentary Series 127 (London: John Weale, 1859), frontispiece

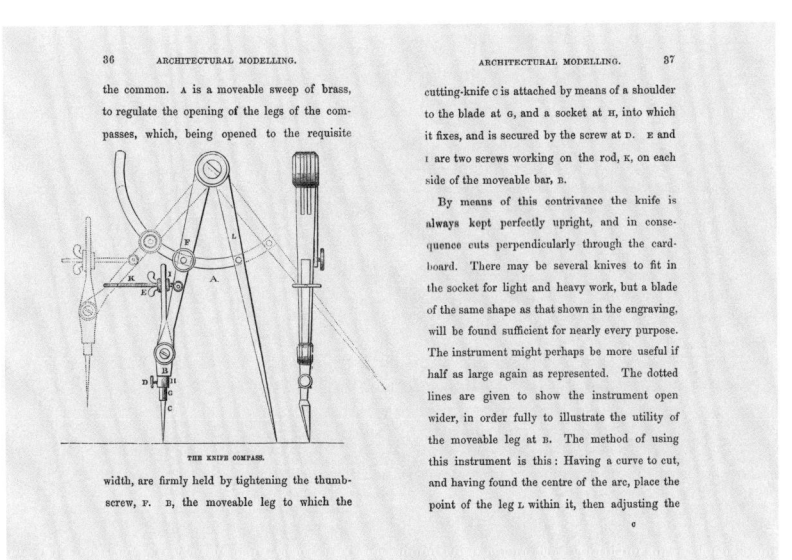

FIG. 58 T. A. Richardson, 'The Knife Compass', *The Art of Architectural Modelling in Paper*, 36–7

course not drawing in the window frames but merely the outline of the square of the window, the side will present the appearance shown in the accompanying elevation, and which is merely sketched and not drawn to any scale.

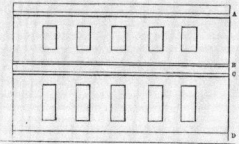

A Lines for cornice.   B Lines of upper string.
c Ditto lower cornice.   D Ditto Plinth.

The four or more elevations having been drawn, proceed to cut out all windows, doors, and other openings cleanly and accurately. The windows and their frames must now be made and gummed at the back of the several openings; where panels occur paper of the same tint must be used, sometimes the pieces cut from the

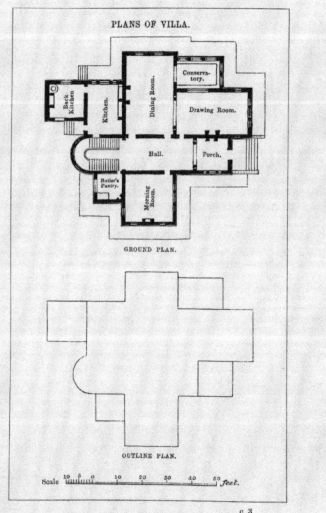

FIG. 59   T. A. Richardson, 'Plans of a Villa', *The Art of Architectural Modelling in Paper*, 44–5

a few trials on waste cardboard are necessary before the operator will perform this skilfully. The straight-edge holding the paper firmly, it may be cut through at two or three strokes, observing to hold the knife always at the same angle. All mitreing work finished, affix the windows at the back, placing the whole under a slight pressure.* Then the model must be blocked up. First cut a number of squares, all sizes, from waste or other cardboard; let them be perfectly square; cut these diagonally, and they will form the blocks to hold the work together at the angles. Now take any two sides that are to be joined at the mitred angle, and fix them accurately together with gum pretty thick, so that it may

* As there are many little matters during the progress of a model requiring a slight pressure, a pressure sufficient to hold the pieces in their several places till dry, I have found weights answer very well. I have pieces of square lead from one pound upwards covered with paper; and by covering, the humble brick may be usefully pressed into this service.

dry while you hold each side in its place. When set, lay them down and work the others in a similar manner. Take now the outline plan, and having previously numbered the sides to correspond with the plan, fix them (by touching slightly their under edge with gum) to it, and

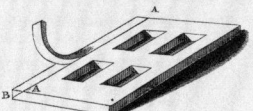

when all are in their places fix, at a distance apart of an inch and half or so, above one another the previously described blocking pieces with gum not so thick in consistency. To make our meaning perfectly plain, we annex an engraving of the appearance of an internal angle when at this stage of the proceedings. A piece of wood (deal) about ½ inch thick, should now be

FIG. 60   T. A. Richardson, 'Making a Door', *The Art of Architectural Modelling in Paper*, 54–5

Assuming that the by now the student had procured the various instruments and materials required, the third part of the book instructs the student in the method of making a model of an Italianate villa (visible in the frontispiece). A description and accompanying diagrams advises first preparing an outline ground plan of the intended building. FIG. 59 Taking the actual thickness of the walls as a guide the student should first paste together individual sheets of paper in a modelling press and then draw each elevation of the building, including the outline of any openings including doors and windows, and mark any horizontal recesses and projections. Once complete the student should carefully cut out the doors and windows in each elevation. Window frames, made with blue-painted paper to represent glass, could then be applied to the rest of the elevation. Additional details such as doors, architraves, and mouldings could be formed using a similar technique with the number of layers of cardboard based on the scale of the model. FIG. 60

In the final chapter Richardson explains how to prepare the model for presentation. First, a wooden base should be covered with cloth or velvet and a small groove made inside the perimeter, designed to receive a glass shade to protect from damage. The model and base should be attached to a timber stand, and additional details could improve the presentation of a model. Richardson warns against turning 'a work of art, [into] a mere toy', through overly colourful materials, candles placed within a model, or unrealistic landscaping.[14] Instead he advises the use of velvet, flock paper, or sand to depict lawns and paths. Water could be represented with glass or mica sheets. Rocks and grottos can be moulded from paper that has been soaked and then dried. Flowerbeds could be made from burned cork to imitate earth; twigs carved to portray trees. Significantly these suggestions for finishing models indicate that Richardson's focus was on presentation models, ostensibly for the clients and competition juries that he describes at the beginning of his book.

Several contemporary architectural journals reviewed Richardson's book positively. For the *Builder* the publication would greatly aid the student in learning how to make models – a medium 'more useful than a perspective view in presenting an architectural idea'.[15] When the second edition was published in 1887 the same journal praised Richardson's 'wise cautions against the temptations that beset the inexperienced modeller'.[16] Another review noted the significance of the work and its role in supporting young architects who were learning how to make models during their pupillage and argued for the RIBA to introduce uniform scales.[17] Instead of the bespoke and time-intensive process of making individual windows and other architectural features with numerous tools, 'many of these could be bought at shops', with their production a potentially profitable business for paper manufacturers. These viewpoints indicate a demand for models and an emerging marketplace for model-making supplies. Equally the proposals for standardization are indicative of a wider movement in the building industry towards proprietary components and prefabrication in construction – ideas that also forced educational establishments across London to respond to changing demands on the architect's technical knowledge. In light of these demands, the three schools of architecture in central London – the Architectural Association, King's College, and University College – offered vital points of reference for the profession.

14 Richardson, *The Art of Architectural Modelling in Paper*, 92.
15 'Books Received', *Builder* 17 (26 March 1859), 227.
16 'Books Received', *Builder* 52 (22 January 1887), 167.
17 'Architectural Modelling', *Building News* 5 (15 April 1859), 346.

EDUCATION AT THE ARCHITECTURAL ASSOCIATION

One evening in the Spring of 1899, the prolific British sculptor Frederick William Pomeroy gave a lecture at the Architectural Association (AA), then based on Great Marlborough Street in Soho.[18] Titled 'Curving and Modelling Applied to Architecture', Pomeroy's lecture considered how 'modelling might be used in architecture for a great variety of purposes', from details of ornament to scaled objects representing 'the whole of a building'.[19] Through these different functions, Pomeroy believed 'a general idea of the general effect of light and shade' could be gained before construction. What distinguished the lecture from others of this time was that Pomeroy demonstrated this approach. On a series of prepared clay surfaces, raised up on a blackboard for the audience to view, Pomeroy, aided by an assistant, gave 'a practical demonstration of both carving and modelling'.[20] To regular attendees of Pomeroy's AA lectures, this was entirely expected – from 1892 the AA curriculum had offered an optional evening class titled 'Instruction in Modelling', taught by Pomeroy and which consisted of making relief copies from existing plaster casts in the AA studios.[21]

Other prominent members of the AA firmly believed in the significance of models in the education of young architects. Among them was the association's president Leonard Stokes who argued, 'Unless [the architect] was able to model in his mind he could never realize what his building would be like',[22] and although the modelling of detail was useful, 'more attention should be paid to form in masses'. The idea of the mental conception of a building as central to the task of the architect was also embraced by contemporary architects outside the AA, such as George Frederick Bodley who told students at the RIBA in 1900 that before designing a building they should close their eyes, and 'with your mind's eye, call up the vision of the edifice as entire and complete as it will stand'.[23] This wider culture of three-dimensional modelling, led by Edward Schroeder Prior's two models at the Royal Academy, contributed to a particular strand of educational practice at the AA. For instance, in a 1903 essay on the AA's pedagogic strategy, the *Architectural Review* argued that the modelling class was 'of great assistance in giving a knowledge of the value of projection, and an appreciation of surface and form' to those at the school.[24] Equally, Arthur T. Bolton, studio master at the AA and later curator of Sir John Soane's Museum, described how models were used by the teaching staff to 'counteract the tendency of students simply to imitate the flat copy' as they learned how to draw.[25] By 1906 fourth-year students were

---

18   The AA would remain in Soho until 1902 when it moved into the Royal Architectural Museum in Tufton Street, Westminster. This episode is discussed in the next chapter, 'The Museum'. In 1917 the AA moved to its present location in Bedford Square.
19   'Architectural Association', *Building News* 76 (21 March 1899), 536.
20   'Architectural Association', (21 March 1899), 536.
21   Pomeroy, previously a Royal Academy Gold Medallist for Sculpture, was active between 1881 and 1924 and worked on a wide range of free-standing and architectural sculpture. 'Obituaries: A Noted English Sculptor Mr F. W. Pomeroy, RA', *The Times* (27 May 1924), 21.
22   'The Architectural Association', *Builder* 53 (19 November 1887), 698.
23   Michael Hall, *George Frederick Bodley and the Later Gothic Revival in Britain and America* (New Haven: Yale University Press, 2014), 234.
24   'Architectural Education – II: The Architectural Association Evening School', *Architectural Review* (June 1903), 217–22, here: 221.
25   'Architectural Education – II', 218. This approach was also one taken in the United States, at universities like Cornell where the ability to draw structural forms (domes, arches) and ornamental details was taught though the copying of models. Charles Babcock, first professor at Cornell, discussed his pedagogic methods when in London in 1887 for the Eighth General Conference of Architects: Charles Babcock, 'Supplement: General Conference of Architects', *Builder* 52 (7 May 1887), 695–6.

making plasticine or clay models of their design projects, complete with scale figures and photographed against manneristic backdrops. FIG. 61 The *Architectural Review* described how these students were at an advanced level and already had a strong knowledge of drawings: it was therefore 'more profitable to devote their energies in the school to questions of architectural form and expression' (the implication being that model-making permitted these aspects to be realized most effectively by the students in a manner similar to Edward Schroeder Prior's approach to the medium).[26]

Before Pomeroy's AA course, students created models to learn about construction. Lawrence Harvey, an architect whose pedagogical principles were based on the study of stereotomy and its material application, taught a practical class in masonry where the students were tasked with constructing models of various structures at 1:96 scale.[27] Harvey, who had been educated first at the Eidgenössisches Polytechnikum by Gottfried Semper in Zurich (1864–67) and then later at the École des Beaux-Arts in Paris, was one of a number of architects who instilled European influence on British architectural education in the late nineteenth century. Since the foundation of the architectural school at Zurich, modelling architectural elements such as walls and vaults in clay, wood, and plaster in order to learn about construction had been an essential part of a student's education.[28] Similar ideas were proposed in London where the president of the AA, George H. Fellowes-Prynne, argued that the first place where an architecture student should learn was a workshop, which would provide, 'precisely the kind of practical training that an architect requires'.[29] This approach would require changes to the AA's premises and pedagogical strategy: with the demonstration workshops accommodating rooms for carpentry, masonry and bricklaying, and metalwork. Fellowes-Prynne recommended that alongside fittings and tools these spaces should be furnished with models of various structural systems and 1:1-scale building elements, which students could study, dismantle, and copy. The initial cost of commissioning the models was considerable, but once the tools and materials had been procured, the integration of a class on construction into the curriculum – led by expert craftsmen and AA members – meant that the students themselves would be assigned particular types of models to produce. Within a few years the AA would have 'a most valuable set of models always ready for reference'.[30] Furthermore, Fellowes-Prynne proposed that while student-architects required knowledge of building trades and technologies, they did not actually need to know *how* to build a brick wall, lay a stone floor, or construct a timber frame. Instead, making a scale model offered students the knowledge of the building site and various crafts without requiring mastery of the technique.

At the AA this approach was taken more broadly in lectures where architectural models were frequently used to communicate technical knowledge regarding building materials or products. A lecture on timber joinery by a builder would be illustrated with models and specimens of doors, windows,

---

26   'Architectural Association School of Architecture', *Architectural Review* 20 (December 1906), 275–9, here: 275.
27   'Architectural Association', *Builder* 51 (2 October 1886), 507. Four years later Harvey would collaborate with the RIBA to establish a prize examination to encourage the study of masonry by students, judged through submitted models and drawings. 'Studentships, Medals, and Prizes Committee', Prizes and Studentships Committees Minutes, 13 February 1890. 7. 4. 2, RIBA, 237.
28   Martin Tschanz, *Die Bauschule am Eidgenössischen Polytechnikum in Zürich: Architekturlehre zur Zeit von Gottfried Semper (1855–1871)* (Zurich: gta Verlag, 2015), 142–3.
29   'Architectural Association', (14 October 1898), 530.
30   'Architectural Association', (14 October 1898), 530.

and skirting boards,[31] while new inventions – for, say, gaskets to keep windows weather- and air-tight – were also presented as models to students and architects. On other occasions, models demonstrated how these new products could be adopted in contemporary architecture. During a lecture on a new type of roof tile one member noted that in the case of a complex roofscape, a model of the roof could be constructed and sent to the tile manufacturer for guidance.[32] Often at the conclusion of these lectures, if the models had caused a particularly profound effect on the audience, the AA membership would request to borrow the item on a long-term basis for use in the classroom. Such examples were especially useful since by the end of the nineteenth century British architectural practice had expanded to include liaising with the manufacturers of new building technologies and products. Consequently, an architecture student's training had to address the demands created by these new relationships and the new types of knowledge embodied within them.

FIG. 61 Arthur Welford, model of design for small mausoleum, in 'Architectural Association School of Architecture', *Architectural Review* 20 (December 1906), 279

---

31 'The Architectural Association', *Builder* 20 (22 March 1862), 202.
32 'Architectural Association', *Building News* 71 (13 November 1896), 693–4.

INSPECTING MODELS OUTSIDE THE ARCHITECTURAL ASSOCIATION

Alongside lectures and instructive classes, the AA curriculum also involved day trips to significant construction sites in London. In February 1899 a group of students and AA members visited Westminster Cathedral, then under construction.[33] Built between 1895 and 1905 to the designs of John Francis Bentley, the cathedral represented a key aspect of Victorian London: the expansion of the metropolis. Previously deprived areas of the capital including neighbourhoods adjacent to the cathedral site were modernized with new roads (Victoria Street), new transport interchanges (Victoria Station), and new building typologies (the mansion block). After visiting in foggy weather, which 'seemed to add to the impressive effect of the mass of the structure', the students were invited to the site offices to inspect the 1:48 model of the cathedral. Made by Farmer and Brindley, a prominent firm of architectural sculptors located across the river Thames in Lambeth, the model took two years to execute due to its detail and size – the extents cover 1.8 × 1.2 metres and the tower rises 2.4 metres in height.[34] FIG. 62 Intricately worked by the firm's principal wood-carver Francis Child, the model was made from Kauri Pine, a softwood native to Oceania and Southeast Asia. The choice of timber indicates one example of how architects and the profession were connected to material flows from the 'periphery' of the British Empire to its 'centre' in the metropolis. Parts of the model, one student noted, could 'be moved to allow the interior to be more thoroughly examined'.[35] A report on the students' visit first described the building and then offered an opinion of the cathedral. In this case the model stood in for the incomplete structure, thereby allowing students to make a judgement about the building without having to concern themselves with the construction site. This line of thinking had been anticipated three years earlier at an AA meeting. In response to a paper on the topic of books as an essential part of the student's education, John Slater, chairman of the meeting, cautioned that no amount of book knowledge would remove the importance of studying buildings in person or 'by the inspection of models'.[36]

    This 'inspection' took on a variety of forms within the instructive confines of a classroom setting. A photograph of the studio on the second floor of the AA's Tufton Street premises from 1904 shows the range of models used in teaching at the school at the turn of the twentieth century. FIG. 63 Mounted on a bench at the front of the classroom are a series of ornamental models. Alongside small-scale sculptural figurines for life drawing, these include a full-size decorative flower, a model of an Ionic capital, and a model of a highly elaborate entablature. On the right-hand bench is a two-sided model of antique columns and an architrave, demonstrating the differing proportional

---

33   At this stage the brick and stonework of the aisles, chapels, transepts, apse and outer walls of the cathedral had been completed but the concrete domes had not yet been cast. Winefride de l'Hôpital, *Westminster Cathedral and Its Architect: The Building of the Cathedral*, vol. 1 (London: Hutchinson, 1919), 85.

34   Patrick Rogers, *Westminster Cathedral: An Illustrated History*. (London: Oremus, 2012), 32–4; 'Model of the Cathedral', *The Westminster Cathedral Record* 9 (June 1899), 7.

35   Philip J. Marvin, 'Roman Catholic Cathedral, Westminster: Second Spring Visit, February 11th 1899', *AA Journal* 14, no. 145 (March 1899), 29–31, here: 29.

36   'Architectural Association: Books', *Builder* 50 (29 May 1886), 777. Slater's belief in the instructive potential of models was demonstrated again at the Eighth General Conference of Architects when, reading a paper on new construction materials, he illustrated his argument with models of specific product including Lindsay's Steel Decking and the correct way to detail the construction of fireproof partitions and ceilings. 'Supplement: General Conference of Architects', *Builder* 52 (7 May 1887), 692–706, here: 704.

relationships of the architectural orders. Next to these are two models of timber trusses that appear very similar to those made by Jacob Schröder, a German lecturer in projective geometry and a model-maker based at the Polytechnisches Arbeits-Institut in Darmstadt. Schröder first presented his work in London at the 1851 Great Exhibition where, after winning a prize medal, the governmental Department of Science and Art purchased five models that showed the construction of roofs in Germany. Exhibited at the South Kensington Museum in the Museum of Construction from at least 1861, these models were made to educate and inform students through observation and the copying of structural archetypes. Established in 1837, Schröder's workshop produced models for mathematicians, mechanical engineers, physicists, civil engineers, and architects. For architects, his models helped to aid in all sorts of artistic and technical education across Europe.[37] Among the many items made by his company were scale models of typical structure elements, such as large-span trusses, or 1:1 examples of timber joints. FIG. 64

Schröder also sold table-top machines to develop skills in drawing. These machines featured screens in front of a model to demonstrate how a platonic or typical house-like form could be projected in lines to create a two-point perspective drawing. Another set of models, a series of ornamental profiles, could be arranged in a classroom or lecture hall to display the shadows created on a backdrop by the refraction of light across them. FIG. 65 As Lucia Allais has recently pointed out, when architects learn how to draw they are instructed not only in techniques but also in the 'vast epistemic scheme' that underpins the absolute certainties of vision in our experiences of the built environment.[38] The microcosm of objects represented in the photograph of the AA studio – at a range of different scales, made of different materials, and at different levels of abstraction – embodies many of the ways that architectural models were used in professional education from technical knowledge around construction to standardized understandings of vision and its two-dimensional representation in drawing.

[37] Schröder also sold 1:1-scale models of machine parts and timber joints alongside models that demonstrated mechanics and forces. See: Jacob Schröder, *Polytechnisches Arbeits-Institut Darmstadt, Preisliste für Unterrichts-Modelle und Apparate* (Hanau: n. p., 1895).
[38] Lucia Allais, 'Rendering: On Experience and Experiments', in Zeynep Çelik Alexander and John May, eds., *Design Technics: Archaeologies of Architectural Practice* (Minneapolis: University of Minnesota Press, 2019), 1–44, here: 1.

FIG. 62   'Model of the Cathedral (from the North-East)', *Westminster Cathedral Record* 9 (June 1899), 7

FIG. 63   Architectural Association evening class studio, Tufton Street premises, 1904

82   Polyt. Arbeits-Institut J. SCHRÖDER, A.-G., Darmstadt.

HOCHBAU und WASSERBAU.   Holzconstructionen.

Dachconstructionen ausgeführter Bauwerke.

Nr.		Mark
1042.	Einfacher stehender Dachstuhl ohne Kehlgebälke	35
1043.	Desgl. mit Kehlgebälke	35
1044.	Desgl. mit Kehlgebälke und Kniestock	40
1045.	Desgl. mit Kehlgebälke und liegendem Stückpfosten	40
1046.	Einfacher liegender Dachstuhl ohne Kehlgebälke	40
1047.	Desgl. mit Kniestock und Kehlgebälke	40
1048.	Doppelt liegender Dachstuhl mit Halbstock, ohne Kehlgebälke	60
1049.	Desgl. mit Kehlgebälke	60

Dachconstructionen.

Zum grösseren Theil nach Dr. Moller's System und von Dr. Moller construirt.

Nach den Vorlegeblättern der Handwerkerschulen des Grossh. Hessischen Gewerbvereins zu Darmstadt von **H. Rössler** zusammengestellt.

Nr.		Tafel	Figur	Mark	Pf.
1050.	Stehender Dachstuhl mit doppelten Kehlzangen ohne Kehlgebälke	5	1—11	35	—
1051.	Desgl. mit einfachen Kehlzangen ohne Kehlgebälke	6	1—5	35	—
1052.	Stehender Dachstuhl mit einfachen Kehlzangen und Kehlgebälke	7	—	35	—
1053.	Desgl. mit doppelten Kehlzangen und Kehlgebälke	7	—	35	—
1054.	Stehender Kniestock-Dachstuhl mit einfachen Kehlzangen ohne Kehlgebälke	8	—	40	—
1055.	Desgl. mit einlaufenden Stichbalken	8	—	40	—
1056.	Stehender Kniestock-Dachstuhl mit einfachen Kehlzangen und Kehlgebälke	9	—	35	—
1057.	Desgl. mit anderem Kniestock-Stichgebälke	9	—	35	—
1058.	Stehender Dachstuhl mit aufgehängtem Kehlgebälke, welches für eine Belastung seine Bestimmung hat	10	—	35	—
1059.	Einfach liegender Dachstuhl	11	—	35	—
1060.	Desgl. mit Seitenverspannung, 2 Binder	11	—	35	—
1061.	Desgl. mit durchlaufenden Bögen und Firstpfette	11	—	35	—
1062.	Liegender Dachstuhl mit Kniestock und doppelten Kehlzangen	12	—	40	—
1063.	Desgl. mit einfacher Kehlzange	12	—	40	—

Hängewerke.

| 1064. | Dachstuhl der Schlosskirche zu Homburg v. d. H. mit 11¼ Meter Spannweite, mit aufgehängtem Gebälke mittelst einer Hängesäule | 13 | 1 | 50 | — |

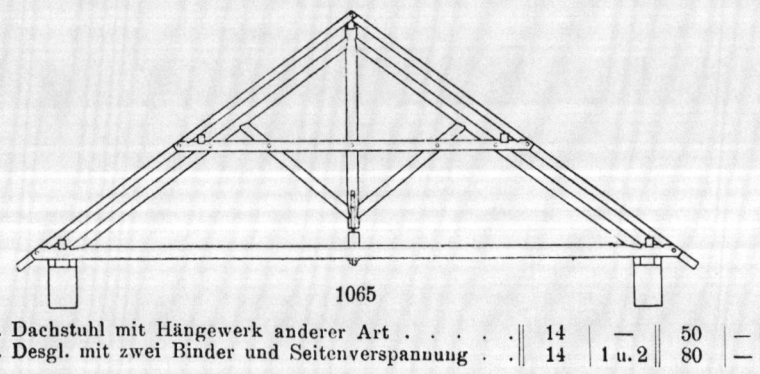

| 1065. | Dachstuhl mit Hängewerk anderer Art | 14 | — | 50 | — |
| 1066. | Desgl. mit zwei Binder und Seitenverspannung | 14 | 1 u. 2 | 80 | — |

FIG. 64   Jacob Schröder, Polytechnisches Arbeits-Institut Darmstadt, *Preisliste für Unterrichts-Modelle und Apparate* (Hanau: n. p., 1895), 82

22   Polyt. Arbeits-Institut J. SCHRÖDER, A.-G., Darmstadt.

MATHEMATIK. Licht- und Schatten-Constructionen.

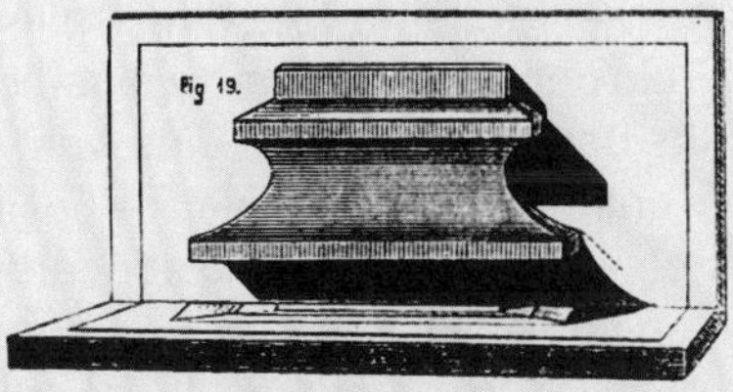

Tafel		Figur	Mark	Pf.
10.	Halbkreishohlkehle mit Platten	19	18	—
11.	Karnisgesims	20	18	—
12.	Karnisgesims als Fussgesims	21	21	—
13.	Gestürzter Karnis	22	21	—
14.	Gestürzter Karnis als Fussgesims	23	25	—
15.	Säulenfuss } auf einer Tafel	24 }	25	—
16.	Säulenkapitäl	25 }		
17.	Gurtengesims	26	18	—
18.	Zusammengesetztes Hauptgesims	27	22	—

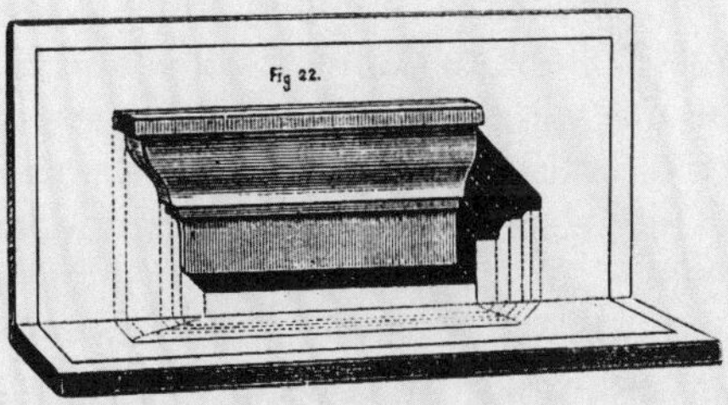

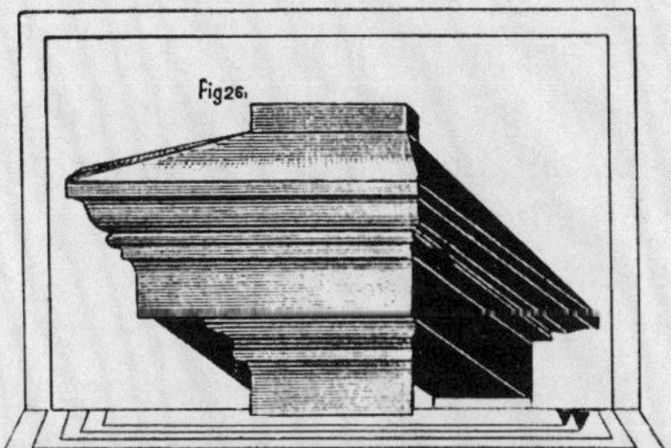

FIG. 65   Jacob Schröder, Polytechnisches Arbeits-Institut Darmstadt, *Preisliste für Unterrichts-Modelle und Apparate* (Hanau: n. p., 1895), 22

BANISTER FLETCHER AND TECHNICAL KNOWLEDGE AT KING'S COLLEGE

In May 1890 the anonymous writer of a regular column in the *Building News* dismissed the effectiveness of a new initiative by Banister Fletcher at King's College (then a constituent college of the University of London).[39] Within months of his appointment as Professor in Architecture (succeeding Robert Kerr), Fletcher had begun to establish a teaching collection with models taking a prominent part.[40] This collection marked a significant juncture in the education of architects at the university. The *Building News*, however, claimed it was 'improbable' that this collection would have any positive effect; instead one might as well spend their afternoons looking at nearby buildings, as any student 'can learn more in an hour's walk through London streets than a day in a museum of examples. Models are mere toys'.[41] The author proposed that an ideal museum should contain photographs of buildings arranged on stylistic and chronological lines, reasoning that photography, not architectural models, was 'the best medium for the illustration of works of architecture.'[42] The following week the journal ran a defence of architectural models by the nineteenth-century model-maker Charles Newson Thwaite. After describing models as 'the only comprehensible representation' to the general public, Thwaite argued for King's College to gather a collection of 'models of executed works, the educational value of which would be very great'.[43]

Under Fletcher's direction the authorities at King's were already assembling a collection of models alongside diagrams, specimens, and material samples.[44] The earliest record of the collection is found in the *Catalogue of the Reference Museum* (1894), which lists 196 models of construction details showing roofs, floors, walls, windows, or the intersection between these elements.[45] The Carpenters' Company, a historic trade association with a long-standing connection to both King's and Fletcher, lent several models representing both typical and exemplary joinery details at full scale. Other models represented particular building products or technical innovations supplied by manufacturers. A report in the press anticipated that the possession of such a 'unique collection of models' would be advantageous for the education of the students.[46] Fletcher also contributed models from his own collection and paid for the additional fittings required in the museum for storage and display.[47] By January 1896 he asked the principal of King's for more space for the ever-expanding collection, claiming that his 'mighty reference museum' was so significant that 'nothing will so add to the prestige of King's College and the addition of students'.[48]

As with the models at the AA, it is important to consider the collection at King's as responsive to the changing demands faced by the profession at

39 'Wayside Notes', *Building News* 58 (16 May 1890).
40 In January 1896 Fletcher described how within months of his election to the professorship, 'I had formed so large a collection of architectural & Building Construction casts, models, drawings, &c. that I applied for more space'. Banister Fletcher, letter to Henry Wace, 7 January 1896. KAS AD3 F7, King's College London [KCL].
41 'Wayside Notes', 687.
42 The author recommended that a collection of photographs should be procured 'to greatly facilitate the student's acquiring a clear knowledge of architectural history'. 'Wayside Notes', 687.
43 Charles Newson Thwaite, 'Architectural Models', *Building News* 58 (13 June 1890), 852.
44 It is likely that the collection was begun in connection with the formation of an evening class for articled pupils in 1892. 'Kings College Architectural Classes', *Building News* 75 (11 October 1898), 495.
45 *Catalogue of the Reference Museum*, 1894, KAS AC2 F11, KCL.
46 'Kings College Architectural Classes', 495.
47 Banister Fletcher, letter to Henry Wace, 1 May 1896, KAS AD3 F7, KCL.
48 Fletcher, letter to Henry Wace, 7 January 1896.

the end of the nineteenth century. A contemporary report in the *Building News* described a transition in the construction industry away from 'simple building operations confined to the traditional trades'.[49] Additional responsibilities were being placed on architects due to the subdivision of existing trades and the emergence of new ones connected to the widespread use of new products, new environmental requirements, and new typologies. In order to prepare for these demands, the architect required access to 'a practical building museum where may be found a collection of the special branches and trades ... described and illustrated by models or specimens'.[50] This is exactly the sort of collection that was assembled at King's to prepare a new generation of architects for the requirements of professional practice at the turn of the twentieth century. Fletcher himself underlined the importance of the collection as a pedagogic aid in 1897 when, writing in the *AA Journal* on the wider context of architectural education, he declared that the museum at King's was 'without anything like its equal in England'.[51] The models of various aspects of construction were organized into different trades (joinery, metalwork, plumbing) and used in both independent study and lectures. Furthermore, because the models were exact in their detail and could be dismantled into their components, a student could learn about modern construction more quickly than from drawings or diagrams.

Following Banister Fletcher's death in July 1899, his son, Banister Flight Fletcher, applied for the now-vacant professorship. Alongside his formal application to the university, the younger Fletcher wrote to the college itself regarding his role in the formation of the museum.[52] He explained that his father's collection of models belonged to him and not the college, although if appointed he would be happy to leave the collection intact and on site. Despite the somewhat threatening offer, in November 1899 Ravenscroft Elsey Smith was appointed professor, and in the subsequent months Banister Flight Fletcher removed a series of models and casts from the museum. The items, which included models of the Pantheon, Hampton Court Palace, and the roof of an unknown church by Alfred Waterhouse, underlined the breadth of the collection's holdings – from antique examples to models of historic and contemporary British buildings.[53]

Elsey Smith's appointment initiated a host of pedagogical changes at King's. For the first time a class in design was introduced and supplemented with new lectures on specification writing, sanitary science, and professional practice. In March 1902 the department recommended, pending approval by the university's council, that students should be awarded a Certificate in Architecture upon completion of the course, and an internal memorandum from March 1905 described how the type of education provided by King's should be restricted 'to more definitive University subjects'.[54] Any provision for classes in building construction, the bedrock of Banister Fletcher's pedagogical approach, as well as the focus on the collection of models, was reduced to a secondary role within a first-year course on drawing. During Elsey

49	'Special Developments', *Building News* 72 (19 February 1897), 261.
50	'Special Developments', 262.
51	Banister Fletcher, 'Architectural Teaching at King's College, London', *AA Journal* 12 (April 1897), 78.
52	Banister Flight Fletcher, letter to Walter Smith, 20 July 1899, KAS AC2 F10, KCL.
53	Ravenscroft Elsey Smith, letter to Walter Smith, 22 January 1900; Ravenscroft Elsey Smith, letter to Banister Flight Fletcher, 24 January 1900, KAS AC2 F11, KCL.
54	Draft copy of Certificate course pasted in with minutes for meeting held on 13 March 1902, KFE/M4, KCL; Memorandum, 27 March 1905, KAS AC2 F10, KCL.

Smith's tenure further changes included the removal of woodcarving classes (led by the Carpenters' Company) from the curriculum.

In London, technical education had been reorganized thanks to the successful establishment of institutes for working-class men and women, such as the polytechnic colleges across the city and the Building Crafts College in Fitzrovia, run directly by the Carpenters' Company. Less academic training was now to be provided outside of universities. Indeed, at King's there was a move away from the practical knowledge provided by the models and classes that the Carpenters' Company supported. Sociologists have argued that a profession is never completely established but continues to undergo renegotiation between different parties and as a part of this renegotiation professional groups must establish and continuously work to maintain the legitimacy of their privileged social position.[55] As the architectural profession developed in the nineteenth century so too did its educational system, and as the newly formed Certificate in Architecture demonstrated, the profession began to value the knowledge developed through drawing, design, and administrative tasks ahead of the study of building construction through models. The 1905 memorandum concluded by stating, 'architecture ought certainly to be a University study'.[56] This conviction led to a reorganization of architectural education within all the colleges of the University of London.

---

[55] Valérie Fournier, 'The Appeal to "Professionalism" as a Disciplinary Mechanism', *Social Review* 47, no. 2 (1999), 280–307, here: 304.

[56] Memorandum, 27 March 1905, KAS AC2 F10, KCL.

EDUCATION AT UNIVERSITY COLLEGE

Another college at the University of London, University College (UCL), based in Bloomsbury, offered a three-year degree in architecture from 1841 under the direction of Thomas Leverton Donaldson. Consisting of a series of courses in the formal and natural sciences, as well as architectural history, construction, and drawing, the education provided was not intended to supersede the conventional mechanism of pupillage but to supplement a student's knowledge.[57] It is unclear whether architectural models were used in the early period of teaching at UCL.[58] However, it is likely that Donaldson used models as teaching aids in his courses. In 1835, at the first meeting of the RIBA, he explained that the institute was forming a museum of 'models, casts, specimens of materials', which would provide visitors with a three-dimensional understanding of antique buildings and allow for public experimentation of materials and their application in design and construction.[59] Donaldson, who was also one of the authors of an 1859 report for the British government on the establishment of a 'National Museum for Architecture' at South Kensington, emphasized the importance of a systematically organized set of scale models in an educational collection.[60] Both episodes indicate Donaldson's belief in the usefulness of architectural models as vital didactic tools.

At UCL new collections of models emerged in two different ways: first, through the acquisition of institutional collections from elsewhere in London. In 1868, on hearing that the RIBA's collection of models was potentially being given away Thomas Hayter Lewis, Donaldson's successor in the Chair of Architecture at UCL from 1865, wrote to the RIBA council requesting some of the casts and models for use in drawing classes at University College.[61] Second, there are also accounts of prominent contemporary architects donating models to the college. For instance, William Tite presented a model to UCL as a 'reference specimen' for use in an architecture course in August 1865, showing a connection between contemporary practice and education.[62]

At the start of the twentieth century a more significant transformation to university architectural education brought with it a new collection of models. Changes to the curriculum followed the appointment of Frederick Moore Simpson as professor in 1903. Evening lectures as a supplement to pupillage were instigated; women were admitted to certain lecture courses; and a series of classes on drawing and architectural history were introduced. While the department was temporarily housed on Gower Street, another major development was the proposed merger of the architectural schools at King's and UCL in 1913.[63] Simpson had requested a new building for the school at UCL while Elsey Smith had complained about the lack of space

---

57   Thomas Leverton Donaldson, 'UCL Curriculum 1847', in: *Architectural Maxims and Theorems in Elucidation of Some of the Principles of Design and Construction* (London: John Weale, 1847), appendix, 1.
58   The architectural course itself was split into two components: one on fine art and the other on construction. A pair of notebooks containing a student's notes on each component of the course from 1863/64 survives in the university's archive but does not mention any models: 'Notes on Lectures given by T. L. Donaldson 1863/64', MS ADD 121, UCL.
59   'Address delivered by Donaldson at the official opening meeting of the [Royal] Institute of British Architects on 15 June 1835', 7, MS.SP/4/1, RIBA.
60   'The Architectural Collections in the Museum at Brompton', *Builder* 17 (17 September 1859), 614–5.
61   Thomas Hayter Lewis, letter to Council, January 1868, LC/5/7/10, RIBA.
62   'University College', *The Illustrated London News* (19 August 1865), 158.
63   Thomas Roger Smith replaced Hayter Lewis as professor in 1882 with few changes made to the course's structure or curriculum. See: Sophie Reed and Rebecca Spaven, '1841–1919 Wandering in a Labyrinth of Experiments', in Jeremy Melvin, ed., *175 Years of Architectural Education at UCL, Architectural Review* (2017), 67–70, here: 70.

at King's and the importance of formalized training for architects. As a result, the senate of the University of London formed an amalgamation committee in July 1910 to examine merging the two schools.[64] Unification with a third school, the AA, was discussed before it withdrew in May 1911.[65] The committee proposed combining both schools on a site adjoining the North Wing of UCL in a new building designed by Simpson, who had been leading the redevelopment of the university's campus since his appointment to the Chair of Architecture.[66] FIG. 66

After the negotiations were complete, in May 1913 Elsey Smith and Simpson recorded and selected the cases of models and building specimens to be transferred to the new school.[67] Following this, in August 1913, the secretary at King's sent a series of lists to the academic registrar at the University of London enumerating the four hundred models that were to be transferred to the newly combined school.[68] The majority depicted typical construction details; others showed technical innovations in building products. Some were scaled objects, such as those that depicted the structure of a timber bridge. Others were full-size models that showed the construction of specific building elements such as doors, windows, and floors. One of these full-sized elements was not in fact a model but an original eighteenth-century doorway and architrave, promised to the new school by Elsey Smith.[69] The objects and models were installed in the recently completed School of Architecture designed by Simpson and provided space for over one hundred students. Fronting onto Gower Street, the new building featured a large dual-aspect museum (232 square metres) on the first floor and a separate cast gallery (125 square metres) on the third floor.[70] As the plan reveals, the museum was the only space in the building where Simpson employed columns to make a large, open-plan space that occupied the most prominent floor of the new building with views onto Gower Street and into the college quadrangle. FIG. 67 The importance of the museum to the school was underlined by a review of the new building that described how the collections of models, samples of materials, and casts were being updated and increased by the university.

64	Minute of a meeting held on 13 July 1910, n.3433, ST/2/2/26, University of London.
65	Arthur Keen, letter to University of London Amalgamation Committee, 1 May 1911, KAS AC2 F10, KCL.
66	'Report of the Committee Appointed by the Senate on the Amalgamation of the Architectural Schools of the University', KAS AC2 F10, KCL. For an in-depth discussion on the redevelopment of UCL see: Amy Louise Spencer, 'University College London: An Architectural History, 1825–1939' (PhD thesis, University College London, 2021), 231–48.
67	'Equipment in the Architectural Department at King's College', KAS AC2 F10, KCL.
68	Additional lists also covered books, casts, and material samples. 'List of Cases, etc. Transferred to University College August 20 to 25 1913: Architecture Museum', KAS AC2 F10, KCL.
69	Secretary of University College London, letter to Secretary of King's College London, 13 October 1913, KAS AC2 F10, KCL; J. Mordaunt Crook, 'Architecture and History', *Architectural History* 27 (1984), 554–78, here: 577, n. 159.
70	'University College. London: New Building for the School of Architecture', *Building News* 105 (5 December 1913), 797.

THE UNIVERSITY

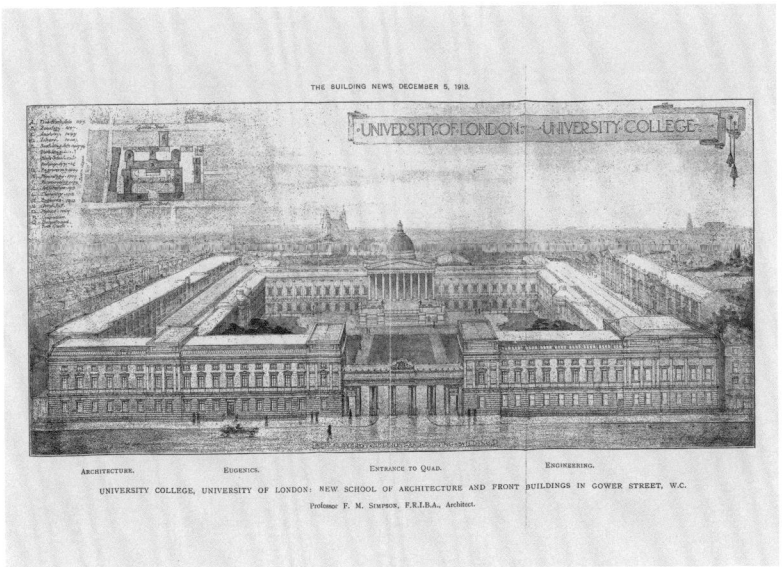

FIG. 66   'University College, University of London: New School of Architecture and Front Buildings in Gower Street', *Building News* 105 (5 December 1913), 801

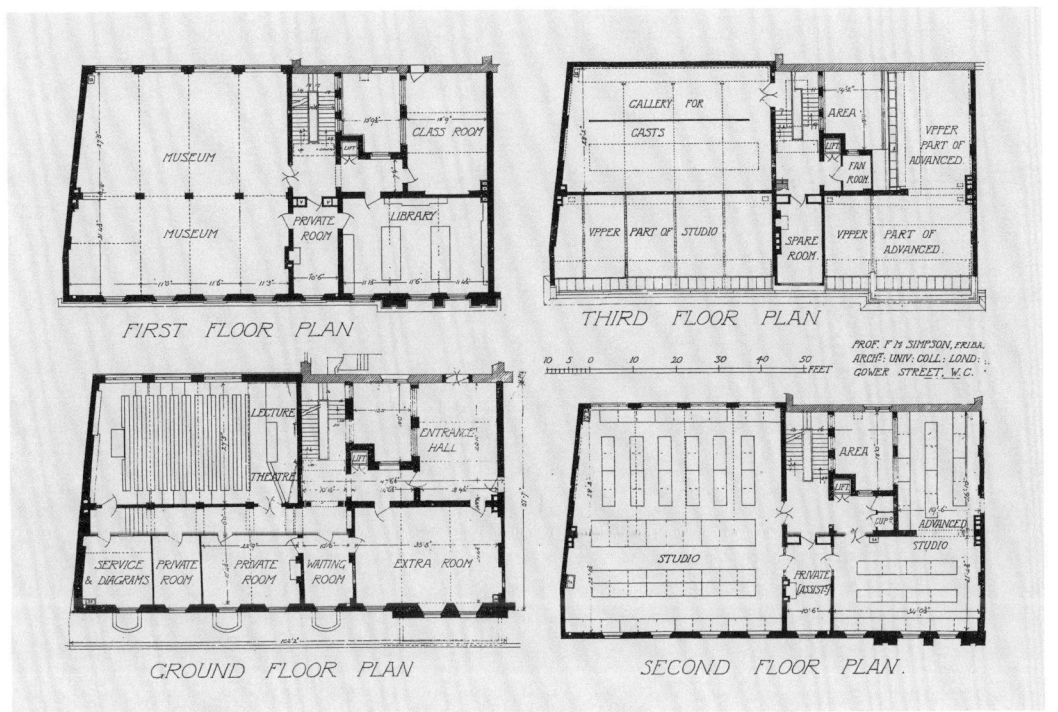

FIG. 67   'University of London: New School of Architecture', *Building News* 105 (5 December 1913), 800

FIG. 68 'School of Architecture – Studio', 'Programme of Conversazione in the New Buildings of the School at University College June 23rd 1914'

FIG. 69 'School of Architecture – Studio', 'Programme of Conversazione in the New Buildings of the School at University College June 23rd 1914'

Beyond the convenience afforded by the merger, the move to the new building at UCL was related to how architecture was reforming as a university subject. This was emphasized in an undated memorandum by the professorial board of the university, probably written in the summer of 1910, suggesting that the presence of the School of Archaeology and the Slade School of Art, also located adjacent to the college quadrangle, created a desirable site for the newly combined School of Architecture.[71] Furthermore the now-combined school's first prospectus described how the presence of engineering laboratories, the School of Hygiene, and other courses offered by the university provided 'facilities for a full and comprehensive Course of Architectural Education on a sound basis not possessed by any other institution in London'.[72] Architecture students benefitted from not only this proximity, but also the long-term social advantages of learning alongside 'engineers, painters, sculptors, and doctors ... and other professions'.

The education offered by the combined school was focused on the classical orders as 'the basis for design', as described in a prospectus from 1913.[73] Whether at an evening class or studying for an undergraduate degree, certificate day course, students were taught design through drawing classes on perspective and orthogonal techniques. Portions of these courses required students to draw from architectural models and casts in the school's museum and at the nearby Slade School.[74] In a 1914 paper on architectural form, Leslie Wilkinson, an assistant professor at the school, discussed the role of models in professional practice: 'A model provides the equivalent of an infinite number of perspective views, and will often settle points with a layman.'[75] The ease of understanding what models can provide, Wilkinson argued, made them suitable for the young architect still in educational formation. This can clearly be seen in two photographs of the school's interiors published in a programme celebrating the opening of the new building in June 1914.[76] In the photograph of the design studio there is a single model of an antique temple, hidden in the shadows and ignored as students in their white smocks draw at their desks. FIG. 68 Treated ornamentally, this model has a symbolic function in its faithful representation of the Beaux-Arts architecture that was being produced at every drawing board, whereas in the photograph of the school's museum there are models strewn across benches: models of arch construction, fragments of structural bays, and full-sized building elements. FIG. 69 Interspersed between these are samples of materials, the glass from a window, and sculptural details carved in wood. These are not design models. Instead, they were there to explain the complicated junctions and detailing required in various forms of construction. Like at the AA and at King's College, these models represent a change in the conception of architecture away from artistic principles towards a logical methodology of practice. These models are to provide students, who are developing their knowledge, with professional and technical authority when interacting with builders, craftsmen, clients, and politicians in the various spatial settings of Victorian London.

71	'Memo by the Professorial Board on the Proposed Scheme for the Amalgamation of the Architectural Schools of the University', KAS AC2 F10, KCL.
72	'University of London School of Architecture 1913–14', 6, KAS AC2 F10, KCL.
73	'University of London School of Architecture 1913–14', 7, KAS AC2 F10, KCL.
74	'University of London School of Architecture 1913–14', 13, KAS AC2 F10, KCL.
75	Leslie Wilkinson, 'The Expression of Form', *Building News* 106 (15 May 1914), 665.
76	These photographs are missing from the UCL archives. The programme they were published in should be found at: 'Programme of Conversazione in the New Buildings of the School at University College June 23rd 1914', Hist V B/14, UCL. My thanks to Sophie Read and Alan Powers for their help with this subject.

MODELLING THE METROPOLIS

THE MUSEUM

North Shields, Northumberland, January 17, 1848. Henry Walker Benson, a provincial architect and model-maker wrote a letter published in the *Builder*. Its subject was a matter of much debate among the architectural press and profession: the absence of a museum of British architecture.[1] Benson proposed London as the home for such a museum that would contain models of cathedrals and churches from all across the country. Each building would be made at three separate standardized scales: one for the overall massing; a larger scale for the interiors; and a third, even larger one, 'for some integral portion' to show its particular characteristics. These three scales would be fixed, Benson believed, in order for the public to better understand the comparative sizes of buildings. For incomplete or ruined buildings Benson proposed making a second model at the same scale, 'to shew the effect to be produced by the completion of the edifice'. Such an institute would be subsidized through sponsorship from the institutional owners of each building.

The idea of art as a means to bring together and reform the social classes was commonplace in the nineteenth century. Equally important was the notion that it was the duty of those in privileged political positions to educate the masses. Therefore the perceived value of an architectural museum was that it could improve society. Only two years before Benson's letter, Charles Heath Wilson, director of the Government School of Design, spoke about need for young designers to study models in order to 'correct' and 'purify' taste.[2] Other writers took on a nationalist agenda about why models

1   Henry Walker Benson, 'Museum of Architectural Models', *Builder* 6 (5 February 1848), 67. Benson later wrote to the *Builder* to discuss various colours of cardboard for models and explained that he had many years' experience as a model-maker. 'Card-board Models', *Builder* 7 (24 March 1849), 141.
2   Charles Heath Wilson, 'Suggestions for Forming a Museum of Casts of the Architecture of Antiquity and of the Middle Ages', *CEAJ* 8 (May 1845), 138–9.

should be collected for public education. Noting that the British Museum's collection of British antiquities was 'bare and miserable', an editorial in the *Builder* advised creating a gallery to represent Stonehenge and other prehistoric sites through plans, sections, models, and paintings.[3] Others saw a clear role for collections of models in the definition of the architectural profession. In an effort to strengthen the RIBA and its mission in London, William Burges proposed that all architectural societies across Britain and their collections should be housed at one location in London to form an architectural museum. This museum would include the 'exhibition of ordinary building materials, another of models, and a third of new inventions', bringing together different types of knowledge for the wider public and architects alike.[4]

FIG. 70   Interior view of Du Bourg's Museum, Grosvenor Street, Westminster, c.1818, aquatint

Before the mid-nineteenth century, collections of models in London consisted of foreign buildings and monuments. The first established collection devoted principally to architectural models was Richard Du Bourg's 'Classical Exhibition', established in 1778 at 24 St Albans Street in Piccadilly and open to the public for a small entrance fee. Du Bourg was both the maker and exhibitor of a collection of cork models of sites associated with classical literature, which were displayed in a large hall and lit from above by a colossal skylight.[5] FIG. 70 Born in London to a French father and an English mother, Du Bourg learned to draw under the well-known engraver Jacob Bonneau.

3   'British Antiquities in the British Museum' (19 March 1853), 179.
4   'The Architectural Association', *The Architect* 14 (25 December 1875), 368.
5   For a fuller discussion on Du Bourg see: Richard Gillespie, 'Richard Du Bourg's "Classical Exhibition", 1775–1819', *Journal of the History of Collections* 29, no. 2.1 (July 2017), 251–69; Richard Gillespie, 'The Rise and Fall of Cork Model Collections in Britain', *Architectural History* 60 (2017), 117–46.

He spent most of the 1760s in Italy, where he studied the sites of antiquity.[6] These locations became the subject of his models in London – Roman monuments along the Via Appia and Greek temples in Paestum. His model of Mount Vesuvius was even designed to erupt with a flow of lava – a feature that caused irreparable damage when one Saturday afternoon in May 1785 the display started a fire that destroyed the whole exhibition. Throughout the nineteenth century Du Bourg's models appeared in collections in London, at Sir John Soane's Museum, at the South Kensington Museum, and in Oxford at the Bodleian Libraries, allowing visitors across England to behold the antique world in ruin before their eyes.

Another prominent set of models commonly found in public collections across Britain and Europe was the plaster-of-Paris series of antique subjects by the French model-makers Jean-Pierre and François Fouquet, a father and son who were active in Paris from the 1790s until the 1830s.[7] Jean-Pierre Fouquet produced seventy-six models of antique buildings in cork and plaster for the collector Louis François Cassas, who exhibited them in a dedicated gallery at 8 Rue de Seine.[8] FIG. 71 British architects including Edward Cresy and John Nash purchased sets of Fouquet models from Cassas in the first few decades of the nineteenth century.[9] Nash's set was displayed in his house at 14–16 Regent Street in about 1820 – the collection impressed Karl Friedrich Schinkel during his visit to London in 1826.[10] FIG. 72 More Fouquet models were purchased by the Bodleian Library in 1823 through public subscription and exhibited alongside paintings and figurative sculpture.[11] These were later joined by further donations, amounting to a collection that the architectural press urged younger readers to visit and study.[12] Within London itself, however, a museum of models had been formed by one of the city's most prominent architects: John Soane.

---

6   As well as being the subject of the models, Italy was also the source of cork model-making techniques, which arrived in Rome from Naples at the end of the eighteenth century. Cork was originally used to make models of Christian nativity scenes (known as *Presepe*) but became adopted by the English Antiquarians and art collectors such as Thomas Jenkins and Charles Townley.

7   Geneviève Cuisset, 'Jean-Pierre et François Fouquet: Artistes modeleurs', *Gazette des Beaux-Arts* 115 (1990), 227–57, here: 224.

8   Louis-Pierre Baltard, *Athenaeum, ou Galerie française des productions de tous les arts. Par une Société d'hommes de lettres et d'artistes, et publié par M. Baltard* (Paris: n. p., 1806) 402–3.

9   Nash told the diarist Joseph Farington that he had paid £1000 for his set of Fouquet models. Valentin Kockel, 'Rom über die Alpen tragen: Korkmodelle antiker Architektur im 18. und 19. Jahrhundert', in Werner Helmberger and Valentin Kockel, eds., *Rom über die Alpen tragen: Fürsten sammeln antike Architektur–die Aschaffenburger Korkmodelle* (Ergolding: Arcos, 1993), 11–31, here: 15–16.

10   Karl Friedrich Schinkel, *The English Journey: Journal of a Visit to France and Britain in 1826*, ed. David Bindman and Gottfried Riemann, trans. F. Gayna Walls (New Haven: Yale University Press, 1993), 90–1.

11   John Norris, *A Catalogue of the Pictures, Models, Busts, &c. in the Bodleian Gallery, Oxford* (Oxford: n. p., 1839), 60. An 1839 catalogue by John Norris, janitor of the Bodleian, recorded the Fouquet models on display alongside one of Du Bourg's models and a model made by one of the Wyatt dynasty.

12   'Leading article', *Builder* 11 (7 May 1853), 289.

FIG. 71 Exhibition of architectural models of Jean-Pierre Fouquet in the gallery of Louis François Cassas, lithograph, in Louis-Pierre Baltard, *Athenaeum, ou Galerie française des productions de tous les arts* (Paris: n.p., 1806), 390

FIG. 72 Augustus Pugin, *Gallery in the House of John Nash, Esq.*, engraving, in John Britton, *Illustrations of the Public Buildings of London*, vol. 2 (London: John Weale, 1825), 348

JOHN SOANE AND THE PRACTICE OF COLLECTING

It all began with the ruin. Alongside antique sculpture and casts, Soane purchased cork models made by the eighteenth-century Neapolitan model-maker Giovanni Altieri in 1804. Initially the models – the Temple of Vesta at Tivoli and the Arch of Constantine in Rome – were displayed as art objects in his house and office in central London on the perimeter of Lincoln's Inn Fields. Others were acquired from auctioneers at Christies from the estate of John Sanders: a model of the 1820 excavations at Pompeii and four cork models of temples at Paestum. Sanders was Soane's first pupil. He had spent two years in Italy with George Ledwell Taylor and Edward Cresy who drew remains of antiquity while Sanders took casts of ornamental details.[13] In the shadow of the Colosseum, Sanders watched as local archaeologists unearthed the Temple of Peace and then recorded their excavations in a model showing each topographic level of the site. When in Pompeii, Sanders wrote to Soane, describing how authentic Roman buildings were 'all to be seen in full view. Everyday something new is brought to light'.[14] Sanders had purchased his model of the theatre district of Pompeii from the model-maker Domenico Padiglione, a member of the archaeological team at Pompeii, who spent decades working on a series of 1:48 models of the antique city. At a workshop in Naples an archaeological plan was copied onto a base board. Slots into the board were cut to insert walls and other vertical elements while cork was laid, cut, and glued down to form the topographic and outlines.[15] But the project remained incomplete and only certain districts of the excavations were made.[16]

On acquiring the model Soane purchased a brass pedestal with two stands to display his collection. On arriving in London, the Pompeii model occupied the entirety of one level of the stand, allowing viewers the chance to transport themselves to a point above the city and look down over the ruins of antiquity. Initially the model stand was not displayed in its own room but in the South Drawing Room on the first floor of 13 Lincoln's Inn Fields between 1826 and 1829. According to Soane's friend, the British antiquarian John Britton, the South Drawing Room had recently been renovated to display a series of cork models – objects, he wrote, that were important to contemporary architectural thought.[17] As he expanded his collection and developed a curatorial strategy, Soane adapted the spaces of display within his house. The museum became both a network of related objects and curated spaces, where the synthesis of architectural arrangement and collections created complex visual effects as part of a particular professional identity. FIG. 73

13	Julia Lenaghan, 'The Cast Collection of John Sanders, Architect, at the Royal Academy', *Journal of the History of Collections* 26, no. 2 (July 2014), 193–205, here: 193.
14	Margaret Richardson, 'Model Architecture: Sir John Soane's Collection of Architectural Models', *Country Life* 183 (21 September 1989), 224–7, here: 224.
15	Kockel, 'Rom über die Alpen tragen', 22.
16	Valentin Kockel, 'Towns and Tombs: Three-Dimensional Documentation of Archaeological Sites in the Kingdom of Naples in the Late Eighteenth and Early Nineteenth Centuries', in Ilaria Bignamini, ed., *Archives and Excavations: Essays on the History of Archaeological Excavations in Rome and Southern Italy from the Renaissance to the Nineteenth Century* (London: The British School at Rome, 2004), 143–62, here: 144–9.
17	John Britton, *The Union of Architecture, Sculpture, and Painting* (London: n. p., 1827), 45.

FIG. 73 Charles James Richardson, Picture Room, Sir John Soane's Museum, engraving, in *Description of the House and Museum* (London: n. p., 1830), plate 10

FIG. 74　Charles James Richardson, Model Room, Sir John Soane's Museum, engraving, in *Description of the House and Museum* (London: n. p., 1830), plate 16

In the Autumn of 1829 when Soane began refurbishing the upper floors of 13 Lincoln's Inn Fields, the models were relocated to the newly renovated attic.[18] Around this time, the end of November 1829, Soane had also begun work on the first edition of his own *catalogue raisonné* of the collection. Published the following year, *Description of the House and Museum* featured an engraving that showed the arrangement of the collection in the attic 'Model Room', illuminated by two sash windows and a thin rectangular roof light, possibly influenced by Du Bourg's museum. FIG. 74 The model stand sits in the middle on the attic's bare timber floorboards. On the upper level of the pedestal are two cork models of temples at Paestum, one on either side of a model of the Temple of Vesta at Tivoli. The model of Pompeii is below, and at the lowest level is a contemporary timber model of Soane's own design for new offices for the Board of Trade on Whitehall. Rendered perspective drawings of Soane's designs for public and private buildings hang on the walls of the room and in recesses formed between the south-facing windows. Additional models were located around the house alongside antique sculptures, casts, and all manner of paintings and decorative art, suggesting a fluidity to the organization of the collection.

The location of the Model Room at 13 Lincoln's Inn Fields was crucial. As Soane noted, the south-facing windows offered panoramic views of London, its monuments, and environs: 'The effect of these models, to be duly appreciated, should be seen under the influence of sunshine'.[19] Earlier, in his Royal Academy lectures, Soane noted how studying an architectural model could replicate the shifting effects of light and shade on a building's facade

18　John Soane, Office Day Book, vol. 1, entries for 23–4, 30–1 October, 4 November 1829, Sir John Soane's Museum, London [SJSM].
19　John Soane, *Description of the House and Museum, on the North Side of Lincoln's Inn-Fields, the Residence of Sir John Soane* (London: n. p., 1830), 25.

across the passage of a day.[20] At Lincoln's Inn Fields the south-facing windows were intended to provide maximum direct sunlight into the room. Entries in Soane's notebook describe how the windows of the attic were altered in 1829.[21] Unlike the typical Georgian window in London, made up of a series of small plate glass rectangles held between sash bars, the newly installed glazing in the Model Room was formed by two long rectangles of glass joined with a single horizontal bar to allow as much sunlight into the interior as possible, thereby replicating the effects of Mediterranean light on the models.

In the following years two new factors would affect the collection and presentation of models at Lincoln's Inn Fields. Soane was keen to create a legacy for his life and work while he was still alive. In April 1833 a Private Act of Parliament passed, ensuring that after Soane's death the collection would be preserved *in situ* in the house-museum and accessible to the public twice a week throughout April, May, and June. Additionally, between 1832 and 1834 Soane expanded his collection of models to include a set of twenty Fouquet models and cork models that had previously been owned by the architect Charles Heathcote Tatham. Meanwhile repairs were made to existing specimens – two plaster models of Soane's work at the Bank of England and Board of Trade were transported across London to the east-end headquarters of the plasterers Robson and Estelle.[22] A new space for the models was created in September 1834: alterations were made to the second floor of 13 Lincoln's Inn, where the bedroom of Soane's late wife was refashioned into a new Model Room, with the collection of models relocated there in March 1835.[23]

FIG. 75 Charles James Richardson, Model Room, Sir John Soane's Museum, watercolour, in *Description of the House and Museum* (London: Levey, Robson, and Franklyn, 1835), plate 38

20 John Soane, 'Lecture III', in David Watkin, ed., *Sir John Soane: The Royal Academy Lectures* (Cambridge: Cambridge University Press, 2000), 63–88, here: 87.
21 John Soane, notebook, vol. 13, no. 211, entries for 6–7 October, 4 November 1829, SJSM.
22 W. Robson and J. Estelle, undated bill to John Soane, Soane XV. K. 3, SJSM.
23 John Soane, notebook, vol. 14, no. 221, entries for 16 September 1834 and 4 March 1835, SJSM.

Following these revisions Soane began a second edition of the *Description* in July 1835.²⁴ As with the first edition, his assistant Charles James Richardson prepared illustrations for the plates, including a watercolour of the second Model Room.²⁵ FIG. 75 Drawn from a viewpoint in the southwest corner, Richardson positioned the model stand in the centre of the second-floor room. It sits on a swath of patterned carpet and is lit by two south-facing windows. New supports have been added to the stand to display the large cork models of various temples at Paestum. Just below are several plaster models in cases. Next to these are two further Fouquet models including a plaster model of the Temple of Zeus or Apollo at Paestum in its idealized form, which sits beneath a ruinous cork version of the same building. The middle level is taken up by the large-scale model of Pompeii (with the cork model of the Temple of Vesta at Tivoli perched on the corner).

Even when displayed as a single collection, materially driven themes emerge among the models. In one set cork was used to replicate the existing ruinous state of the antique monuments (minus the alterations and changes to their structure since antiquity), while in the other set, plaster of Paris reconstructed the monuments in their idealized forms. These two materials allowed for different perspectives on the same subjects: cork emphasized the picturesque and temporal character of antique monuments while the flawless, pure-white plaster models presented a classical idea that could be reconstructed through contemporary scholarly study. None of the models displayed in either incarnation of the Model Room attempted to directly replicate the materiality of the buildings they represented. As Mari Lending describes in her recent cultural history of the plaster monument, throughout the nineteenth century there were many discussions about the replication of colour, texture, and weathering on collections of architectural casts.²⁶ Several contemporaries of Soane discussed the effects of particular model-making materials in order to convey ideas about a building's construction or its present condition. An encyclopaedia entry on models noted that although beautiful, plaster was 'a fault … because it prepossesses the eye too much' and shows the building in a pure uniform hue, 'whiter than the whitest stone'.²⁷ As one architectural writer claimed, the material character of plaster models revealed 'a degree of beauty which is desirable, [rather] than one which is attainable'.²⁸ Another article offering advice to young architects described how the whiteness of newly finished stone on the building site was distinct from 'the unnatural chalky complexion of a plaster model'.²⁹ The article proposed that instead of ice-white examples shown to the public and other members of the profession, plaster models should be mixed with colour or exposed to dirt to simulate the environmental conditions of the smoke-filled metropolis. Commentators also discussed the qualities and difficulties of model-making with cork. According to the same encyclopaedia entry faulting plaster, cork was often used for antique subjects – 'reconstructions of the original structures or dilapidated by time' – in order 'to express of itself the ruggedness and flaws of decay'.³⁰ An article on model-making techniques

---

24 John Soane, notebook, vol. 14, no. 223, entry for 24 July 1835, SJSM.
25 John Soane, Office Day Book, vol. 8, entries for 28 August to 26 December 1835, SJSM.
26 Mari Lending, *Plaster Monuments: Architecture and the Power of Reproduction* (Princeton: Princeton University Press, 2017), 94–5.
27 'Models, Architectural', in George Long, ed., *The Penny Cyclopaedia of the Society for the Diffusion of Useful Knowledge*, vol. 15, (London: Charles Knight, 1839), 294.
28 William Henry Leeds, 'Modes of Architectural Representation', *Architectural Magazine* 2 (October 1835), 452–9, here: 454.
29 'Advice and Counter-Advice', *Building News* 6 (3 February 1860), 69, n.*.
30 'Models, Architectural', 294.

suggested that cork held the advantage of being easily worked but was 'more suitable for models of old buildings and ruins than for new buildings'.[31] While quick to carve, the accuracy and detail of buildings, including pinnacles, spires, and mouldings, could easily be lost or altogether ignored due to the material quality of cork.

On the lowest level of Soane's model stand were examples relating to his own architectural practice. These included construction technology (a model of an engine for driving foundation piles), presentation models, and working design models. How then should the multiplicity of subjects, materials, and scales in the Model Room be interpreted? Why display a mix of antique and his own contemporary buildings in one place? One argument is that the models of antique buildings are the sources from which Soane's prized architectural fragments and casts (exhibited throughout the rest of his house-museum) were taken. If his strategy for collecting architectural fragments was a way of using part of a building to represent the whole, then Soane's approach in the Model Room was to create a microcosm where the scale models could stand in for the real buildings. The result is an alternative history of antiquity that distorts both geography and time. And yet both in the materiality of the models and Soane's text in the *Description* there is a distinction between the ruined model and the idealized one. Similarly, the models related to Soane's practice are allocated their own portion of the stand, their own paragraph in the *Description,* and their own material (timber) – assignations that serve to partially separate them from the plaster and cork models of antique buildings. And so while there is no singular history visualized by the collection there are still distinct categories created by the curation of the models on the stand. At the same time it is impossible to miss an attempt by Soane to connect the legacy of his work with the classical canon. Through the accumulation and deployment of objects, antiquarians and collectors constructed spaces that never existed in the past to evoke a world that similarly only existed in their imagination. Surrounded by these symbols of classicism – which were often contemporary depictions rather than 'original material' – the collector was able to realize in physical form his dreams and fantasies. United by a common medium Soane was able to construct a world where the canonical monuments of antiquity are comparable to his own buildings – both the complete and unrealized.

31 'Architectural Modeling', *Building News* 14 (16 December 1867), 851.

THE ROYAL INSTITUTE OF BRITISH ARCHITECTS: MODELS FOR THE PROFESSION

At the same time, less than a mile away in Covent Garden, the Institute of British Architects was considering how to form an architectural collection of its own, part of a mission to define the profession as a coherent group with a clearly demarcated body of knowledge. At the opening meeting of the institute in 1835, Thomas Leverton Donaldson, one of the founding members, explained that the institute was forming a museum of 'models, casts, specimens of materials', which would be both 'instructive and interesting' for visitors. Crucially this museum of models would allow a three-dimensional understanding of buildings in Greece and Rome from 'different points of view'.[32] The importance of architectural models to the RIBA's cause was reinforced by another member who provided a definitive rationale for displaying architectural models ahead of other forms of representation, as a 'model conveys so perfect an idea of the object contemplated'.[33] It emerged that the RIBA had even greater ideas for the scope of its collection, which it was hoped would contain models of 'celebrated buildings' of antiquity, combined with domestic examples, all made to the same scale.[34] Later described as 'model rooms', British buildings, when arranged alongside antique monuments, would acquire a position in the lineage of European architectural history. Through the medium of models, the visiting public would acquire knowledge of architecture, a discipline 'classed by universal consent among the most liberal'.[35]

In reality however the RIBA's acquisition of models was more contingent than its original intentions. Donations and bequests from members, exhibitors at monthly meetings, and other benefactors were the main sources for the collections. Thomas de Grey, RIBA president, described how although each individual donation to the institute might appear small, these gifts would 'form a valuable collection in the aggregate'.[36] During the initial stages of the RIBA's establishment there was a belief that collecting models would benefit professional practice, especially to foster public understanding. Through these multiple aspects, models offered clear benefits to the institute's aim to disseminate architectural knowledge. Furthermore, by forming a canon of models which relied on scale and miniaturization to make comparisons between buildings in different physical locations and temporal epochs, the RIBA sought to situate the nation's architecture within a broader historical narrative and establish a British School (or style) of architecture.

Models also played a role in discussions of ethnography at the institute – discussions that were interwoven with British colonial power. In addition to their role within a formal collection of physical objects, models contributed to the formation of a library, or archive of thinking, about other architectural cultures, albeit from a Western, imperial perspective. Displayed at particular meetings, models aided in the collective examination of cultural responses to other environments and social practices through the design and construction of buildings. For example, in June 1847 Donaldson exhibited 'A curious

---

32   'Address delivered by Donaldson at the official opening meeting of the [Royal] Institute of British Architects on 15 June 1835', 7, MS.SP/4/1, RIBA.
33   'Report of the Council', *RIBA Transactions* (1835–36), 24.
34   'Report of the Council', 24–5.
35   'Report of the Council', 26–7.
36   'Address delivered by Donaldson at the official opening meeting of the [Royal] Institute of British Architects on 15 June 1835', 7, MS.SP/4/1, RIBA.

Model of a Chinese Chemist's House and Shop'.[37] The model had been produced for a prominent London pharmacist keen to know more about one of his Guangzhou counterparts in the wake of the First Opium War (1839–42).[38] Accurate and comprehensive drawings were difficult to obtain, so a model was made by local craftsmen to convey key information about non-Western building practices in relation to the local climate and social habits. Its formal expression – derived from 'the tents of their herdsmen-ancestors' – met with the condescension typical of the time, but the architectural press used the model to make a broader point regarding the enduring power of vernacular building forms, noting their persistence in contemporary London, where even 'ugly' buildings were copied, and every repetition played its part 'in further vitiating public taste'.[39] Similarly in 1854 the art historian James Fergusson gave two lectures on fifteenth- and sixteenth-century monuments constructed by the Adil Shahi dynasty in the city of Bijapur in southern India. The second lecture focused on the Gol Gumbaz, the tomb of Mohammad Adil Shah (1601–56), which featured an immense hemispherical dome forty-four metres in diameter (the second largest in the world after St Peter's in Rome). Following the use of structural domes in Britain was debated, and members who owned drawings or models of domes were asked to bring them to the institute's next meeting.[40] At that meeting, one member unveiled a plaster model of the tomb at Bijapur to enable the opportunity to understand the formal and structural effects of the dome. As Itohan Osayimwese has recently explored in a German context, in the nineteenth century these discussions were a part of a new form of architectural research, where ethnographic study increased the existing body of knowledge and helped contribute to contemporary debates on European architectural practice.[41]

In 1837 the RIBA moved from its first premises at 43 King Street in Covent Garden to 16 Grosvenor Street in Mayfair. However, by May 1838 its library and collection were threatening to outgrow the new apartments. An appeal to the government for more accommodation in a public building was unsuccessful.[42] Instead the institute moved again (this time only 200 metres) to 9 Conduit Street. With ample space, there was even a large room dedicated to the display of models. While the collection survived the RIBA's relocation to Conduit Street, there are no further recorded discussions about the arrangement of models. In fact, it appears that the collection quickly became redundant, relegated to the basement of 9 Conduit Street (a request was made in June 1867 for shelving to store more models).[43] Although models were emerging as important objects in architectural education (as mentioned in the previous chapter, in 1868 University College requested the loan of casts and models for use in drawing classes), the redundancy of the RIBA's collection was directly connected to the formation of new national collections elsewhere in London.[44]

37 '28 June 1847', *RIBA Proceedings* (1842–49), 213–4; 'Institute of British Architects', *Athenaeum* (31 July 1847), 818.
38 'Forensic Medicine', *Edinburgh Medical and Surgical Journal* 65 (May 1847), 865.
39 'Influence of Early Buildings on the Architecture of all Countries – The Chinese Model of a House Now in this Country', *Builder* 5 (6 March 1847), 105.
40 '11 December 1854', *RIBA Proceedings* (1854–55), 7.
41 Itohan Osayimwese, 'The Irresistible Call of Adventure: German Architects and Ethnography', in *Colonialism and Modern Architecture in Germany* (Pittsburgh: University of Pittsburgh Press, 2017), 61–96.
42 Minute of a meeting, 7 May 1838, vol. 1, 1.2.1, RIBA.
43 Charles Charnock Nelson, letter to RIBA Council, 3 June 1867, LC/5/7/10, 1.2.3, RIBA.
44 Thomas Hayter Lewis, letter to RIBA Council, 14 January 1868, LC/5/7/10, 1.2.3, RIBA. According to a letter from Albert Richardson these models appear to have survived an air raid in 1941 but were probably removed from the university in the 1960s by Richard Llewelyn-Davis. My thanks to Charles Hind for this information.

ARCHITECTURAL MODELS AT THE SOUTH KENSINGTON MUSEUM

> The object of a Metropolitan Establishment was to create, exhibit, and distribute the most improved illustrations, models, and diagrams, both in Science and Art, which should be readily accessible to the public at large, but especially to all persons throughout the country interested in education.[45]

Following the Great Exhibition in 1851 there were calls to reform art and design education in the United Kingdom. Henry Cole, a crucial figure in both the organization of the Great Exhibition and British cultural life, believed that innovative design education could be provided through a new national museum.[46] Following the example of museums in Dresden, Berlin, and Vienna, the medium for the new museum's didactic message would be the copy. The copy, in the unified display of models and casts, was central to the curatorial approach of the architectural collections. Models are a form of reproduction – they are not the object itself but hold the potential to represent it in new settings to new audiences. Through scale and material abstraction, a model can present architecture in a way that becomes more legible than the original object, in part because a viewer is not limited by geography, time, or space. Cole believed that by engaging with models museum visitors would in turn be able to engage with buildings, objects, and concepts that existed in both the past and present, or would exist in the future. With the ability to transcend physical and temporal limitations while still offering a reality to visitors, the medium fitted perfectly within both the museum's didactic agenda and its communicative techniques.

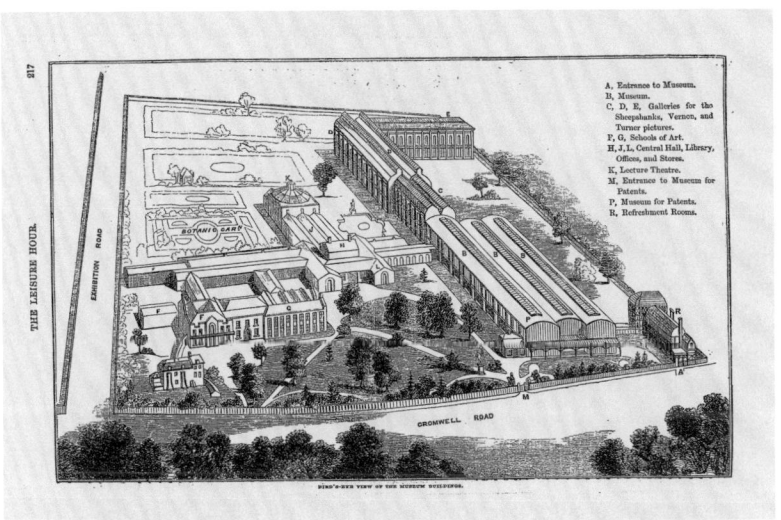

FIG. 76 'Bird's Eye View of the Museum Buildings', *Leisure Hour* 380 (7 April 1859), 217

---

45 Science and Art Department, *First Report of the Art and Science Department of the Committee of Council on Education* (London: Eyre and Spottiswoode, 1854), x.

46 Cole was the first superintendent of the Department of Practical Art (later Science and Art Department), an offshoot of the Board of Trade that supervised the new South Kensington Museum alongside the Royal Dublin Society, the School of Mines, the Geological Museum, and the provincial Government Schools of Design. See: Anthony Burton, *Vision and Accident: The Story of the V&A* (London: V&A Publications, 1999); Giles Waterfield, *The People's Galleries: Art Museums and Exhibitions in Britain, 1800–1914* (New Haven: Yale University Press, 2015).

Using the profits from the Great Exhibition, an estate of 86 acres was purchased by a royal commission led by Prince Albert who hoped to form a complex of exhibitions, schools, and learned institutions in the newly named district: South Kensington. Located close to Hyde Park, the southeast corner of the estate was occupied by the large, dilapidated Brompton Park House and its grounds, which constituted the site for the new museum. A view of the museum from 1858 shows the initial layout with Brompton Park House repurposed as the Art School. FIG. 76 To the northeast was James Pennethorne's 'Junction', a low single-storey building that contained offices, storerooms, and a circular lecture theatre, which led to the exposed iron galleries commonly known as the Brompton Boilers that housed the collections from 1857 until the early 1860s. FIG. 77

FIG. 77   J. C. Lanchenick, *South Kensington: South End of the Iron Museum* [the 'Brompton Boilers'], c.1860, watercolour

In 1857 the temporary buildings of the museum were the setting for a lecture by the art historian James Fergusson titled 'On a National Collection of Architectural Art'. Modern art, Fergusson declared, had narrowed to become 'the reproduction of some technical or archaeological form of art, rather than becoming the expression of the nation's wants and feelings'.[47] To address this gap it was necessary to establish a new national museum in the metropolis. The existing private collections, including Sir John Soane's Museum, though useful, were limited in their ability 'to improve the taste of the nation', while existing institutional collections, including the RIBA, were 'far too small' to fully represent the array of subjects required.[48] Instead a new architectural museum would consist of a collection of casts of ornaments of every style with models of entire buildings located nearby to contextualize the displays. Alongside these examples, Fergusson argued that a 'National

47   James Fergusson, 'On a National Collection of Architectural Art', *Builder* 16 (2 January 1858), 8–10, here: 8.
48   Fergusson, 'On a National Collection of Architectural Art', 9.

Museum of Architecture' would be incomplete without a portion dedicated to the technical aspects of construction. This would include structural and construction models of roofs, floors, and foundations as well as samples of building materials and new inventions related to sanitation and hygiene. The synthesis of these two aspects 'would convey a mass of information which has never yet been accessibly to the public ... in a form which all could comprehend'.[49] It was this content and form that became the basis for the architectural collections at the South Kensington Museum.

Initially the museum was not a single entity but formed by a series of independent collections including the Museum of Ornamental Art, Education Collections, the (Royal) Architectural Museum, and Sculpture. In this early incarnation, the South Kensington Museum displayed its architectural models in two distinct galleries. First, the Museum of Ornamental Art, a permanent national collection consisting of donations from Queen Victoria and other prominent private collectors alongside existing objects transferred from the National Art Training School at Marlborough House. FIG. 78 The collection, as the guidebook explained, was 'intended for the instruction of the public in decorative or ornamental art'.[50] With this goal in mind objects were displayed in one of seventeen classifications based either on technical skill or material. The first objects a visitor saw on entering the museum were an assemblage of ornamental plaster casts, hung in bays from projecting screens that ran perpendicular to the row of iron columns in the west corridor of the Brompton Boilers. These screens were labelled to show their chronological period and stylistic genre – the one in the photograph reads 'Antique – Greek & Roman'. Set between the screens were glass cases on pedestals containing plaster-of-Paris models of antique monuments made by Fouquet, accompanied by contemporary photographs of the buildings in their current 'state of ruin and dilapidation'.[51] Beyond this bay were sections containing examples of Renaissance and neoclassical architecture from Italy and France. Shortly after the museum's opening the *Builder* wrote that by comparing the models with the casts and photographs, a visitor would, 'without travelling', be able 'to form a good idea of those works which by name are so familiar'.[52] A few months earlier the same journal had stressed the informative aspects of the architectural display and its instructional potential on art education in the United Kingdom.[53]

49	Fergusson, 'On a National Collection of Architectural Art', 9.
50	Science and Art Department, *Guide to the South Kensington Museum* No. 1 (London, William Clowes: June 1857), 2.
51	Science and Art Department, *Guide to the South Kensington Museum*, 2, 71. This set of Fouquet models was the one previously owned by John Nash, as described at the beginning of the chapter, and purchased by the Office of Works in 1857.
52	'The Brompton Museum', *Builder* 15 (29 August 1857), 496.
53	'Leading Article', *Builder* 15 (27 April 1857), 358.

FIG. 78 Museum of Ornamental Art, South Kensington Museum, 1857

THE ORIGINS OF THE
ROYAL ARCHITECTURAL MUSEUM

This didactic agenda was further supported by a second display of models within the Architectural Museum, a collection located in the upper gallery of the Brompton Boilers. Formed in 1851 as a National Museum of Architecture, the collection quickly gained royal patronage, becoming the Royal Architectural Museum (RAM) in 1856. The aim of this collection was to provide a three-dimensional catalogue of ornamental designs to be used in contemporary architectural practice. This ambition was fostered by an advisory committee of leading British architects, including George Gilbert Scott, Charles Barry, and Philip Hardwick.[54] In addition to its function as a physical reference library the RAM's self-stated purpose was 'to improve and perfect the art workmanship so deficient at the present time'.[55] Scott argued that the creation of a repository of Gothic specimens would result in 'architecture and sculpture [becoming once more] the living product of the present time, instead of the dead repetition of the past'.[56] Originally located in the upper storeys (a 'cock loft') of a wharf along Canon Row, Westminster, by January 1853 some 6,500 items were on display, including 3,500 plaster casts, 130 original specimens in stone, wood, and metal, and an impressive array of original drawings, prints, and models.[57] Organized chronologically, the museum was geographically divided, with specimens from France, Italy, and Germany separated from native British examples. The majority of these items had been donated (a number of architectural models from the Ecclesiological Society depicted English churches and decorated stone monuments),[58] but the museum soon began to commission its own objects depicting buildings from across Britain and Ireland.

While the museum itself expanded and thrived, the educational part of its mission floundered. A 'School of Art' was established with evening classes scheduled from 7 to 9 o'clock in the evening to suit the working patterns of the artisans and craftsmen who would attend the sessions. However, by November 1853 only eleven students were enrolled in the museum's programme of study, who were to draw the cast collection before progressing onto relief modelling in clay or wax, eventually executing a final piece in stone.[59] By March 1854 the school was closed, causing further problems for the RAM, which had large debts due to the acquisition of specimens and the cost to instal these in the museum. In August 1856 Henry Cole suggested that the RAM might like to apply for rent-free accommodation in the South Kensington Museum, and by the following spring it had moved. The 1857 guide to the collection listed sixty-one 'specimens' that were arranged in the central bay of the West Gallery of the Brompton Boilers. Alongside whole building elements, figural sculptures, and casts were a number of architectural models. On one table was a model of Windsor Castle and another of Karl Friedrich Schinkel's Schloss Ehrenburg at Coburg, both exhibited by

---

54   Edward Bottoms, 'The Royal Architectural Museum in the Light of New Documentary Evidence', *Journal of the History of Collections* 19, no. 1 (May 2007), 115–39; Isabelle Flour, 'On the Formation of a National Museum of Architecture: The Architectural Museum Versus the South Kensington Museum', *Architectural History* 51 (2008), 211–38.
55   *Architectural Museum, Prospectus* (London: n.p., 1856), 2.
56   George Gilbert Scott, 'On the Formation of the Medieval Museum', *Builder* 9 (15 February 1851), 104.
57   The Architecture Museum: *Catalogue* (London: n.p., 1855), vii.
58   The Architecture Museum: *Catalogue*, 44.
59   Royal Architectural Museum [RAM], minute books, Sub-committee, 21 November 1853, B401, Architectural Association [AA], London. My thanks to Ed Bottoms for his help with the RAM archive.

Queen Victoria.[60] FIG. 79 On another table was a suite of unnamed models of cathedrals and churches, donated by the Ecclesiological Society.[61] These models were at the centre of the royal opening of the museum in June 1857 where Thomas de Grey, president of the RIBA, gave a tour of the collection to Queen Victoria and Prince Albert, Prince Friedrich of Prussia, and Archduke Maximilian of Austria.

Despite the formal opening of the museum, the presentation and displays were not long term. Several key members of the architectural profession were consulted by the government as to the format, layout, and organization of this 'National Museum for Architecture' at South Kensington. Two reports written by George Godwin, Thomas Leverton Donaldson, and Francis Penrose were published in the *Builder* (Godwin was the journal's editor) following requests by readers in September 1859. The first report focused on the collections of architectural casts, describing 'an educational series illustrative of the progress of architectural detail and decoration'.[62] The authors recommended maintaining stylistic distinctions (Greek, Roman, Renaissance, etc.) within a chronological sequence. They proposed that both the Museum of Ornamental Art and the Royal Architectural Museum would be more useful for public instruction if they were categorized systematically with 'specimens arranged in a like sequence'.[63] The role of the architectural models within this curatorial structure was clear. As the first report described, 'the system', which situated full-size casts and scale models side-by-side along with photographs showing the contemporary condition of a building, was 'excellent' and should be deployed throughout the museum. The display of the models alongside photographs offered a reference point for the surrounding cast fragments, thereby allowing connections to be made by visitors between near and distant objects. At the same time the idealized condition of the models allowed for the representation of existing narratives in a new visual form capable of distorting both geography and time. The purpose of both approaches and the collection itself was clear: 'as affecting the progress of art and … the improvement of taste in the application of art'.[64]

---

60   'Model of Windsor Castle', *Illustrated London News* (14 November 1857), 475. The model of Windsor Castle was probably made by John Bellamy, who the *Illustrated London News* recorded as having exhibited a model of Windsor Castle that covered nearly ninety square feet to the Royal family in November 1857. Bellamy was the son of a Gloucestershire farmer who began to work on card and cork models of English country houses from c. 1830. A series of these models formed a travelling show with elaborate models housed in specially built caravans that toured England. Queen Victoria and Prince Albert attended the show at Windsor Great in 1857 as reported by the *Illustrated London News*. For further details on Bellamy see: Christies, *The Collection of Professor Sir Albert Richardson, PRA.*, auction catalogue, 18, 19 September 2013, lot 153, 160.

61   It is likely that these models were a group donated by the Ecclesiological Society, and included models of Salisbury Cathedral and St Mary's Redcliffe, Bristol, as well as models of memorial crosses and the font at Winchester Cathedral. These models were also displayed on a table when the museum was at Canon Row. Ed Bottoms suggests that these models are the models of St Mary's Bristol (V&A SCP L.7) and Salisbury Cathedral (V&A SCP L.9), which remain in the care of the Sculpture Department at the V&A. *Architectural Museum, Catalogue* (London: n.p., 1855), 44.

62   'The Architectural Collections in the Museum at Brompton', *Builder* 17 (17 September 1859), 614–15, here: 614. The second report consisted of a series of questions in response to the Committee of Council on Education about the collection and arrangement of casts.

63   'The Architectural Collections in the Museum at Brompton', 614.

64   'The Architectural Collections in the Museum at Brompton', 614.

FIG. 79 Architectural Museum, South Kensington Museum, 1857

CHANGE AT THE SOUTH KENSINGTON MUSEUM

Those involved in the foundation of the South Kensington Museum took a keen interest in its architectural collections. Henry Cole, in his introductory address at the formation of the Science and Art Department, had bemoaned the fact that the greater public had been deprived of the two collections during their time in other locations, but uniting these collections and supplementing them with new additions would 'betoken what an Architectural Museum may become, if the individuals and the State will act together'.[65] While a united museum remained unrealized, over the years Cole and other museum administrators made alterations to the collection and its layout. These changes affected how architectural models were displayed, used, and understood by public and profession alike. Museums, collections, and curatorial strategies are never static entities, but dynamic processes driven by the attitudes and intentions of particular individuals and organizations. Just as the South Kensington Museum was an agglomeration of buildings (some new and purpose-built, others found and appropriated for a new function), the collections of the museum were an overlapping and contradictory series of objects, something Henry Cole identified when he later described the museum as a temporary refuge for transient collections.[66] John Ruskin, however, was less kind, describing the cumulative effect of these different collections in a contingent setting as a 'Cretan labyrinth of military ironmongery, advertisements of spring blinds, model fish-farming, and plaster bathing nymphs with a year's smut on all the noses of them'.[67]

By 1860 a major change was instigated in how the South Kensington Museum classified and organized its collections. Moving forward, the museum would be divided into two parts, marking a clear distinction between art and science. The Art Division still included seven thousand 'specimens' separated stylistically into the (Classical) Museum of Ornamental Art and the (Gothic) Royal Architectural Museum, whereas the Science Division included a newly formed Museum of Construction. Within a year all of the models were relocated from the Museum of Ornamental Art to the Museum of Construction, which was complemented with a growing collection of domestic and foreign building materials.[68] Curators also tried to make sense of the objects held by the museum and offer a coherent direction to their display. Captain Francis Fowke, the Royal Engineer now in charge of the Museum of Construction, noted how the exhibits had been impeded by a lack of space but were now rearranged and 'classified with a view to its utility for immediate reference'.[69] Under the control of Fowke and his deputy Henry Sandham (another engineer), the collection was embellished with donations and purchases following the 1855 Paris Exhibition. Other objects were donated by the Royal Commission for the Exhibition of 1851 or lent by inventors and companies (who were obliged by the museum's regulations to provide their objects for a minimum of twelve months).[70]

---

65   Henry Cole, 'Address on the Functions of a Science and Art Department', in *Fifty Years of Public Work*, vol. 2, (London: George Bell, 1884), 285–95, here: 292.

66   Henry Cole, *Fifty Years of Public Work*, vol. 1 (London: George Bell, 1884), 310–12.

67   John Ruskin, 'A Museum of Picture Gallery: Its Functions and its Formation', *Art Journal* 6 (1880), 215–7, here: 216.

68   South Kensington Museum, *Guide to the South Kensington Museum* 8 (London, April 1860), 2.

69   Science and Art Department, *Sixth Report of the Art and Science Department of the Committee of Council on Education* (London: Eyre and Spottiswoode, 1859), 430.

70   Science and Art Department, 'Construction and Building Materials', in *Catalogue of the Collection Illustrating Construction and Building Materials in the South Kensington Museum* (London: Eyre and Spottiswoode, 1861), 7.

The curatorial logic of the Museum of Construction was based on thematic or material groupings rather than chronology or stylistic genre. The section devoted to architectural models included John Nash's set of Fouquet models, displayed alongside a newly acquired plaster model of the Marble Arch, the state entrance to Buckingham Palace designed by Nash in 1827. Beside these were twelve models that depicted roof construction, including a pair of sectional models of the roof covering King's Cross station, on loan from Lewis Cubitt. Interspersed were several models for new inventions in building technology including innovative sash windows and steel shutters, the latest developments in ventilation systems and fireplaces. Seen as a whole, the rearrangement of the Museum of Construction offered visitors a different educational experience to the earlier and stylistically organized Museum of Ornamental Art.

In 1861 Fowke discussed the perceived audience and proposed that the new classification had rendered the Museum of Construction valuable to architects and builders, 'from whom frequent inquiries are received for various building contrivances'.[71] This idea connected to an wider pedagogical strategy that rejected the museum as 'a passive, dormant institution, an encyclopedia', and proposed instead that the collection should be 'an active, teaching institution, officiously useful and suggestive'.[72] However, the active nature of the collection was under threat. Fowke warned that the current arrangement and recent contributions to the Museum of Construction had almost exhausted the space allotted to it within the wider museum complex. Without additional space for new models, new inventions and devices used in construction would not be represented, thus rendering the collection 'incapable of competing with the various and increasing demands now placed upon it' by visitors.[73]

During the 1860s the collection expanded and was often reframed by the museum through changes to its name, layout, and juxtaposition of particular objects. The sequence of architectural objects was rebranded as the 'Museum of Building Materials' and relocated to the East Corridor adjacent to the refreshment rooms and entrance to Cromwell Road. FIG. 80 Displayed on a series of tables were models of technical inventions and a model of a wooden bridge in Sri Lanka.[74] Beside these were models of a memorial at Kanpur dedicated to British casualties following the First War of Indian Independence. Next to these were raw materials from around the world, such as 'model' specimens of native timber from Canada and New Zealand, potential resources for the construction of new buildings in the metropolis.[75] Whether colonial memorials, infrastructure, or extracted materials, these displays reveal another way in which imperial societies represented the extra-European world within the confines of the metropole. At the time however, the purpose of the collection was seen differently. In 1864 the *Builder* declared that the models of the Museum of Building Materials were 'of the greatest importance to architects'.[76] In this setting, models of construction techniques and new technologies were crucial to informal learning and professional

---

71   Science and Art Department, *Eighth Report of the Art and Science Department* (London: Eyre and Spottiswoode, 1861), 140.
72   Science and Art Department, 'Appendix G: Report on the Museum of Ornamental Art, by Curator', *First Report of the Art and Science Department* (London: Eyre and Spottiswoode, 1854), 228.
73   Science and Art Department, *Eighth Report*, 141.
74   *Guide to the South Kensington Museum* (London, 1866), 11.
75   *Guide to the South Kensington Museum* (London, 1866), 11–12.
76   'The South Kensington Museum and Schools', *Builder* 22 (26 November 1864), 859.

practice in London as they transmitted developments in building and material science and educated visitors with differing levels of understanding.

Despite this important intellectual role, the museum itself still lacked a systematic curatorial approach – such was the difficulty of creating a coherent display from a mismatched collection of models. To rectify this the Science and Art Department actively collected further specimens and models more suited to a contemporary museum of construction. New acquisitions included architectural models that gave an insight into the wider social and infrastructural developments that affected the built environment of contemporary London. By 1876, the collection had grown – with seventy-seven models among 167 objects.[77] There were, for instance, four cardboard models of 'dwellings for the working classes' in Bethnal Green and Pimlico, two London districts with reformist strategies for housing and sanitation. A pair of models was produced for each location: one presented the elevations and the other depicted the internal arrangement of a typical floor. The public could therefore see what the building would look like from the street and how its internal layout functioned to provide a modern standard of dwelling. Other models nearby represented designs for more recognizable and contemporary buildings as well as unrealized projects. Within the collection were also two large models, one of the Victoria Embankment from Westminster to Blackfriars, and another of the area around the Embankment, 'Made by the Department 1869, by order of the Treasury, to show the several sites proposed for the New Law Court Buildings'. With these urban examples (last encountered in the first two chapters), the museum could position itself as a site for the discussion of public building works and the expansion of London during the nineteenth century.[78] New acquisitions further emphasized this function and expanded its geographic remit. These included models of Cleopatra's Needle and the scaffolding used to erect the obelisk on the Victoria Embankment (as discussed in the chapter 'The Commons'). Donated by the civil engineer John Dixon, the model of the obelisk and the technical apparatus used to raise it were a major monument of trans-regional power erected in Victorian London.[79]

Despite the prominent objects on show, in 1881 the Committee of Council on Education examined the Museum of Building Materials to advise on whether 'this collection should be developed, and what specimens might with advantage be removed'.[80] This was the first mention of the possible removal of models from the collections. The report began by noting the great reference value of the collection and citing developments in the contemporary use of mosaics, terracotta, and ceramics in the decoration of buildings. In particular the committee argued that the collection could operate as a conduit between British and European building technologies, and that the exhibition of building materials and models from overseas would 'enlarge the views and improve the practice of our own manufacturers and workmen'.[81] Though 'highly desirable on public grounds' the collection still required the

77 These other objects included material samples, specimens, and full-sized fragments of particular building technologies. Science and Art Department, *Catalogue of the Collection Illustrating Construction and Building Materials* (London: Eyre and Spottiswoode, 1876), 203–27.
78 *Catalogue of the Collection Illustrating Construction and Building Materials*, 209, 41.b.Y; p. 222, 134Y.
79 *Lists of Bequests and Donations to the Department of Science and Art to 31 December 1888* (London, 1889).
80 Science and Art Department, 'Structural Collection of the South Kensington Museum', in *Twenty-Ninth Report of the Department of Science and Art* (London: Eyre and Spottiswoode, 1882), 13–4, here: 13. The committee of four included James Abernethy and Charles Hutton Gregory (both civil engineers), George Edmund Street (architect), and Major H. C. Seddon (examiner for building construction in the Science and Art Department).
81 Science and Art Department, 'Structural Collection', 14.

government to support its development. This entailed the removal of specimens deemed out of date and models, 'which may not be of practical value'. The committee also proposed rearranging the objects in new galleries and bringing 'the collection up to the present date' to promote contemporary 'technical knowledge' on 'public grounds' – the costs of which 'would be greatly outweighed by the public advantage'.[82] Running throughout the collection's life was the idea that it should be an active educational resource, and there were attempts to acquire aspects of construction that were unrepresented. This active role put the Museum of Construction in a significant position, as an institution responsible for developments in several areas of building technology. On the other side of the arc of technological development, this led to obsolete specimens.

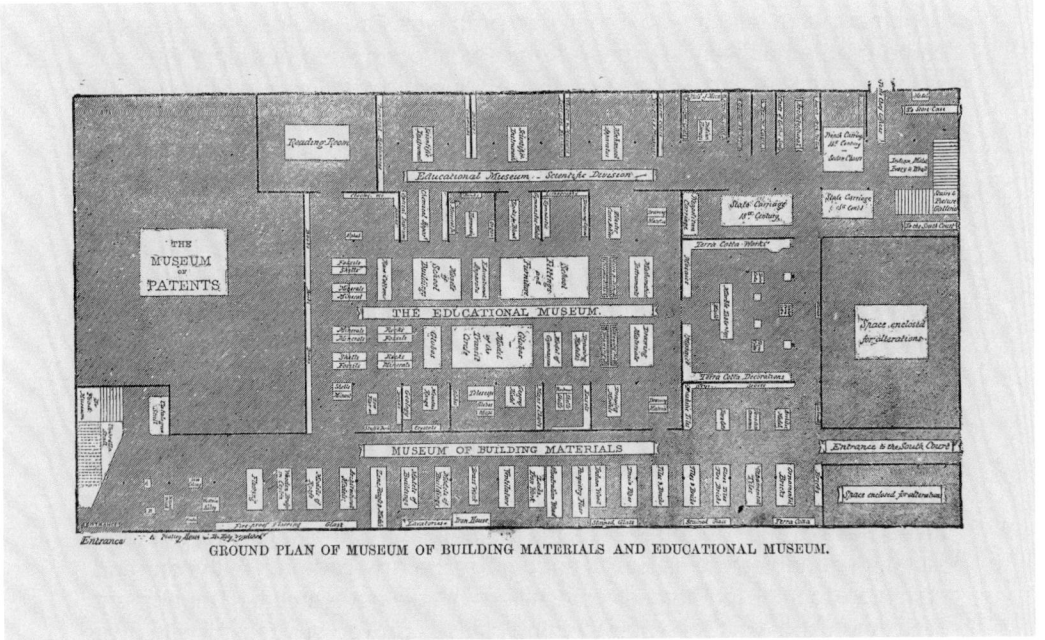

FIG. 80   Ground plan of Museum of Building Materials and Educational Museum, *Guide to the South Kensington Museum* (London: Eyre and Spottiswoode, 1866), 6

82   Science and Art Department, 'Structural Collection', 14.

In the other collections at the South Kensington Museum obsolescence was founded more in cultural redundancy than in technical development. Following the 1860 curatorial reorganization, the Royal Architectural Museum's collection of didactic objects was replaced by contemporary models, technical devices, and material specimens provided by architects, builders, and subcontractors. In a confidential report Henry Cole described how the museum 'prefers original works in architecture' and would accept representations 'only as substitutes for original works'.[83] This attitude was at odds with the Royal Architectural Museum's conception of a directly instructional collection for the benefit of young architects and artisans, and so new opportunities were sought beyond South Kensington. Advertisements ran in the press and institutions including University College and the RIBA were approached to house the collection.

In 1869, after twelve years at South Kensington, the Royal Architectural Museum's collection of casts, fragments, models, and other building-related ephemera were relocated to brand new premises. The site for a new museum came from an unlikely source. A firm of builders owned by Henry Poole, a stonemason who had a close working relationship with George Gilbert Scott, had recently leased a 600-square-metre site in Tufton Street, behind Westminster Abbey. FIG. 81 Offered at a cost-price sublease for thirty years, Poole permitted the Royal Architectural Museum to demolish the existing buildings on the site and sell any salvaged materials for profit. Members of the museum began to raise funds and collect materials from across London. The basic structural frame of the new building – six iron supports spanning fifty feet each – came from the 1862 International Exhibition building, donated by the building firm Lucas Brothers. Other firms of artisans and craftsmen were approached for sculptural ornament, tiles, and stained glass to feature on the museum's facade. Completed in June 1869, the building housed not only the collection but also a new school of architecture. The curriculum was based around evening classes on drawing – from copying three-dimensional and relief models to learning perspective and orthographic techniques. Through these classes and a lecture series the ultimate aim of the Royal Architectural Museum remained the same: 'to encourage the Art-Workmen of the day and train them to think for themselves'.[84] Allied with the governmental Department of Science and Art, these new evening classes proved successful with over 130 subscribers in 1877. This was complemented by a rapidly expanding collection and a new guide to the casts and models published by Scott. Two albums of photographs of the galleries and selected objects, taken by Bedford Lemere & Co, were published in 1872 and 1874, thus propagating the collection far beyond the physical spaces of the new museum. FIG. 82 After the death of Scott in 1878, John Pollard Seddon purchased the lease of the Tufton Street site from Henry Poole thereby allowing the museum to remain for a further forty-two years. Plots of land adjacent to the museum were purchased in 1896 for the construction of new classrooms, with the intention of furthering the excellent reputation of the museum's educational remit.

---

83   Royal Architectural Museum [RAM], minute books, Sub-committee, 21 November 1853, B401, AA, London.

84   Royal Architecture Museum, *Catalogue of Collection with a Guide to the Museum by Sir G. Gilbert Scott, RA* (London: n.p., 1877), 5.

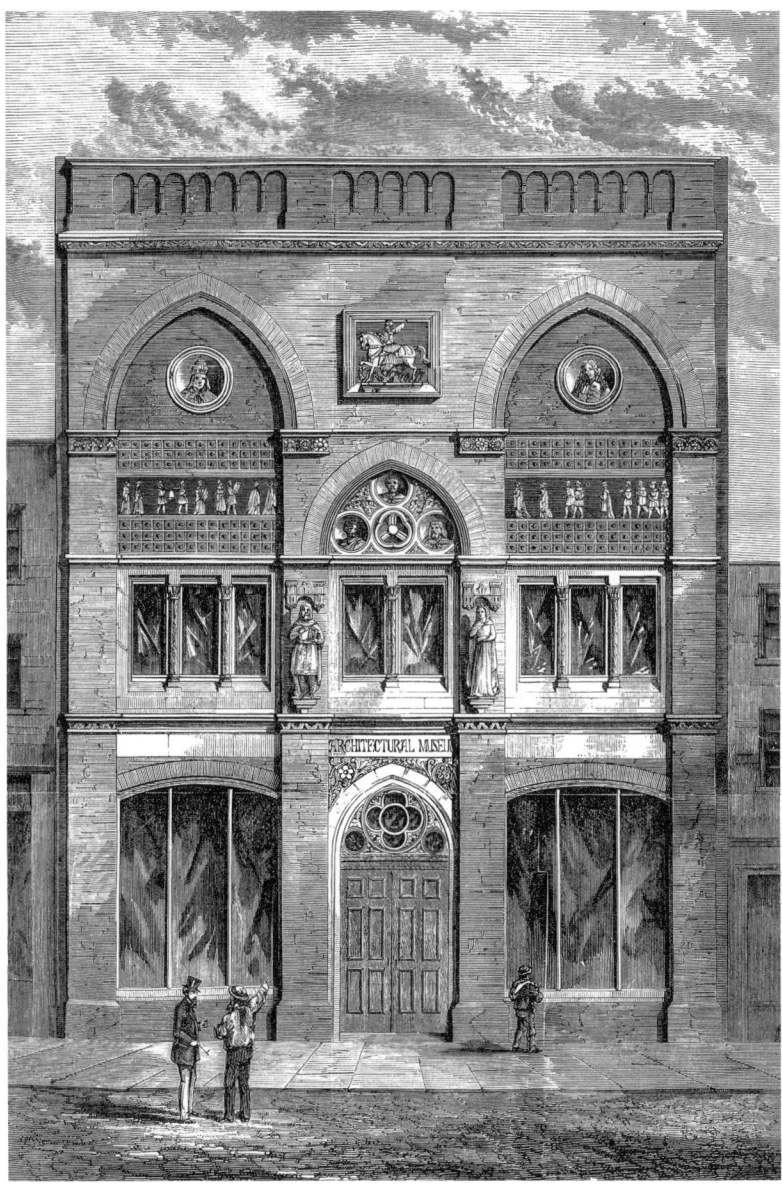

FIG. 81 'Royal Architectural Museum, Bowling-Street, Dean's Yard, Westminster', *Builder* 27 (24 July 1869), 587

FIG. 82   Interior view of the first-floor galleries, central court, Royal Architectural Museum, *Architectural Photographs* (London: Bedford Lemere, 1872)

Surprisingly, in 1902 the honorary secretary of the museum, the architect Maurice B. Adams, proposed to transfer the Tufton Street building and RAM collection to the Architectural Association (AA), where he was a prominent member. The AA had been searching for new premises, estimated by *The Times* to cost some £20,000.[85] Instead, for £700, the AA acquired the complex at Tufton Street with the newly constructed classrooms and extensive teaching collection. But architectural education had changed by the turn of the twentieth century. While a generation of students had been taught by copying casts from the museum lent on a weekly basis to the AA in the 1880s, the focus now turned towards Arts and Crafts or Beaux-Arts visual styles and working methods connected to increasing technical specialization (see chapter 'The University'). Instead, the collection assumed a minor role in a single class for first- and second-year students. Titled 'Freehand Drawing', participants were required to make large-scale drawings from casts in the collection. But outside of this course the collection of casts and models had become a dingy nuisance, taking up most of Tufton Street, with its old-fashioned presentation of the Gothic Revival at odds with the primary focus of teaching or even contemporary exhibitions on classical decoration held elsewhere in the building. Having lost both its autonomy and its purpose, the remaining collections of the RAM were offered as a gift to the Victoria & Albert Museum (the former South Kensington Museum from 1899). Cecil Harcourt Smith, then director of the V&A, acknowledged 'the desirability of preserving [the collection] for the Nation'.[86] Although the museum's curatorial strategy had been fixed on original objects rather copies, museum staff noted how the RAM's Romanesque and Gothic items would complement the V&A's collection of antique or Renaissance specimens. At the V&A's expense, three horse-drawn vans returned almost four thousand objects to South Kensington from Tufton Street one morning in January 1916.

85   Bottoms, 'The Royal Architectural Museum', 131 cites *The Times* (26 April 1902), 190.
86   Royal Architectural Museum [RAM], minute books, Sub-committee, 21 November 1853, B401, AA, London.

Another round of changes to the display of models in South Kensington had occurred while the RAM's collections had been in Tufton Street. In 1885 there was a major restructuring as artistic and scientific objects were divided not just into different collections but two independent museums. Subsequently a separate director was appointed to the Science Museum. By 1909 the divorce of the two institutions was formalized and the Science Museum began to organize its galleries and storerooms prior to moving across the road to new premises. When curators at the Science Museum found to their dismay storerooms filled with architectural models they wrote to their colleagues at the V&A. There was no longer 'any use for [models] in the newly independent Science Museum'.[87] Instead it was proposed that all objects that had originated in the Museum of Ornamental Art or Museum of Construction should be returned to the V&A. All of the architectural models were enumerated, their origin and condition documented.[88] Even at this stage certain models, such as the model of Whitehall showing sites for important public works, were recorded as missing. While ultimately the V&A agreed to reaccession of the models, internally there were doubts as to their function in a modern art and design museum. Certain curators questioned the status of the models as art objects. Others argued that the antique examples should be offered to the British Museum. Eric Maclagan, Keeper of the Architecture and Sculpture Department, believed that 'such models are really very little use to students in a well equipped museum.'[89] Ultimately it was agreed that certain objects, in particular the antique models and casts, could be transferred to the Circulation Department, whose role was to provide provincial museums throughout Britain with design objects on permanent loan. Another curator argued that 'models of modern work ... might usefully be destroyed'.[90] Over the years the purpose of the museum had steadily but decisively shifted from public education through copies to connoisseurship and the rise of the art-object. Despite all this, most of the architectural models in the V&A's collection remained. A few were lent to other museums around Britain, but the majority languished in various storerooms until they were rediscovered by John Physick, an assistant keeper at the museum, who returned them to public attention in *Marble Halls*, a highly significant exhibition on secular Victorian architecture held at the V&A in 1973. Both then and in the nineteenth century, models allowed curators to take visitors through a series of carefully choreographed cultural journeys, presenting and representing the world in a single place: London.

87   Science Museum Nominal File, 19 November 1912, MA/1/5851, Victoria & Albert Museum [VAM], London.
88   'Lists of Architectural Objects in the Store Room of Southern Galleries Science Museum', 11 June 1912, MA/1/5851, VAM.
89   Eric Maclagan memo, 17 May 1912, MA/1/5851, VAM.
90   R. F. Martin memo to Mr Bailey, 24 July 1912, MA/1/5851, VAM.

CONCLUSION

As cultural artefacts, architectural models have proven to be an effective means of exploring how the nineteenth-century metropolis was comprehended by its inhabitants. In Parliament, the museum, or even the courtroom, models depicted existing situations or potential futures, enabling these visions to be debated by architects, politicians, and the wider public. In the popular press, articles and their illustrations enabled models to travel from interiors to the public sphere, facilitating open discussion on the built environment, its conditions, and its goals. In particular, the legibility of the medium was central to its exhibition and display in nineteenth-century London. But even a model held the potential to cause problems since it allowed non-architects the opportunity to criticize a proposed design, thereby threatening the privileged position and legitimacy of the profession. In 1867 the *Building News* observed this precise issue during the Royal Courts of Justice competition and suggested that this was exactly why a model was attractive to an uninitiated public: it enabled both the comprehension of an as-yet unbuilt project and the formation of collective and individual judgements about the development of London.[1] In response to these collective judgements, by the end of the nineteenth century there was a shift in how models were perceived by architects. The use of a model as a tactile design tool by E. S. Prior in 1895 indicates a moment where architects attempted to gain conceptual control and authorship over the medium, connecting the model to other artistic disciplines such as sculpture. FIG. 83

Despite this shift in use, questions of miniaturization and scale crept into discussions about the role of models in urban expansion. By the end of the century there was increased awareness within the profession that politicians were using models as 'toys' to criticize prominent building projects on

---

1   'Courts of Justice Competition', *Building News* 14 (25 January 1867), 57.

behalf of the public. 'We have the highest opinion of the value of models', an article in the *Builder* noted when the statutory use of models for public building projects was debated in Parliament – as long as they were not deployed 'as toys for public amusement'.[2] For many commentators, the toy-like nature of a model was related to its scale, size, and how it was viewed. Often the criticism of a model's size was connected to what the profession perceived as its correct use in practice. In another critique the press proposed that the 'real value of a model' was to show part of the detail of a building at a large scale, 'so that its effect and projection can be estimated'.[3] A small model of the building, the writer suggested, was only able to amuse an interested public audience. These debates indicate a belief in 'right' and 'wrong' uses for models that depended on the discernment and knowledge of the viewer. On other occasions the scale of a model apparently reduced the effectiveness of its presentation when exhibited to the wider public. When J.B. Bunning displayed a model of the new Coal Exchange at the 1847 Royal Academy Exhibition, its size prompted one journal to describe it as a 'toy' that was 'impossible' to judge any more than the general form of the building.[4] FIG. 84 Model-maker John Thorp's depiction of Old London, however, was celebrated not as a 'sensational toy' but for its realistic and accurate presentation of the historic structures and districts. His was a model with educational value for architects, artists, and 'all classes of people'.[5]

Throughout the nineteenth century London was never depicted in a single unified scene, but a series of distinct fragments, each at a different scale and with different intentions. Instead of presenting a single image of the city, architectural models enabled it to be visualized in a modern and historic light. As London expanded and was rebuilt, the highly finished and elaborate work of model-makers such as Richard Day, Thorp, and others allowed broad audiences of non-architects to comprehend and engage with the design of proposed buildings or legal cases. These models also remained a key part of professional practice in the metropolis: they had a clear role in explaining designs to lay audiences of decision makers, shaping the public perception of an architect's work, and offering an immediately legible and detailed version of a design, unlike in the slow and chaotic business of construction.

2	'Lord Wemyss and the Government Offices', *Builder* 81 (20 July 1901), 46.
3	'Architecture at the Royal Academy', *Builder* 74 (30 April 1898), 407–9, here: 408.
4	'Royal Academy Exhibition: Architecture', *CEAJ* 61 (30 April 1898), 408.
5	'Notes of the Month', *Architectural Review* 12 (November 1907), 212.

CONCLUSION

FIG. 83   Edward Walter Hobbs, *Pictorial House Modelling: A Practical Manual Explaining How to Make Models of Buildings* (London: C Lockwood, 1926), 12–13

FIG. 84   James Bunstone Bunning, model of the Coal Exchange, London, 1847

Models also held a symbolic role in the nineteenth-century city through their public exhibition and presentation, operating as markers of identity for individuals, institutions, and governments in London. Models of antique buildings validated architects' knowledge of the artistic canon and helped to differentiate them from the builder or engineer. Similarly the exhibition of a model was a way in which the profession could present work to the public, framed by either an individual, collective, or national agenda. At the Royal Academy Exhibition architects displayed models to show their individual abilities as well as new ideas about the decoration, form, and technological expression of architecture. In institutional settings, such as at the South Kensington Museum, in Parliament, or on ceremonial occasions, models were used in a performative capacity, as a testimony and proxy for buildings and the political authorities responsible for procurement. At various international exhibitions held in London, models were also used as a part of the construction of local and national identities. For instance, the presentation of Thorp's models of Brook Hospital for the Metropolitan Asylum Board at the 1900 Exposition Universelle in Paris presented the image of a modern city and the refinement of its building programmes in response to the hygiene and sanitation problems of the metropolis. National identity was often also a concern: throughout London various groups and individuals proposed the construction of a museum of architecture with a nationalist agenda, where models would be used to signify and promote a particular 'British' style and identity.

Models were also an important vehicle for displaying and marketing new technical products. Many of these examples suggest that the overall value of models in the nineteenth century became focused more on their rhetorical power than their practical application. At King's College, the Architectural Association, and the South Kensington Museum, models were collected and shown to prepare a new generation of architects for the requirements of practice at the turn of the twentieth century. Their content was also indicative of the standardization of the architectural profession, building trades, and construction techniques in the expansion of nineteenth-century London. In addition to architects there were other individuals who used and made architectural models. Various governmental and private clients who were able to understand orthographic drawings were actively involved in the architectural models representing the buildings they were commissioning.

The production of models, combined with their use and display was a central part of architectural practice, anchored in the emergence of professionalism. This was a crucial vehicle for the public debates surrounding the appearance of the metropolis: its image, its infrastructure, its institutions, and its buildings. Models were a primary mechanism through which architects, clients, and the wider public made sense of and acted upon both their material lives and society at large. As architecture was still in the midst of shaping its identity, models were both creative tools and contested sites for architects to draw on in the construction of their authority. Finally, *Modelling the Metropolis* does not just provide new insights into nineteenth-century London or the subject of architectural models. It calls into question the traditional understanding of architecture as a discipline defined primarily in terms of authorship. In its place, a multi-layered narrative of architectural production through objects that recorded, altered, and remade the built environment of the nineteenth-century metropolis is established.

BIBLIOGRAPHY

PRIMARY SOURCES

ARCHIVAL MATERIAL

ARCHITECTURAL ASSOCIATION (AA), LONDON
- B401, Royal Architectural Museum minute books
- Brown Book, 1860–1911 [AA Prospectus]
- C101, Meetings of the Class for the Study of Architectural Science, minute books
- C201–205, General AA Meetings minute books
- C401, Schools Committee minute books

KING'S COLLEGE LONDON (KCL)
- KCL KA IC H18, Letters to William Hoskins
- KCL KAS AC2, Secretary's files relating to academic schools, faculties, and departments
- KCL KAS AD3, Secretary's general administration files
- KCL KFE M1-3, Engineering/Applied Sciences minute books

LONDON METROPOLITAN ARCHIVES (LMA)
- 4435/A/01, Meux Brewery: Company records
- CLA/062/02, Royal Exchange and Gresham Trusts Committee: Minute Books
- CLA/062/04/019, Royal Exchange: Extracts and Reports
- CLA/062/04/039, Royal Exchange: Audit of Accounts
- CLC/521/MS04952, Joseph Gwilt: Volume of papers relating to the Royal Exchange
- COL/CC/04/01/21, Coal, Corn, and Finance Committee: Minute books and reports
- COL/CC/CCF/01/006, Court of Common Council: Coal, Corn, and Finance Committee Journals

MERCERS' COLLECTION (MC), LONDON
- GC, Joint or Grand Gresham Committee minute books

NATIONAL GALLERY (NG), LONDON
- NG5, papers relating to building of gallery

ROYAL ACADEMY OF ARTS (RA), LONDON
- RA SP/4, Material concerning the Royal Academy Schools

ROYAL INSTITUTE OF BRITISH ARCHITECTS (RIBA), BRITISH ARCHITECTURAL LIBRARY, LONDON
- 1.2.1, General Meeting Minutes
- 1.2.2, Council Minutes & Papers
- 1.2.3, Letters to Council
- 1.2.4, Annual Reports of Council
- 5.3.1, (Early) New Premises Committees Papers
- 5.3.2, Title Deeds & Agreements RIBA Premises
- 6.1, Library Catalogues
- 6.8, Competition Conditions Collection
- 11.5.2, Architectural Competitions Committee Papers
- BuW/1, William Burges' journal recording the history of his proposed scheme for the interior decoration of St Paul's Cathedral, London
- CoC/3/16, C. R. Cockerell's report to Joint or Grand Gresham Committee
- DB/7/2/3, 'Specification of works [...] Chapel of the Holy Trinity, Knightsbridge'
- MS.SP/1, Unbound volume of manuscripts of papers read at meetings 1834–54
- MS.SP/2, Bound volume of manuscripts of papers read at meetings 1844–53
- MS.SP/3, Bound volume of manuscripts of papers read at meetings 1835–49
- MS.SP/4, Papers by Thomas Leverton Donaldson, read at the RIBA, 1835–45
- MS.SP/8, Bound volume of manuscripts of papers read at meetings 1834–54
- VOL/77, John Eastly Goodchild, album 'Reminiscences... of my twenty-six years association with the late Professor C. R. Cockerell Esq. with a supplement of the late F. P. Cockerell Esq. to 1878'.
- VuL 1, Lewis Vulliamy Dorchester House letters from Robert Holford
- VuL 13, Lewis Vulliamy Dorchester House letters from tradesmen
- VuL 33, Lewis Vulliamy Westonbirt House letters from Robert Holford
- VuL 42, Lewis Vulliamy Westonbirt House letters from tradesmen

SIR JOHN SOANE'S MUSEUM (SJSM)
- George Bailey Diaries
- Office Day Book
- Soane Journal
- Soane Notebook
- Soane XV. K. 1, Private Correspondence
- Soane XV. K. 2, Private Correspondence
- Soane XV. K. 3, Private Correspondence

ST PAUL'S CATHEDRAL ARCHIVES (SPC)
- AA/A/1, William Burges Album

THE NATIONAL ARCHIVES (TNA), LONDON
- WORK 1/20, Office of Works, letter book
- WORK 2/33, Treasury, letter book
- WORK 12/33, Office
- WORK 12/88, Office of Works New War Office and Admiralty registered files
- WORK 12/115, Office of Works New War Office and Admiralty registered files
- WORK 17/10/1, Office of Works, Letters relating to the National Gallery
- WORK 22/2, Office of Works papers relating to establishment, organization and finance
- WORK 33/910, Office of Works, National Gallery drawings

UNIVERSITY COLLEGE LONDON (UCL)
- MS ADD 121, 'Notes on Lectures given by T. L. Donaldson 1863/64'
- MS ADD 367, 'Specification of Work to be done ... in erecting a studio in rear of No 7 Gordon Street, Gordon Square for T. Roger Smith', August 1899.

UNIVERSITY OF LONDON (UOL)
- UoL ST/2, Minutes and related papers of Senate meetings

VICTORIA & ALBERT MUSEUM (V&A), LONDON
- MA/1, Nominal Files
- MA/32, Guard Books
- RF, Registry Files
- SCP, Sculpture departmental files

PARLIAMENTARY RECORDS

- Barrow, John Henry, ed. *Mirror of Parliament, Second Session of the Tenth Parliament of Great Britain and Ireland (Commencing 6th December 1831)*. London: 3 Abingdon Street Westminster, Vol. 4. 1832.
- *Hansard's Parliamentary Debates*, 3rd series. Vols. 1–350. London: Hansard, 1830–1891.
- *Hansard's Parliamentary Debates*, 4th series. Vols. 1–77. London: Hansard, 1892–1908.
- *Report from the Select Committee on Admiralty and War Office (Sites)*. Vol. 184. London: Hansard, 1887.

JOURNALS AND NEWSPAPERS

- *AA Journal*
- *AA Notes*
- *The Architect*
- *The Architects' Magazine*
- *Architectural Magazine*
- *Architectural Review*
- *Arnold's Magazine of the Fine Arts*
- *The Art Journal*
- *The Athenaeum*
- *British Architect*
- *The Builder*
- *The Builders' Journal*
- *Building News*
- *The Burlington Magazine*
- *The Civil Engineer and Architect's Journal (CEAJ)*
- *City Press*
- *Chelmsford Chronicle*
- *Country Life*
- *The Estates Gazette Digest of Land and Property Cases*
- *Fraser's Magazine for Town and Country*
- *The Gentleman's Magazine*
- *The Illustrated London News*
- *The Ipswich Journal*
- *Journal of the Royal Society of Arts*
- *Leisure Hour*
- *Magazine of Art*
- *The Morning Chronicle*
- *Morning Post*
- *Observer*
- *The Pall Mall Magazine*
- *Popular Science Monthly*
- *RIBA Journal (3rd Series 1894–)*
- *RIBA Proceedings (1st Series 1834–84; 2nd Series 1885–93)*

- RIBA Transactions (1st Series 1835–84; 2nd Series 1885–92)
- RICS Professional Notes
- RICS Transactions
- The Strand Magazine
- The Surveyor
- Tatler
- The Times
- Westminster Cathedral Record
- Westminster Review
- The World's Work

CATALOGUES

ROYAL ARCHITECTURAL MUSEUM
- Architectural Museum Catalogue. London: Joseph Masters, 1855.
- The Architecture Museum Prospectus. London: n.p., 1856.
- The Architecture Museum Report. 3 vols. London: n.p., 1860, 1863–64.
- Lewis N. Cottingham, Descriptive Memoir of the Museum of Mediaeval Architecture and Sculpture Formed by the Late L.N. Cottingham, etc. London: J. Davy, 1850.
- Royal Architecture Museum Catalogue of Collection with a Guide to the Museum by Sir G. Gilbert Scott, RA. London: n.p., 1877.
- Scott, George Gilbert. A Guide to the Royal Architecture Museum. London: Harrisons, 1876.

SCIENCE AND ART DEPARTMENT
- Catalogue of the Collection Illustrating Construction and Building Materials. London: Eyre and Spottiswoode, 1862, 1876.
- Catalogue of Models of Machinery, Drawing, Tools, etc. London: Eyre and Spottiswoode, 1880.
- Guide to the South Kensington Museum. London, William Clowes, No. 1, June 1857; No. 7, September 1859; No. 8, April 1860; No. 9, October 1860.
- A Guide to the South Kensington Museum. 2nd ed. London: William Clowes, 1866.
- Guide to the South Kensington Museum. London: Spottiswoode, February 1869; July 1869.
- Guide to the Victoria and Albert Museum, South Kensington. London: Spottiswoode, 1905.
- Inventory of the Objects Forming the Collections of the Museum of Ornamental Art at South Kensington. London: Eyre and Spottiswoode, 1860.
- Italian Wall Decorations of the 15th and 16th Centuries: A Handbook to the models, illustrating Interiors of Italian Buildings in the Victoria and Albert Museum, South Kensington. London, Chapman and Hall, 1901.
- Lists of Bequests and Donations to the Department of Science and Art to 31 December 1888. London: Eyre and Spottiswoode, 1889.
- Reports of the Department of Science and Art of the Committee of Council on Education. London: Eyre and Spottiswoode, First Report, 1854; Fifth Report, 1858; Eighth Report, 1861; Twenty-Ninth Report, 1882.

OTHER
- Great Exhibition of the Works of Industry of all Nations, 1851: Official Descriptive and Illustrated Catalogue. 4 vols. London: William Clowes, 1851.
- International Exhibition 1862: Official Catalogue of the Fine Art Department. London: Truscott and Summons, 1862.
- Paris Exhibition, 1900: British Official Catalogue. London: Royal Commission, 1900.
- Shaw, Henry. Catalogue of the Museum of Mediaeval Art Collected by the Late L. N. Cottingham, FSA Architect. London: John Davy, 1850.
- Royal Academy of Arts, Catalogue of the Exhibition of the Royal Academy. London: William Clowes, 1830–1916.

PUBLISHED PRIMARY SOURCES

Architects', Engineers' and Building Trades' Directory. London: Wyman & Sons, 1868.
Austin, Henry. Thoughts on the Abuses of the Present System of Competition in Architecture. London: John Weale, 1839.
Baltard, Louis-Pierre. Athenæum, ou Galerie française des productions de tous les arts. Par une Société d'hommes de lettres et d'artistes, et publié par M. Baltard. Paris: no publisher, 1806.
Beckett Denison, Edmund. A Book on Building, Civil and Ecclesiastical. London: Crosby Lockwood, 1880.
Bedford Lemere & Co.: Architectural Photographs. London: Bedford Lemere & Co, 1872.
Blasche, Bernhard Heinrich. The Art of Working in Pasteboard. 3rd ed. Translated by Daniel Boileau. London: Boosey, 1831.
Briggs, John Henry. Naval Administrations 1827 to 1892. Edited by Elizabeth Briggs. London: Sampson Low & Co, 1897.
Brimley, George. Essays. London: Macmillan, 1858.
Britton, John. The Union of Architecture, Sculpture, and Painting. London: no publisher, 1827.
Cole, Henry. Fifty Years of Public Work. 2 vols. London: George Bell, 1884.
A Description of Mr Burges' Models for the Adornment of St Paul's Now Exhibited at the Royal Academy. London: E. Stanford, 1874.
The Dictionary of Architecture. Vol. 5. Edited by Architectural Publication Society. London: Thomas Richards, 1875.
Dictionary of Architecture and Building. Vol. 2. Edited by Russell Sturgis. London: Macmillan, 1901–2.
A Dictionary of Architecture; Historical, Descriptive, Topographical, Decorative, Theoretical and Mechanical. Vol. 2. Edited by Robert Stuart. London: Jones & Co, 1830.
Donaldson, Thomas Leverton. Architectural Maxims and Theorems in Elucidation of Some of the Principles of Design and Construction. London: John Weale, 1847.
Fergusson, James. Proposal for the Completion of St Paul's Cathedral. London: Bush, 1874.
Hobbs, Edward Walter. Pictorial House Modelling: A Practical Manual Explaining How to Make Models of Buildings. London: C. Lockwood, 1926.
Hopper, Thomas. A Letter to Lord Viscount Melbourne on the Rebuilding of the Royal Exchange. London: John Weale, 1839.
Kelly's Directory of the Building Trades. London: Kelly & Co, 1870.
Kerr, Robert. The Consulting Architect: Practical Notes on Administrative Difficulties and Disputes. London: John Murray, 1886.
Long, George, ed. The Penny Cyclopædia of the Society for the Diffusion of Useful Knowledge. Vol. 15. London: Charles Knight, 1839.
Milman, Henry Hart. Annals of St Paul's Cathedral. London: John Murray, 1868.
Muthesius, Hermann. Das englische Haus. 3 vols. Berlin: Ernst Wasmuth, 1904–5.
New Courts of Justice. London: no publisher, 1867.
Norris, John. A Catalogue of the Pictures, Models, Busts, &c. in the Bodleian Gallery, Oxford. Oxford: no publisher, 1839.
Parker, John Henry. A Hand-book for Visitors to Oxford. Oxford: John Henry Parker, 1875.
Pullan, Richard Popplewell. The Designs of William Burges, ARA. London: Batsford, 1885.
Post Office Directory of London. 17 vols. London: Kelly & Co, 1840–56.
The Queen's London: A Pictorial and Descriptive Record of the Streets, Buildings, Parks, and Scenery of the Great Metropolis in the Fifty-ninth Year of Reign of Her Majesty Queen Victoria. London: Cassel, 1896.
Richardson, T. A. The Art of Architectural Modelling in Paper. Weale's Rudimentary Series 127. London: John Weale, 1859.
Round London: An Album of Pictures from Photographs of the Chief Places of Interest in and round London. London: George Newnes, 1895.
Schröder, Jacob. Polytechnisches Arbeits-Institut Darmstadt, Preisliste für Unterrichts-Modelle und Apparate. Hanau: no publisher, 1895.
Soane, John. Description of the House and Museum, on the North Side of Lincoln's Inn-Fields, the Residence of Sir John Soane. London: no publisher, 1830.
Soane, John. Description of the House and Museum, on the North Side of Lincoln's Inn-Fields, the Residence of Sir John Soane. London: Levey, Robson, and Franklyn, 1835.
The Stranger's Guide through the University and City of Oxford. Oxford: no publisher, 1852.
Street, Arthur Edmund, ed. Memoir of George Edmund Street, RA., 1824–1881. London: John Murray, 1881.

Thorp, John. *Concerning Models of Buildings, Estates, Works, etc. for Exhibitions or Law Cases*. London: n. p., 1913.

Vulliamy, Lewis. *Examples of Ornamental Sculpture in Architecture Drawn from the Originals of Bronze, Marble and Terra Cotta in Greece Asia Minor and Italy*. 3 vols. London: Lewis Vulliamy and Henry Moses, 1823–4, 1827.

Walford, Edward. *Old and New London*. Vol. 4. London: Cassell, 1878.

Weale, John. *Rudimentary Dictionary of Terms Used in Architecture, Civil, Architecture, Naval, Building and Construction, Early and Ecclesiastical Art, Engineering, Civil, Engineering, Mechanical, Fine Art, Mining, Surveying, Etc.* London: John Weale, 1850.

Wilson, Effingham. *Description of the New Royal Exchange*. London: no publisher, 1844.

SECONDARY LITERATURE

A

Adams, Ellen. 'Shaping Collecting and Displaying Medicine and Architecture: A Comparison of the Hunterian and Soane Museums'. *Journal of the History of Collections* 25, no. 1 (2013), 59–75.

Alberti, Samuel. 'Conversaziones and the Experience of Science in Victorian England'. *Journal of Victorian Culture* 8, no. 2 (Autumn 2003), 208–30.

Alberti, Samuel. 'Objects and the Museum.' *Isis* 96, no. 4 (2005), 559–71.

Altick, Richard. *The Shows of London*. Cambridge, Mass.: Belkamp, 1979.

Amsellem, Guy, ed. *La Maquette: Un outil au service du projet architectural*. Paris: Editions des Cendres, 2015.

Anderson, Richard. 'Connoisseurship, Pedagogy or Antiquarianism? What Were Instruments Doing in the Nineteenth-Century National Collections in Great Britain?' *Journal of the History of Collections* 7, no. 2 (January 1995), 211–25.

Arnold, Dana, ed. *The Metropolis and Its Image: Constructing Identities for London, c. 1750–1950*. Oxford: Blackwell, 1999.

Arscott, Caroline. 'The Representation of the City in the Visual Arts.' In Martin Daunton, ed., *The Cambridge Urban History of Britain, Volume III: 1840–1950*. Cambridge: Cambridge University Press, 2001, 809–32.

Arscott, Caroline, and Griselda Pollack, 'The Partial View: The Visual Representation of the Early Nineteenth-Century Industrial City'. In Janet Wolff and John Seed, eds., *The Culture of Capital: Art, Power, and the Nineteenth-Century Middle Class*. Manchester: Manchester University Press, 1988, 191–234.

Aspinal, Arthur. 'The Circulation of Newspapers in the Early Nineteenth Century'. *The Review of English Studies* 22, no. 85 (January 1946), 29–43.

Auerbach, Jeffrey. *The Great Exhibition of 1851: A Nation on Display*. New Haven: Yale University Press, 1999.

Ayers, Gwendoline Margery. *England's First State Hospitals and the Metropolitan Asylums Board, 1867–1930*. London: Wellcome Institute of the History of Medicine, 1971.

B

Barringer, Tim. 'The World for a Shilling: The Early Panorama as Global Landscape, 1787–1830.' In Katie Trumpener and Tim Barringer, eds., *On the Viewing Platform: The Panorama Between Canvas and Screen*. New Haven: Yale University Press, 2020, 83–106.

Bassin, Joan. *Architectural Competitions in Nineteenth-Century England*. Ann Arbor: UMI Research Press, 1984.

Bates, Alan William. '"Indecent and Demoralising Representations": Public Anatomy Museums in Mid-Victorian England.' *Medical History* 52, no. 1 (January 2008), 1–22.

Beattie, Susan. *The New Sculpture: Aspects of a Nineteenth-Century English Renaissance*. London: Yale University Press, 1983.

Bennett, Tony. *The Birth of the Museum: History, Theory, Politics*. London: Routledge, 1995.

Bergdoll, Barry. 'Competing in the Academy and the Marketplace: European Architecture Competitions, 1401–1927'. In Helene Lipstadt and Barry Bergdoll, eds., *The Experimental Tradition: Essays on Competitions in Architecture*. New York: Princeton Architectural Press, 1989, 21–52.

Bergdoll, Barry. '"The Public Square of the Modern Age": Architecture and the Rise of the Printed Press in the Early Nineteenth Century.' In Mari Hvattum and Anne Hultzsch, eds., *The Printed and the Built: Architecture, Print Culture and Public Debate in the Nineteenth Century*. London: Bloomsbury, 2018, 27–50.

Bingham, Neil, ed. *The Education of the Architect: Proceedings of the 22nd Annual Symposium of the Society of Architectural Historians of Great Britain*. No publisher, 1993.

Bois, Yves-Alain. 'Metamorphosen der Axonometrie'. *Daidalos* 1 (1981), 40–58.

Bois, Yves-Alain. 'Montage and Architecture'. *Assemblage* 10 (December 1989), 110–31.

Bottoms, Edward. 'The Royal Architectural Museum in the Light of New Documentary Evidence'. In *Journal of the History of Collections* 19, no. 1 (May 2007), 115–39.

Bradley, Simon, and Nikolaus Pevsner, *The Buildings of England, London 1: The City of London*. London: Yale University Press, 1997.

Brejzek, Thea, and Lawrence Wallen. *The Model as Performance: Staging Space in Theatre and Architecture*. London: Bloomsbury, 2018.

Briggs, Asa. *England in the Age of Improvement*. A History of England. London: Folio Society, 1999.

Briggs, Martin. *The Architect in History*. Oxford: Clarendon Press, 1927.

Briggs, Martin. 'Architectural Models–I'. *The Burlington Magazine for Connoisseurs* 54, no. 313 (1929), 174–5, 178–81, 183.

Briggs, Martin. 'Architectural Models–II'. *The Burlington Magazine for Connoisseurs* 54, no. 314 (1929), 245–7, 250–2.

Brownlee, David. *The Law Courts: The Architecture of George Edmund Street*. Cambridge, Mass.: The MIT Press, 1984.

Brownlee, David. 'That "Regular Mongrel Affair": G. G. Scott's Designs for the Government Offices'. *Architectural History* 28 (1985), 159–97.

Bryant, Julius. *Art and Design for All: The Victoria & Albert Museum*. London: V & A Publishing, 2012.

Buchanan, Robert Angus. *The Engineers: A History of the Engineering Profession in Britain, 1750–1914*. London: Kingsley, 1989.

Burton, Anthony. *Vision and Accident: The Story of the V & A*. London: V & A Publications, 1999.

C

Calhoun, Craig. *The Roots of Radicalism: Tradition, the Public Sphere, and Early Nineteenth-Century Social Movements*. Chicago: University of Chicago Press, 2012.

Carile, Maria Cristina. 'Buildings in Their Patrons' Hands? The Multiform Function of Small Size Models Between Byzantium and Transcaucasia'. *Kunsttexte* 3 (2014), 1–15.

Carlisle, Janice. 'On the Second Reform Act, 1867'. *BRANCH: Britain, Representation and Nineteenth-Century History*. https://branchcollective.org/?ps_articles=-janice-carlisle-on-the-second-reform-act-1867.

Carlisle, Janice. *Picturing Reform in Victorian Britain*. Cambridge: Cambridge University Press, 2012.

Carr-Saunders, Alexander Morris, and P. A. Wilson. *The Professions*. Oxford: Clarendon Press, 1933.

Caygill, Marjorie, and Christopher Date. *Building the British Museum*. London: British Museum Press, 1999.

Çelik Alexander, Zeynep, and John May, eds. *Design Technics: Archaeologies of Architectural Practice*. Minneapolis: University of Minnesota Press, 2019.

Chadarevian, Soraya de, and Nick Hopwood eds. *Models: The Third Dimension of Science*. Stanford: Stanford University Press, 2004.

Christies, *The Collection of Professor Sir Albert Richardson, PRA*, auction catalogue, 18, 19 September 2013.

BIBLIOGRAPHY

Cole, David. *The Work of Gilbert Scott*. London: Architectural Press, 1980.

Cole, Emily, Susan Skedd, Jonathan Clarke, and Sarah Newsome, eds. *The Rotunda (former Royal Artillery Museum), Woolwich Common, London Borough of Greenwich: History, Structure and Landscape*. Research Report Series nos. 251–2020. Portsmouth: Historic England, 2020.

Coltman, Viccy. 'Classicism in the English Library'. *Journal of the History of Collections* 11, no. 1 (1999), 35–50.

Colvin, Howard. *Biographical Dictionary of English Architects*. 3rd ed. New Haven: Yale University Press, 1995.

Colvin, Howard. *English Architectural History: A Guide to Sources*. London: Pinhorns, 1967.

Colvin, Howard. 'Fifty New Churches'. *Architectural Review* 107, no. 639 (March 1950), 189–96.

Cook, Chris. *The Routledge Companion to Britain in the Nineteenth Century, 1815–1914*. London: Routledge, 2005.

Cook, Edward Tyas, and Alexander Wedderburn, eds. *The Works of John Ruskin*. Vol. 2. London: George Allen, 1903.

Cook, Martin Godfrey. *Edward Prior: Arts and Crafts Architect*. Marlborough: Crowood Press, 2015.

Crinson, Mark, and Jules Lubbock. *Architecture: Art or Profession? Three Hundred Years of Architectural Education in Britain*. Manchester: Manchester University Press, 1994.

Crook, J. Mordaunt. 'Architecture and History'. *Architectural History* 27 (1984), 554–78.

Crook, J. Mordaunt. 'The Pre-Victorian Architect: Professionalism and Patronage'. *Architectural History* 12 (1969), 62–78.

Crook, J. Mordaunt. 'William Burges and the Completion of St Paul's'. *The Antiquaries Journal* (September 1980), 285–307.

Crook, J. Mordaunt. *William Burges and the High Victorian Dream*. 2nd ed. London: Frances Lincoln, 2013.

Crook, J. Mordaunt, and Michael Port. *The History of the King's Works*. Vol. 6, 1782–1851. London: HMSO, 1973.

Cuisset, Geneviève. 'Jean-Pierre et François Fouquet. Artistes modeleurs'. *Gazette des Beaux Arts* 115 (1990), 227–57.

Curl, James Stevens. *Victorian Architecture: Diversity and Invention*. Reading: Spire, 2007.

D

Darley, Gillian. *John Soane: An Accidental Romantic*. New Haven: Yale University Press, 1999.

Dennis, Richard. *Cities in Modernity: Representations and Productions of Metropolitan Space, 1840–1930*. Cambridge: Cambridge University Press, 2008.

Deriu, Davide. 'Transforming Ideas into Pictures: Model Photography and Modern Architecture'. In Andrew Higgott and Timothy Wray, eds., *Camera Constructs: Photography, Architecture and the Modern City*. Burlington: Ashgate, 2012, 159–78.

Dixon, Roger, and Stefan Muthesius. *Victorian Architecture*. 2nd ed. London: Thames & Hudson, 2008.

Dorey, Helen. 'Sir John Soane's Model Room'. *Perspecta* 41 (2008), 26, 46, 92–3, 170–1.

Downes, Kenny. 'Wren and the New Cathedral'. In Derek Keene, Arthur Burns, and Andrew Saint, eds., *St Paul's: The Cathedral Church of London 604–2004*. London: Yale University Press, 2004, 190–206.

E

Elsner, John. 'A Collector's Model of Desire: The House and Museum of Sir John Soane'. In John Elsner and Roger Cardinal, eds., *The Cultures of Collecting*. London: Reaktion, 1994, 155–76.

Elser, Oliver, and Peter Cachola Schmal, eds. *Das Architekturmodell: Werkzeug, Fetisch, kleine Utopie / The Architectural Model: Tool, Fetish, Small Utopia*. Exhibition catalogue. Zurich: Scheidegger & Spiess, 2012.

Esdaile, Katherine Ada. 'Battles Royal: No. 1. The Royal Exchange'. *Architect and Building News* (9 January 1931), 47–9.

F

Fankhänel, Teresa. *The Architectural Models of Theodore Conrad: The 'Miniature Boom' of Mid-century Modernism*. London: Bloomsbury, 2021.

Feinberg, Susan. G. 'The Genesis of Sir John Soane's Museum Idea: 1801–1810'. *Journal of the Society of Architectural Historians* 43, no. 3 (October 1984), 225–37.

Felstead, Alison, Jonathan Franklin, and Leslie Pinfield. *Directory of British Architects 1834–1900*. 2 vols. London: Mansell, 1993.

Flour, Isabelle. 'On the Formation of a National Museum of Architecture: The Architectural Museum Versus the South Kensington Museum'. *Architectural History* 51 (2008), 211–38.

Freidson, Elliot. *Professional Powers: A Study of the Institutionalization of Formal Knowledge*. Chicago: University of Chicago Press, 1986.

Freidson, Elliot. *Professionalism: The Third Logic*. Chicago: University of Chicago Press, 2001.

Frommel, Sabine, and Raphaël Tassin, eds. *Les maquettes d'architecture: Fonction et évolution d'un instrument de conception et de réalisation*. Paris: Picard, 2015.

Fournier, Valérie. 'The Appeal to "Professionalism" as a Disciplinary Mechanism'. *Social Review* 47, no. 2 (1999), 280–307.

Fournier, Valérie. 'Boundary Work and the (Un)Making of the Professions'. In Nigel Malin, ed., *Professionalism, Boundaries and the Workplace*. London: Routledge, 2000, 67–86.

G

Geppert, Alexander C. T. *Fleeting Cities: Imperial Expositions in Fin-de-siècle Europe*. Basingstoke: Palgrave Macmillan, 2010.

Geppert, Alexander C. T. 'True Copies: Time and Space Travels at British Imperial Exhibitions, 1880–1930'. In Hartmut Berghoff, Barbara Korte, Ralf Schneider, and Christopher Harvie, eds., *The Making of Modern Tourism: The Cultural History of the British Experience, 1600–2000*. Basingstoke: Palgrave Macmillan, 2002, 223–48.

Gillespie, Richard. 'Richard Du Bourg's "Classical Exhibition", 1775–1819'. *Journal of the History of Collections* 29, no. 2 (July 2017), 251–69.

Gillespie, Richard. 'The Rise and Fall of Cork Model Collections in Britain'. *Architectural History* 60 (2017), 117–46.

Gnehm, Michael, and Sonja Hildebrand, eds. *Architectural History and Globalized Knowledge: Gottfried Semper in London*. Mendrisio: Mendrisio Academy Press; Zurich: gta Verlag, 2021.

Godfrey, Walter. *Survey of London*. Volume 4: Chelsea, Pt II. London: London County Council, 1913.

Godfrey, Emil W. 'Crosby Hall and Its Re-Erection'. *Transactions of the Ancient Monuments Society* (1982), 227–43.

Golinski, Jan. *Making Natural Knowledge: Constructivism and the History of Science*. 2nd ed. Cambridge: Cambridge University Press, 2005.

Gotch, John Alfred, ed. *The Growth and Work of the Royal Institute of British Architects, 1834–1934*. London: Royal Institute of British Architects, 1934.

Greenhalgh, Paul. *Ephemeral Vistas: The Expositions Universelles, Great Exhibitions and World's Fairs, 1851–1939*. Manchester: Manchester University Press, 1988.

H

Habermas, Jürgen. *The Structural Transformation of the Public Sphere: An Inquiry into a Category of Bourgeois Society*. Translated by Thomas Burger with Frederick Lawrence. Oxford: Polity, 1992.

Hall, Michael. *George Frederick Bodley and the Later Gothic Revival in Britain and America*. New Haven: Yale University Press, 2014.

Halliday, Terence C. *Beyond Monopoly: Lawyers, State Crises, and Professional Empowerment*. Chicago: University of Chicago Press, 1987.

Hanson, Brian. *Architects and the 'Building World' from Chambers to Ruskin: Constructing Authority*.

Cambridge: Cambridge University Press, 2003.

Harper, Roger. *Victorian Architectural Competitions: An Index to British and Irish Architectural Competitions in The Builder 1843–1900*. London: Mansell, 1983.

Harrison, Charles, Paul Wood, and Jason Gaiger, eds. *Art in Theory, 1815–1900: An Anthology of Changing Ideas*. Oxford: Wiley-Blackwell, 2001.

Harrison, Mark. *Crowds and History: Mass Phenomena in English Towns, 1790–1835*. Cambridge: Cambridge University Press, 2002.

Hilaire-Pérez, Liliane. *La pièce et le geste: Artisans, marchands et savoir technique à Londres au XVIIIe siècle*. Paris: Albin Michel, 2013.

Hitchcock, Henry-Russell. *Early Victorian Architecture in Britain*. 2 vols. London: Architectural Press, 1954.

Hobhouse, Hermione, ed. *Survey of London*. Monograph 17: *County Hall*. London: Athlone, 1991.

Hobsbawm, Eric. *Nations and Nationalism since 1780: Programme, Myth, Reality*. Cambridge: Cambridge University Press, 1990.

Hopwood, Nick. *Embryos in Wax: Models from the Ziegler Studio*. Cambridge: Whipple Museum of the History of Science, 2002.

Horsfall Turner, Olivia, Simona Valeriani, Matthew Wells, Teresa Fankhänel, eds. *An Alphabet of Architectural Models*. London: Merrell, 2021.

Houghton, Walter E. *The Victorian Frame of Mind: 1830–1870*. New Haven: Yale University Press, 1985.

Hussey, Christopher. 'London Houses: Dorchester House–I. London'. *Country Life* (5 May 1928), 646–53.

Hussey, Christopher. 'London Houses: Dorchester House–II. London'. *Country Life* (12 May 1928), 684–9.

Hvattum, Mari, and Anne Hultzsch, eds. *The Printed and the Built: Architecture, Print Culture and Public Debate in the Nineteenth Century*. London: Bloomsbury, 2018.

Hyde, Timothy. *Ugliness and Judgement: On Architecture in the Public Eye*. Princeton: Princeton University Press, 2019.

I

Ingold, Tim. *Making: Anthropology, Archaeology, Art and Architecture*. London: Routledge, 2013.

J

James, Henry. 'London'. In *Essays in London and Elsewhere*. London: Osgood & McIlwaine, 1893, 1–43.

Jenkins, Frank. *Architect and Patron: A Survey of Professional Relations and Practice in England from the Sixteenth Century to the Present Day*. London: Oxford University Press, 1961.

Jenkins, Frank. 'Nineteenth-Century Architectural Periodicals'. In John Summerson, ed., *Concerning Architecture: Essays on Architectural Writers and Writing presented to Nikolaus Pevsner*. London: Allen Lane, 1968, 153–60.

Jenkins, Frank. 'The Victorian Architectural Profession'. In Peter Ferriday, ed., *Victorian Architecture*. London: Jonathan Cape, 1963, 37–50.

K

Kaye, Barrington. *The Development of the Architectural Profession in England: A Sociological Study*. London: George Allen & Unwin, 1960.

Keene, Derek, Arthur Burns, and Andrew Saint, eds. *St Paul's: The Cathedral Church of London 604–2004*. London: Yale University Press, 2004.

Knight, Charles. 'Crosby Place'. In *London*. Vol. 1. London: Charles Knight, 1841, 317–32.

Knox, Tim. 'Ecclesiastical models'. *RIBA Journal* 99, no. 8 (August 1992), 30–1.

Kockel, Valentin. 'Rom über die Alpen tragen: Korkmodelle antiker Architektur im 18. und 19. Jahrhundert'. In Werner Helmberger and Valentin Kockel, eds., *Rom über die Alpen tragen: Fürsten sammeln antike Architektur–die Aschaffenburger Korkmodelle*. Ergolding: Arcos, 1993, 11–31.

Kockel, Valentin. 'Plaster Models and Plaster Casts of Classical Architecture and its Decoration'. In Rune Frederiksen and Eckhart Marchand, eds., *Plaster Casts: Making, Collecting and Displaying from Classical Antiquity to the Present*. Berlin: De Gruyter, 2010, 419–34.

Kockel, Valentin. 'Towns and Tombs: Three-Dimensional Documentation of Archaeological Sites in the Kingdom of Naples in the Late Eighteenth and Early Nineteenth Centuries'. In Ilaria Bignamini, ed., *Archives and Excavations: Essays on the History of Archaeological Excavations in Rome and Southern Italy from the Renaissance to the Nineteenth Century*. London: The British School at Rome, 2004, 143–62.

Kostof, Spiro. *The Architect: Chapters in the History of the Profession*. New York: Oxford University Press, 1977.

Knox, Tim. 'Cockerell's Model for Langton: A House for the Dorsetshire Nimrod'. *The Georgian Group Journal* 3 (1993), 62–7.

Kucich, John. *The Power of Lies: Transgression in Victorian Fiction*. Ithaca, NY: Cornell University Press 1994.

L

Larson, Magali Sarfatti. *The Rise of Professionalism: A Sociological Analysis*. Berkeley: University of California Press, 1979.

Lenaghan, Julia. 'The Cast Collection of John Sanders, Architect, at the Royal Academy'. *Journal of the History of Collections* 26, no. 2 (July 2014), 193–205.

Lending, Mari. *Plaster Monuments: Architecture and the Power of Reproduction*. Princeton: Princeton University Press, 2017.

Lending, Mari, and Mari Hvattum, eds. *Modelling Time: The Permanent Collection 1925–2014*. Oslo: Torpedo Press, 2014.

Lepik, Andres. *Das Architekturmodell in Italien, 1335–1550*. Worms: Wernersche, 1994.

Leslie, Fiona. 'Inside Outside: Changing Attitudes Towards Architectural Models in the Museums at South Kensington'. *Architectural History*, 47 (2004), 159–200.

Lever, Jill. *Catalogue of the Drawings Collection of the Royal Institute of British Architects L–N*. Farnborough: Gregg, 1973.

L'Hôpital, Winefride de. *Westminster Cathedral and its Architect*. 2 vols. London: Hutchinson, 1919.

Lightman, Bernard, ed. *Victorian Science in Context*. Chicago: University of Chicago Press, 1997.

Lillie, Amanda, and Mauro Mussolin. 'The Wooden Models of Palazzo Strozzi as Flexible Instruments in the Design Process'. In Amedeo Belluzzi, Caroline Elam, and Francesco Paolo Fiore, eds., *Giuliano da Sangallo: Disegni degli Uffizi*. Milan: Officina Libraria, 2017, 210–29.

Linstrum, Derek. *Catalogue of the Drawings Collection of the Royal Institute of British Architects: The Wyatt Family*. Farnborough: Gregg, 1973.

Liptau, Ralf. *Architekturen bilden: das Modell in Entwurfsprozessen der Nachkriegsmoderne*. Bielefeld: transcript, 2019.

Liptau, Ralf. 'Selber kneten. Modellbasiertes Entwerfen zwischen Originalität und Nachbildung'. In Eva von Engelberg-Dočkal, Markus Krajewski, and Frederike Lausch, eds., *Mimetische Praktiken in der neueren Architektur Prozesse und Formen der Ähnlichkeitserzeugung*. Heidelberg: arthistoricum.net. 2017, 131–43.

Liscombe, Rhodri Windsor. *William Wilkins 1778–1839*. Cambridge: Cambridge University Press, 1980.

Lucey, Conor. *Building Reputations: Architecture and the Artisan, 1750–1830*. Manchester: Manchester University Press, 2018.

M

Mace, Angela. *Architecture in Manuscript 1601–1996. Guide to the British Architectural Library Manuscripts and Archive Collection*. London: Mansell, 1998.

Mace, Angela. *RIBA Guide to its Archive and History*. London: Mansell, 1986.

Maerker, Anna. 'Between Profession and Performance: Displays of

BIBLIOGRAPHY

Anatomical Models in London, 1831–32'. *Histoire, médecine et santé* 5 (Spring 2014), 47–59.

Malafouris, Lambros. *How Things Shape the Mind: A Theory of Material Engagement*. Cambridge, Mass.: The MIT Press, 2013.

Martin, Gregory. 'Wilkins and the National Gallery'. *The Burlington Magazine* 113, no. 819 (June 1971), 318–26, 329.

Martini, Manuela, Liliane Hilaire Pérez, and Giorgio Riello. 'Practices of Fixed-Price Work: Trades, Techniques and Subcontracting in a Eurasian Perspective, Eighteenth to the Twentieth Century. An Introduction'. *Revue de Synthèse* 140, nos. 1–2 (December 2019), 1–12.

Matheson, Suzanne. 'A Shilling Well Laid Out: The Royal Academy's Early Public'. In David Solkin, ed., *Art on the Line: The Royal Academy Exhibitions at Somerset House 1780–1836*. New Haven: Yale University Press, 2002, 39–54.

Millon, Henry A. 'Models in Renaissance Architecture'. In Henry A. Millon and Vittorio Magnago Lampugnani, eds., *The Renaissance from Brunelleschi to Michelangelo: The Representation of Architecture*. London: Thames and Hudson, 1994, 19–74.

Mindrup, Matthew. *The Architectural Model: Histories of the Miniature and the Prototype, the Exemplar and the Muse*. Cambridge, Mass.: The MIT Press, 2019.

Mindrup, Matthew, and Matthew Wells. 'The Architectural Model as Tool, Medium and Agent of Change'. *Architectural Theory Review* 24, no. 3 (May 2020), 221–23.

Minkenberg, Michael, ed. *Power and Architecture: The Construction of Capitals and the Politics of Space*. New York: Berghahn, 2014.

Moon, Karen. *Modelling Messages. The Architect and the Model*. New York: Monacelli Press, 2005.

Morgan, Mary. 'Learning from Models'. In Mary Morgan and Margaret Morrison, eds., *Models as Mediators: Perspectives on Natural and Social Science*. Cambridge: Cambridge University Press, 1999, 347–88.

Morris, Mark. *Models: Architecture and the Miniature*. London: Wiley, 2006.

Morris, Mark. 'Worlds Collide: Reality to Model to Reality'. In Andrew Higgott and Timothy Wray, eds., *Camera Constructs: Photography, Architecture and the Modern City*. Burlington: Ashgate, 2012, 179–94.

Morris, Pam. *Imagining Inclusive Society in Nineteenth-Century Novels: The Code of Sincerity in the Public Sphere*. Baltimore: Johns Hopkins University Press, 2004.

Muirhead, Findlay. *London and Its Environs*. London: Macmillan, 1927.

N

Nead, Lynda. *Victorian Babylon: People, Streets and Images in Nineteenth-Century London*. New Haven: Yale University Press, 2000.

Norman, Philip. 'Crosby Place'. *London Topographical Record* 6 (1909), 1–22.

Norman, Philip, and William Douglas Caröe. *Survey of London. Monograph 9: Crosby Place*. London: Guild & School of Handicraft, 1908.

O

Oechslin, Werner. 'Le modèle architectural. "Idea materialis"'. In Sabine Frommel and Raphaël Tassin, eds., *Les maquettes d'architecture: Fonction et évolution d'un instrument de conception et de réalisation*. Paris: Picard, 2015, 103–17.

Olsen, D. J. 'The Changing Image of London in "The Builder"'. *Victorian Periodicals Newsletter* 19 (March 1973), 4–9.

Osayimwese, Itohan. *Colonialism and Modern Architecture in Germany*. Pittsburgh: University of Pittsburgh Press, 2017.

Otter, Chris. *The Victorian Eye: A Political History of Light and Vision in Britain, 1800–1910*. Chicago: University of Chicago Press, 2008.

P

Palmer, Susan. 'Sir John Soane and the Design of the New State Paper Office, 1829–34'. *Archivaria* 60 (2005), 39–70.

Pearce, Susan. *Museums, Objects, and Collections: A Cultural Study*. Leicester: University Press, 1992.

Perkin, Harold. *The Rise of Professional Society: England since 1880*. London: Routledge, 1989.

Physick, John. *The Victoria and Albert Museum: The History of its Building*. London: Phaidon, 1982.

Physick, John, and Michael Darby. *Marble Halls: Drawings and Models for Victorian Secular Buildings*. Exhibition catalogue. London: Victoria & Albert Museum, 1973.

Pillsbury, Joanne, Patricia Joan Sarro, James Doyle, and Juliet Wiersema. *Design for Eternity: Architectural Models from the Ancient Americas*. New Haven: Yale University Press, 2015.

Port, Michael. 'Destruction, Competition and Rebuilding: The Royal Exchange, 1838–1884'. In Ann Saunders, ed., *The Royal Exchange*. London: London Topographical Society, 1997, 286–93.

Port, Michael. 'From Carey Street to the Embankment–and back again!' *London Topographical Record* 24 (1980), 167–90.

Port, Michael. 'Government and the Metropolitan Image: Ministers, Parliament, and the Concept of a Capital City, 1840–1915'. In Dana Arnold, ed., *The Metropolis and Its Image: Constructing Identities for London, c. 1750–1950*. Oxford: Blackwell, 1999, 101–27.

Port, Michael. 'Hyde Park Corner: Resolving a Nineteenth Century Traffic Block'. *London Topographical Record* 28 (2001), 167–86.

Port, Michael. *Imperial London: Civil Government Buildings in London 1851–1915*. New Haven: Yale University Press, 1995.

Port, Michael. 'The New Law Courts Competition, 1886–67', *Architectural History* 11 (1968), 75–93.

Port, Michael. 'A Regime for Public Buildings: Experiments in the Office of Works, 1869–75'. *Architectural History* 27 (1984), 74–85.

Powell, Christopher G. *An Economic History of the British Building Industry 1815–1979*. London: Architectural Press, 1980.

Powers, Alan. 'Architectural Education in Britain 1880–1914'. PhD thesis, University of Cambridge, 1982.

Powers, Alan. 'Edwardian Architectural Education: A Study of Three Schools of Architecture'. *AA Files* 5 (1984), 49–59.

Price, Richard. *British Society, 1680–1880: Dynamism, Containment, and Change*. Cambridge: Cambridge University Press, 1999.

Puff, Helmut. *Miniature Monuments: Modeling German History*. Media and Cultural Memory. Berlin: De Gruyter, 2014.

Q

Quinault, Roland. 'From National to World Metropolis: Governing London, 1750–1850'. *The London Journal* 26, no. 1 (May 2001), 38–46.

R

Read, Donald. *The Age of Urban Democracy: England 1868–1914*. London: Longman, 1994.

Reed, Sophie, and Rebecca Spaven. '1841–1919 Wandering in a Labyrinth of Experiments'. in Jeremy Melvin, ed., *175 Years of Architectural Education at UCL, Architectural Review* (2017), 67–70.

Richardson, Albert. 'Architectural Causerie: Architectural Models'. *Architect's Journal* (5 May 1920), 582.

Richardson, Margaret. 'Model Architecture: Sir John Soane's Collection of Architectural Models'. *Country Life* 183 (21 September 1989), 224–27.

Richmond, Lesley, and Alison Turton, eds. *The Brewing Industry: A Guide to Historical Records*. Manchester: Manchester University Press, 1990.

Riley, William Edward, and Laurence Gomme, eds. *Survey of London. Volume 3: St Giles-in-The-Fields, Pt I: Lincoln's Inn Fields*. London: London County Council, 1912.

Riva, Alessandro. 'The Evolution of Anatomical Illustration and Wax Modelling in Italy from the 16th to Early 19th Centuries'. *Journal of Anatomy Publication* 216, no. 2 (February 2010), 209–22.

Roehrig, Catherine H. 'Life Along the Nile: Three Egyptians of Ancient Thebes'. *The Metropolitan Museum of Art Bulletin,* 60, no. 1 (Summer 2002).

Rogers, Patrick. *Westminster Cathedral: An Illustrated History*. London: Oremus, 2012.

Roscoe, Ingrid, M. G. Sullivan, and Emma Hardy. *A Biographical Dictionary of Sculptors in Britain 1660–1851*. New Haven: Yale University Press, 2009.

S

Saint, Andrew. *Architect and Engineer: A Study in Sibling Rivalry*. New Haven: Yale University Press, 2008.

Saint, Andrew. 'Ashbee, Geddes, Lethaby and the Rebuilding of Crosby Hall'. *Architectural History* 34 (1991), 206–23.

Saint, Andrew. *The Image of the Architect*. New Haven: Yale University Press, 1983.

Saint, Andrew. *London 1870–1914: A City at Its Zenith*. London: Lund Humphries, 2021.

Saint, Andrew. 'The Marble Arch'. *The Georgian Group Journal* 7 (1997), 75–93.

Salmon, Frank. 'British Architects, Italian Fine Arts Academies and the Foundation of the RIBA, 1816–43'. *Architectural History* 39 (1996), 77–113.

Salmon, Frank. *Building on Ruins: The Rediscovery of Rome and English Architecture*. Aldershot: Ashgate, 2000.

Saunders, Robert. *Democracy and the Vote in British Politics, 1848–1867: The Making of the Second Reform Act*. Farnham: Ashgate, 2011.

Savage, Nicholas. 'Exhibiting Architecture: Strategies of Representation in English Architectural Exhibition Drawings, 1760–1836'. In David Solkin, ed., *Art on the Line: The Royal Academy Exhibitions at Somerset House 1780–1836*. New Haven: Yale University Press, 2002, 201–16.

Sawyer, Sean. 'Processional Route'. In Margaret Richardson and Mary-Anne Stevens eds., *John Soane Architect: Master of Space and Light*. Exhibition catalogue. London: Royal Academy of Arts, 1999, 252–64.

Sawyer, Sean. 'Sir John Soane's Symbolic Westminster: The Apotheosis of George IV'. *Architectural History* 39 (1996), 54–76.

Schinkel, Karl Friedrich. *The English Journey: Journal of a Visit to France and Britain in 1826*. Edited by David Bindman and Gottfried Riemann. Translated by F. Gayna Walls. New Haven: Yale University Press, 1993.

Schneider, Wendie Ellen. *Engines of Truth: Producing Veracity in the Victorian Courtroom*. New Haven: Yale University Press, 2015.

Sheppard, Francis, ed. *Survey of London*. Volume 40: *The Grosvenor Estate in Mayfair*, Part 2: *The Buildings*. London: London County Council, 1980.

Sheppard, Francis. *The Treasury of London's Past: A Historical Account of the Museum of London and its Predecessors, the Guildhall Museum and the London Museum*. London: HMSO, 1991.

Sladen, Teresa. 'Embellishment and Decoration, 1696–1900'. In Derek Keene, Arthur Burns, and Andrew Saint, eds., *St Paul's: The Cathedral Church of London 604–2004*. London: Yale University Press, 2004, 233–57.

Smith, Albert. *Architectural Model as Machine*. Oxford: Architectural Press, 2004.

Solkin, David, ed. *Art on the Line: The Royal Academy Exhibitions at Somerset House 1780–1836*. New Haven: Yale University Press, 2002.

Spencer, Amy Louise. 'University College London: An architectural history, 1825–1939'. PhD thesis, University College London, 2021.

Spooner, Rosemary. 'Day-Tripping: Urban Excursions and the Architecture of International Exhibitions'. *Architectural Theory Review* 23, no. 3 (2019), 326–44.

Stalder, Laurent, and Moritz Gleich. 'Stirling's Arrows'. *AA Files* 72 (2016), 57–67.

Stewart, Susan. *On Longing, Narratives of the Miniature, the Gigantic, the Souvenir, the Collection*. Baltimore: Johns Hopkins University Press, 1984.

Summerson, John. *The Architectural Association, 1847–1947*. London: Pleiades Books, 1947.

Summerson, John. 'IV. A Victorian Competition: The Royal Courts of Justice'. In *Victorian Architecture: Four Studies in Evaluation*. New York: Columbia University Press, 1973, 77–117.

Summerson, John. *The London Building World of the Eighteen-Sixties*. London: Thames and Hudson, 1973.

Summerson, John. 'The London Building World of the 1860s'. *The Unromantic Castle and Other Essays*. London: Thames and Hudson, 1990, 175–92.

T

Thom, Colin, ed. *Survey of London*. Volume 50: *Battersea: Homes and Housing*. London: Yale University Press, 2013.

Thomas, Sophie. 'A "Strange and Mixed Assemblage": Sir John Soane, Archivist of the Self'. *Studies in Romanticism* 57, no. 1 (Spring 2018), 121–42.

Thompson, Denys. 'A Hundred Years of The Higher Journalism'. *Scrutiny* 4, no. 1 (June 1935), 25–34.

Thornton, Peter, and Helen Dorey. *A Miscellany of Objects from Sir John Soane's Museum*. London: Laurence King, 1992.

Thornton, Peter, and Helen Dorey. *Sir John Soane: The Architect as Collector*. New York: Abrams, 1992.

Tilbrook, Adrian. *Truth, Beauty and Design: Victorian, Edwardian and Later Decorative Art*. London: Fischer, 1986.

Tschanz, Martin. *Die Bauschule am Eidgenössischen Polytechnikum in Zürich: Architekturlehre zur Zeit von Gottfried Semper (1855–1871)*. Zurich: gta Verlag, 2015.

Tschudi, Victor Plahte. 'Plaster Empires: Italo Gismondi's Model of Rome'. *Journal of the Society of Architectural Historians* 71, no. 3 (September 2012), 386–403.

Tyack, Geoffrey. *Sir James Pennethorne and the Making of Victorian London*. Cambridge: Cambridge University Press, 1992.

V

Valeriani, Simona. 'Three-dimensional Models as "in-between-objects": The Creation of in-between Knowledge in Early Modern Architectural Practice'. *History of Technology* 31 (2011), 26–46.

Valinsky, David. *An Architect Speaks: The Writings and Buildings of Edward Schröder Prior*. Exeter: Shaun Tyas, 2014.

W

Walker, Lynne. 'E. S. Prior 1852–1932'. PhD thesis, Birkbeck College, University of London, 1978.

Waterfield, Giles. *The People's Galleries: Art Museums and Exhibitions in Britain, 1800–1914*. New Haven: Yale University Press, 2015.

Watkin, David. 'Holford, Vulliamy, and the Sources for Dorchester House'. In Sarah Macready and Frederick Hugh Thompson, eds., *Influences in Victorian Art and Architecture*. London: Society of Antiquaries of London, 1985, 81–92.

Watkin, David. *The Life and Work of C. R. Cockerell*. London: Zwemmer, 1974.

Watkin, David. *Sir John Soane: Enlightenment Thought and the Royal Academy Lectures*. Cambridge: Cambridge University Press, 1996.

Watkin, David, ed. *Sir John Soane: The Royal Academy Lectures*. Cambridge: Cambridge University Press, 2000.

Weaver, Thomas. 'Model-maker Grimm'. *AA Files* 73 (2016), 94–100.

Weber, Christiane. 'Technical Nation Building: German Professional Organizations and Their Journals in the Nineteenth Century'. *The Journal of Architecture* 25, no. 7 (October 2020), 924–47.

Webster, Christopher. 'The Architectural Profession in Leeds 1800–50: A Case Study in Provincial Practice'. *Architectural History* 38 (1995), 176–91.

Wells, Matthew. 'Architectural Models and the Rebuilding of the Royal Exchange, 1839–1844'. *Architectural History* 60 (2017), 219–41.

Wells, Matthew. 'Carpenters and Craftsmen, Architects and Collectors: A Short History of the Architectural Model'. In Maureen Cassidy-Geiger, ed., *Living with Architecture as Art: The Peter W. May Collection of Architectural Drawings, Models and Artefacts*. London: Paul Holberton, 2020, 64–81.

BIBLIOGRAPHY

Wells, Matthew. '1847: J. B. Bunning and the Coal Exchange Model'. In Mark Hallett, Sarah Victoria Turner, and Jessica Feather eds., *The Royal Academy of Arts Summer Exhibition: A Chronicle, 1769–2018*.

Wells, Matthew. *Survey: Architecture Iconographies.* Zurich: Park Books, 2021.

Wenger, Etienne. *Communities of Practice: Learning, Meaning, and Identity.* Cambridge: Cambridge University Press, 1998.

Whitehead, Christopher. *Museums and the Construction of Disciplines: Art and Archaeology in Nineteenth-Century Britain.* London: Bloomsbury, 2009.

Williams, Matthew. 'Lady Bute's Bedroom, Castell Coch: A Rediscovered Architectural Model'. *Architectural History* 46 (2003), 269–76.

Wilton-Ely, John. 'The Architectural Model'. *Architectural Review* 142 (July 1967), 26–32.

Wilton-Ely, John. 'The Architectural Model: English Baroque'. *Apollo* 88 (October 1968), 250–9.

Wilton-Ely, John. 'The Architectural Models of Sir John Soane: A Catalogue'. *Architectural History* 12 (1969), 5–38, 81–101.

Wilton-Ely, John. 'The Rise of the Professional Architect in England'. In Spiro Kostof, ed., *The Architect: Chapters in the History of the Profession*. New York: Oxford University Press, 1977, 180–208.

Wilton-Ely, John. 'The Role of Models in Church Design'. *Country Life Annual* (1969), 76–7, 79.

White, Jerry. *London in the Nineteenth Century: A Human Awful Wonder of God.* London: Vintage, 2008.

Wood, Jane. 'A Culture of Improvement: Knowledge, Aesthetic Consciousness, and the Conversazione'. *Nineteenth Century Studies* 20 (2006), 79–98.

Wylde, Peter. 'The First Exhibition: The Architectural Association and the Royal Architectural Museum'. *Architectural Association Annual Review* (1981), 8–14.

Y

Yaneva, Albena. *The Making of a Building: A Pragmatist Approach to Architecture.* Bern: Peter Lang, 2009.

Yorke, James. 'Tiny Temples of Mr Nash'. *Country Life* (8 February 2001), 66–7.

IMAGE CREDITS

COVER TOP
Model of the Southwest Tower of the Admiralty and War Office, 1885. AFC 000006, by permission of the Architectural Fabric Collection, UK Parliament. Photo: © Victoria and Albert Museum

COVER MIDDLE
Model of Westminster Cathedral, *Westminster Cathedral Record* (1899)

COVER BOTTOM
Model of the Admiralty and War Office, 1885. AFC 000005, by permission of the Architectural Fabric Collection, UK Parliament. Photo: © Victoria and Albert Museum

BACK COVER
West Elevation of Model for Meux Brewery, Wandsworth, 1907, *Concerning Models of Buildings, & c.* Courtesy Thorp Archive, AUB

FIG. 1	Presented by Georges A. Mevil-Blanche 1947, Tate
FIG. 6	British Museum, 1954,1103.12. © Trustees of the British Museum
FIG. 8	London Metropolitan Archives, Plan 27. J.2. © London Metropolitan Archives
FIG. 9	London Metropolitan Archives, p5349658. © London Metropolitan Archives
FIG. 10	COLL 0217. Courtesy the Mercers' Company Archive
FIG. 11	COLL 0116. Courtesy the Mercers' Company Archive
FIG. 12	Victoria & Albert Museum, 1069–1873. Courtesy Victoria and Albert Museum
FIG. 13	London Metropolitan Archives, q8023029. © London Metropolitan Archives
FIG. 15	RIDA, SD09/1(4)
FIG. 16	Architectural Association Archives
FIG. 18	National Archives, PRO.1–2003. Photo: © Victoria and Albert Museum
FIG. 19	AFC 000006, by permission of the Architectural Fabric Collection, UK Parliament. Photo: © Victoria and Albert Museum
FIG. 20	AFC 000005, by permission of the Architectural Fabric Collection, UK Parliament. Photo: © Victoria and Albert Museum
FIG. 27	London Metropolitan Archives, q3698573. © London Metropolitan Archives
FIG. 28	Courtesy Thorp Archive, AUB
FIG. 29	Yale Center for British Art, Paul Mellon Collection, New Haven
FIG. 32	St Paul's Cathedral 4628
FIG. 33	St Paul's Cathedral, AA/A/1, 11
FIG. 34	RIBA, PB731/4 1
FIG. 35	RIBA, PB731/4 2A
FIG. 37	Architekturmuseum, TU Berlin, 2745
FIG. 40	RIBA VuL 1/2/5
FIG. 42	RIBA, VuL 13 1 38a
FIG. 44	Courtesy Thorp Archive, AUB
FIG. 45	Courtesy Thorp Archive, AUB
FIG. 46	Courtesy Thorp Archive, AUB
FIG. 50	Courtesy Thorp Archive, AUB
FIG. 51	Private collection
FIG. 52	Private collection
FIG. 53	London Metropolitan Archives, 4435/A/03/006. © London Metropolitan Archives
FIG. 54	Courtesy Thorp Archive, AUB
FIG. 55	Courtesy Thorp Archive, AUB
FIG. 63	Architectural Association Archives
FIG. 64	Courtesy Rare Books, ETH Zurich
FIG. 65	Courtesy Rare Books, ETH Zurich
FIG. 70	London Metropolitan Archives, p5416254. © London Metropolitan Archives
FIG. 73	Private collection
FIG. 74	Private collection
FIG. 75	© British Library Board
FIG. 77	Victoria and Albert Museum, 2816. © Victoria and Albert Museum
FIG. 78	Victoria and Albert Museum, 32053. © Victoria and Albert Museum
FIG. 79	Victoria and Albert Museum, 32054. © Victoria and Albert Museum
FIG. 82	© Victoria and Albert Museum
FIG. 84	RIBA MOD/BUNN/1

INDEX

A

AA (Architectural Association), 43, 57, 65, 119, 125–9, 134–5, 138, 141, 168, 174
Adams, Maurice B., 168
Admiralty and War Office, 51–3, 57–9, 62–3
Aitchison, George, 15, 49, 61–3
Alberti, Leon Battista, 11, 31
Altieri, Giovanni, 147
l'Anson, Edward, 73
Architectural Association. See AA
Architectural Review, 126–7
Architectural Society, 36, 119
Arch of Constantine, Rome, 147
Assize Courts, Durham, 67
Austin, Henry, 29

B

'The Barn' cottage, Exmouth, 88
Barry, Charles, 33, 41, 159
Barry, Edward Middleton, 41
Beckett Denison, Edmund (Lord Grimthorpe), 13
Belcher, John, 15
Benson, Henry Walker, 143
Bentley, John Francis, 129
Beresford Hope, Alexander, 77, 80
Bijapur tomb, 154
Bishop, John P., 113
Blasche, Bernhard Heinrich, 121–2
Blythe, John, 119–20
Bodley, George Frederick, 126
Bolton, Arthur T., 126
Bonneau, Jacob, 144
British Museum, 119, 144, 169
Britton, John, 147
Brook Hospital, Greenwich, 103, 174
Building Crafts College, Fitzrovia, 136
Bunning, James Bunstone, 172
Burges, William, 75–7, 80–2, 84, 144
Burton, Decimus, 101

C

Carlton House, 14
Child, Francis, 129
Christian, Ewan, 52, 58
Clarke, Andrew, 50–2, 62
Cleopatra's Needle, 61, 164
Coal Exchange, 172
Cockerell, Charles Robert, 10, 33–7, 97
Cole, Henry, 155, 159, 162, 166
Cresy, Edward, 145, 147
Crystal Palace, 112
Cubitt, Lewis, 163

D

Davies, Horatio, 73
Day, Richard Jr, 26, 93–101
Day, Richard Sr, 14, 26, 37, 93, 107, 172
Department of Science and Art, 130, 166
Dighton, Thomas Dibdin, 14
Dixon, John, 164
Donaldson, Thomas Leverton, 80, 137, 153, 160
Dorchester House, 93–6, 98–101, 113
Du Bourg, Richard, 144–5, 149

E

Eastlake, Charles, 77
Ecclesiological Society, 159–60
Elsey Smith, Ravenscroft, 70, 135, 137–8
Etherington-Smith, Henry, 113
Exposition Universelle, Paris 1900, 103, 174

F

Farmer and Brindley, 129
Fellowes-Prynne, George H., 127
Fergusson, James, 43, 81, 154, 156–7
Festival of Empire, 112
Finsterlin, Hermann, 89
Fletcher, Banister, 134–5
Fletcher, Banister Flight, 135
Fouquet, François, 145
Fouquet, Jean-Pierre, 145, 157
Fowke, Francis, 162–3
Franco-British Exhibition 1908, 107–8, 112

G

Gallery of Practical Science (Adelaide Gallery), 26
Garling, Henry Bayley, 40
Godwin, Edward William, 80, 160
Godwin, George, 160
Gol Gumbaz (tomb of Mohammad Adil Shah), 154
Goodchild, John Eastly, 33
Government School of Design, 143
Gower Street, 137–38
Great Exhibition 1851, 10, 101, 130, 155–6
Gwilt, Joseph, 33

H

Haig, Axel, 82, 84
Hamo Thornycroft, 15
Hardwick, Philip, 33, 52, 58, 159
Harvey, Lawrence, 57, 127
Hoetger, Bernhard, 89
Holford, Robert, 93, 96–8, 101
Hopper, Thomas, 32
Houses of Parliament, 61
  House of Commons, 42, 50, 52, 56, 58–9
  House of Lords, 50, 52–3, 59, 61–5
Hyde Park, London, 10, 93, 156

I

Imperial International Exhibition 1909, 103, 112

J

James, Henry, 7
Jerdan, William, 22, 25

K

Kerr, Robert, 61, 65–6, 68, 134
King's College, London, 70, 119, 125, 134, 141, 174
King William IV, 28

L

Lansdowne, Fifth Marquess of, Henry Petty-Fitzmaurice, 62–63
Layard, Austin, 42–3, 52, 62
Leeds, William Henry, 25, 34, 36
Leeming, John, 52–3, 56–9
Leeming, Joseph, 52–3, 56, 58–9
Lewis, Thomas Hayter, 137
Liverpool Architectural Society, 10
London and Westminster Bank building, London, 33
London Bridge, 107–8
London Building Acts, 66
Longman, William, 77, 80, 84
Lonsdale, Horatio Walter, 77
Lucas Brothers, building firm, 166
Luckhardt, Hans, 89
Luckhardt, Wassili, 89

M

Mabey, Charles Henry, 14, 56, 58
Mabey, Charles Henry Jr, 14
Mabey, James, 14
Maclagan, Eric, 169
Maddox, George, 120
Marble Arch, 163
Metropolis Management Act 1855, 66
Metropolitan Asylum Board, 103, 174
Meux's Brewery Company, 113–15
Mould, Jacob Wray, 98
Mountford, Edward William, 15
Mount Vesuvius, 145
Museum of London, 8, 112
Muthesius, Hermann, 88–9

N

Nash, John, 14, 145, 163
National Art Training School, Marlborough House, 157
National Gallery, 22, 25–8, 37, 40–1, 75, 96
New Law Courts (Royal Courts of Justice), 39–41, 43–6, 67
Nicholl, William Grinsell, 34, 97

O

Office of Works, 40, 42, 45, 52–3, 56, 58, 63

P

Padiglione, Domenico, 147
Paestum temples, 145, 147, 149, 151
Pantheon, 135
Paris Exhibition 1855, 162
Park Lane, London, 93–4
Pennethorne, James, 101, 156
Penny Cyclopædia, 13
Penrose, Francis, 160
Perrault, Claude, 31
Physick, John, 169
Plunkett, David, 58
Pomeroy, Frederick William, 15, 126–7
Pompeii, 147, 149, 151
Poole, Henry, 166
Princess Mary Village Homes, Addlestone, 107
Prior, Edward Schroeder, 85, 88–9, 126–7
Pugin, Edward Welby, 43

Q

Quatremère de Quincy, Antoine-Chrysostôme, 31
Queen Victoria, 39, 157, 160

R

RAM (Royal Architectural Museum), 157, 159–62, 166–9
Randoll, Robert, 73
Reform Act 1832, 21,

INDEX

Reform Act 1867, 49
RIBA (Royal Institute of British Architects), 17, 29, 31, 36, 39, 41, 49, 57–8, 61–3, 67, 125–6, 137, 153–4, 156
Richardson, Charles James, 151
Richardson, T. A., 122, 125
Robson and Estelle plasterers, 150
Royal Academy, 15, 75, 81–2, 84–5, 88–9, 119–20, 126, 149
    Royal Academy Schools, 102, 120
    Summer Exhibition, 80, 82, 85, 88
Royal Architectural Museum. See RAM
Royal Exchange, 31–9, 41, 97, 112
Royal Military Repository (the Rotunda), 14
Ruskin, John, 30, 162

S

Salter, Stephen, 14
Sanders, John, 147
Sandham, Henry, 162
Schinkel, Karl Friedrich, 145, 160
Schröder, Jacob, 130
Scott, George Gilbert, 57, 59, 159, 166
Seddon, John Pollard, 40, 166
Semper, Gottfried, 10, 127
Shaw Lefevre, George, 52–3, 58
Simpson, Frederick Moore, 137–8
Sir John Soane's Museum, 126, 145, 156
    Model Room, 149–52
Slater, John, 129
Smirke, Robert, 33
Smith, Cecil Harcourt, 168
Smith, T. Roger, 80–1
Soane, John, 120, 145, 147–52
Somerset House, 57, 75
South Kensington Museum, 8, 43, 101, 130, 145, 155–68, 174
    Brompton Boilers, 156–7, 159
    Museum of Building Materials, 163–4
    Museum of Construction, 130, 162–3, 165, 169
    Museum of Ornamental Art, 157, 160, 162–3, 169
St Martin-in-the-Fields, 26
Stokes, Leonard, 126
Storey's Gate, Westminster, 14, 56
St Paul's Cathedral, 76–7, 80–5
Street, George Edmund, 41–3, 45
Sutherland MacColl, Dugald, 88

T

Tatham, Charles Heathcote, 150
Taylor, George Ledwell, 147
Temple of Vesta, Tivoli, 147, 149, 151
Thomas, Alfred Brumwell, 15
Thomas, Clement, 98, 100, 153, 160
Thorp, Annie Farish, 107
Thorp, John, 14, 69–70, 73, 102–3, 107–8, 112–15, 172, 174
Thwaite, Charles Newson, 14
Tite, William, 33–7, 39, 137
Treadwell, Henry John, 70

U

University College London, 119, 125, 137–41, 154, 166

V

Victoria Embankment, 42–3, 61, 164
Victoria Station, 129
Victoria Street, 129
Voewood, Norfolk, 88
Vulliamy, Benjamin, 97
Vulliamy, Lewis, 93–4, 96–101

W

Walden, John, 77
Waterhouse, Alfred, 56, 135
Wemyss, Tenth Earl of, Francis Richard Charteris, 52–3, 59–65
West End, London, 14, 69
White City, Hammersmith, 103, 108, 112
Whitehall, 50, 52–3, 57–8, 61, 149, 169
Wilkins, William, 22, 25–6, 28, 41
Wilkinson, Leslie, 141
Wilson, Charles Heath, 143
Worshipful Company of Mercers, 31
Wren, Christopher, 31

ACKNOWLEDGEMENTS

It would not have been possible to undertake and write this book without the assistance and support of many generous people, only some of whom it is possible to thank here. At the Victoria & Albert Museum, this project would not have happened had Simona Valeriani and Olivia Horsfall Turner not created it. I wish to thank both of them for their continued advice, enthusiasm, and knowledge for which I am eternally grateful. I only hope that I have managed to write a book that lives up to the potential of the project before my involvement. During my viva, Mari Lending and William Whyte drew out aspects of the work that I had not seen before, thereby providing the frame for this book. I am also indebted to a number of staff at the Royal College of Art including Brian Dillon, Chantal Faust, Jane Pavitt, Sarah Teasley, and Elaine Tierney. My most heartfelt thanks go to my fellow comrades: Lauren Fried, Rujana Rebernjak, Miranda Clow, Juliana Kei, and Yongkeun Chun. Our friendship, encouragement, and complaints supported me at every stage of this work.

A number of conversations with other scholars have provided precious insights and assistance. I would also like to thank Neil Bingham, the late Geoff Brandwood, Teresa Fankhänel, Michael Hall, Niall Hobhouse, Peter Howell, Tim Knox, Todd Longstaffe-Gowan, Joshua Mardell, Jeremy Musson, Mark Morris, Nicholas Olsberg, Will Palin, Alan Powers, Sophie Read, Frank Salmon, and Amy Spencer. I have also had a number of remarkable teachers: the late David Dunster, Neil Jackson, and Torsten Schmiedeknecht, and later Biba Dow, Alun Jones, and Georgia Clarke. I am deeply grateful to them all.

The research would have been impossible without the support and assistance of a number of archives, libraries, and special collections. Particular thanks go to Charles Hind, Fiona Orsini, Suzie Pugh, Jason Canham, Lauren Alderton, and the staff of the British Architectural Library at the RIBA; James Sutton, Melissa Hamnett, Emma Rogers, and Danielle Thom at the V&A; Fran Sands, Helen Dorey, and Susan Palmer at the Sir John Soane's Museum; Ed Bottoms at the Architectural Association; the staff of the London Metropolitan Archives. A number of other collections have also offered support including David Lund at Arts University Bournemouth; Charlotte Drew and Jane Ruddell at the Mercers' Company; Mark Pomeroy at the Royal Academy archive; Sarah Radford at St Paul's Cathedral; Jane Pendlebury and Jeremy Parrett at Manchester Metropolitan University; Mark Collins at the Parliament's Heritage Collections. I would also like to thank the staff of the libraries that I have made my home over the last seven years, in particular at the Baubibliothek at ETH Zurich, the British Library, the National Art Library, the Zentralinstitut für Kunstgeschichte in Munich, and the Zentralbibliothek in Zurich.

This book was written during my time at ETH Zurich, where I owe several people an enormous debt of gratitude. Laurent Stalder gave me both the space to write the book and new ways to think about its content. Andreas Kalpakci, Rainer Schützeichel, Carla Peca, Davide Spina, Tobias Erb, and Barbara Bitterli all generously listened and supported the project. Chiara Gloor helped me gather several of the images. In discussions on their own studies Giulia Boller, Lukas Ingold, and Maxime Zaugg helped me consider my own research from new perspectives.

Failure is a part of realisation, and Mark Eastment, Mark Hallett, and Thomas Weaver all gave me advice during the difficult transition from dissertation to manuscript. I am particularly grateful to the two anonymous readers for their remarkably meticulous reading of the manuscript at an early crucial stage, while thanks are also due to the review board of Eve Blau, Mari Hvattum, Caroline A. Jones, and Markus Krajewski. The support and direction that I received from Moritz Gleich and Jennifer Bartmess at gta Verlag has been invaluable. So too was Sarah Handelman's copyediting in preparing the manuscript for publication.

Needless to say, any mistakes that remain despite their best efforts are my own. I was also very lucky that this project was generously supported by several institutions at various stages: the Arts and Humanities Research Council, the Victoria & Albert Museum, the Zentralinstitut für Kunstgeschichte in Munich, and the Institute for the History and Theory of Architecture (gta) at ETH Zurich. The School of Environment, Education and Development at the University of Manchester provided much-appreciated support in the final stages of the book's production.

Finally, I would like to thank my family, in particular my father, mother, and sister, for their continued support in all manner of ways. I would like to thank my wife, India Whiteley, for her understanding and encouragement. Without her all of this might have been possible, but it certainly would not have been worthwhile. I dedicate this book to her.

The series Architectural Knowledge is published by the Department of Architecture (D-ARCH) and the Institute for the History and Theory of Architecture (gta), ETH Zurich.

SERIES REVIEW BOARD
Eve Blau
Mari Hvattum
Caroline A. Jones
Markus Krajewski

The printing of this book was kindly supported by the Peter und Waltraud Betsche-Fonds in memory of the architect Egon Eiermann.

PROJECT MANAGEMENT
AND PROOFREADING
Jennifer Bartmess

COPYEDITING
Sarah Handelman

GRAPHIC CONCEPT,
TYPESETTING, AND DESIGN
Salzmann Gertsch

PREPRESS AND PRINTING
Merkur Druck

BINDING
Buchbinderei Grollimund

TYPEFACE
Suisse Int'l

PAPER
Keaykolour Lichen, 300 gm²
Munken Lynx, 100 gm²

© 2023
gta Verlag, ETH Zurich
Institute for the History and
Theory of Architecture
Department of Architecture
8093 Zurich, Switzerland
www.verlag.gta.arch.ethz.ch

© Texts: by the author
© Illustrations: by the image authors and their legal successors; for copyrights, see image credits

Every reasonable attempt has been made by the author and publisher to identify owners of copyrights. Should any errors or omissions have occurred, please notify us.

The entire contents of this work, insofar as they do not affect the rights of third parties, are protected by copyright. All rights are reserved. No part of this publication may be reproduced, stored in a retrieval system, or transmitted, in any form or by any means, electronic, mechanical, photocopying, recording, or otherwise, without the written permission of the publisher.

Creative Commons License
CC BY-NC-ND

ISBN (print) 978-3-85676-435-7
ISBN (PDF) 978-3-85676-449-4
ISSN (print) 2813-2521
ISSN (PDF) 2813-253X
https://doi.org/10.54872/gta/4494